GHOSTS OF BAGHDAD

MARINE CORPS GUNSHIPS ON THE OPENING DAYS OF THE IRAQ WAR

COLONEL ERIC "FERRIS" BUER, USMC (RET.)

Ballast Books, LLC
www.ballastbooks.com

ISBN: 978-1-955026-67-3

Printed in Hong Kong

Published by Ballast Books
www.ballastbooks.com

For more information, bulk orders, appearances, or speaking requests, please email: info@ballastbooks.com

DEDICATION

To the Marine Medium Helicopter Squadron 268 "Red Dragons" crew of Major Jay Aubin, Captain Ryan Beaupre, Staff Sergeant Kendall Waters-Bey, and Corporal Brian Kennedy.

To the Marine Light Attack Helicopter Squadron 169 "Vipers" crew of Captain Aaron Contreras, Sergeant Michael Lalush, and Sergeant Brain McGinnis.

To the Marine Light Attack Helicopter Squadron 267 "Stingers" crew of Captain Benjamin Sammis and Captain Travis Ford.

To all who gave their lives flying and fighting in support of US Marine forces during *Operation Iraqi Freedom.*

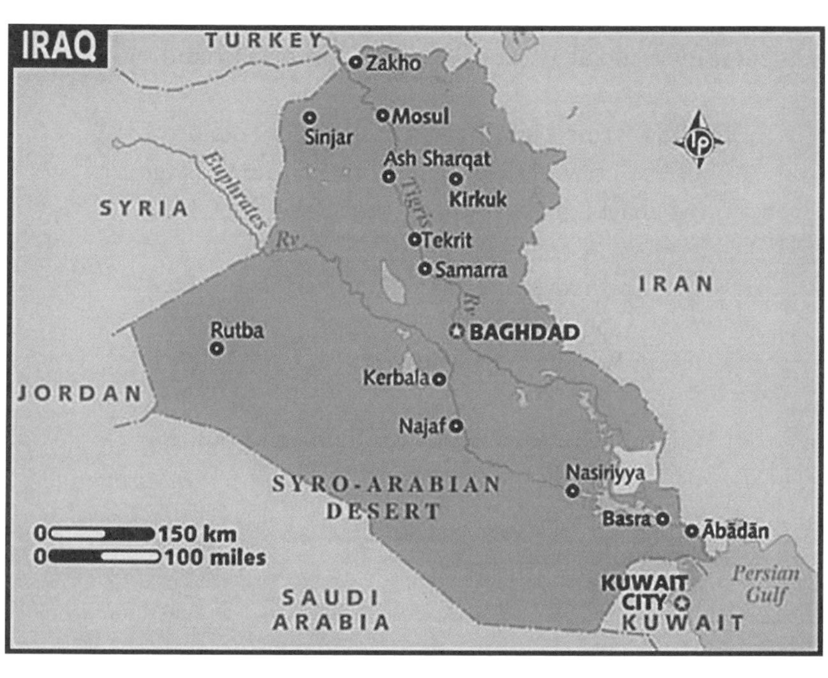
IRAQ
TURKEY
Zakho
Mosul
Sinjar
Ash Sharqat
Kirkuk
Euphrates
Tigris
SYRIA
Rv.
Tekrit
Samarra
IRAN
Rv.
Rutba
BAGHDAD
Kerbala
JORDAN
Najaf
Nasiriyya
SYRO-ARABIAN
DESERT
Basra
Ābādān
0 150 km
0 100 miles
Persian
Gulf
KUWAIT
CITY
KUWAIT
SAUDI
ARABIA

March 2003

1st Marine Division (REIN)

Commanding General's Message to All Hands

For decades, Saddam Hussein has tortured, imprisoned, raped and murdered the Iraqi people; invaded neighboring countries without provocation; and threatened the world with weapons of mass destruction. The time has come to end his reign of terror. On your young shoulders rest the hopes of mankind.

When I give you the word, together we will cross the Line of Departure, close with those forces that choose to fight, and destroy them. Our fight is not with the Iraqi people, nor is it with members of the Iraqi army who choose to surrender. While we will move swiftly and aggressively against those who resist, we will treat all others with decency, demonstrating chivalry and soldierly compassion for people who have endured a lifetime under Saddam's oppression.

Chemical attack, treachery, and use of the innocent as human shields can be expected, as can other unethical tactics. Take it all in stride. Be the hunter, not the hunted: never allow your unit to be caught with its guard down. Use good judgement and act in best interests of our Nation.

You are part of the world's most feared and trusted force. Engage your brain before you engage your weapon. Share your courage with each other as we enter the uncertain terrain north of the Line of Departure. Keep faith in your comrades on your left and right and Marine Air overhead. Fight with a happy heart and strong spirit.

For the mission's sake, our country's sake, and the sake of the men who carried the Division's colors in past battles-*who fought for life and never lost their nerve*-carry out your mission and *keep your honor clean.* Demonstrate to the world there is "No Better Friend, No Worse Enemy" than a U.S. Marine.

J.N. Mattis
Major General, U.S. Marines
Commanding

BOOK ONE

The Ghosts

We'd stared into the face of Death, and Death blinked first. You'd think that would make us feel brave and invincible. It didn't.

—Rick Yancey

GHOSTS OF BAGHDAD

GOB

CHAPTER 1

Location: 12 Miles from Safwan Hill, Iraq
Date: 20MAR03
Time: 1725L

I hated the desert. I despised its emptiness. The complete lack of contrast, the heat, the unpredictable weather, and the sand. It seemed as if a Ghost lived in every desert. A Ghost that devoured aircraft and snatched the lives of their crews. The Ghost had found us. I felt her presence. If I looked long enough and hard enough into the darkness, I could see her faint silhouette. I had pretended not to notice her on my flight from the ship into Joe Foss Field in the Kuwaiti desert. I had pretended to not see her earlier on the endless nighttime training missions in the Persian Gulf. Yet I knew she was here. I could smell her. She knew whenever we flew, where we flew, and why we flew. This wasn't any ghost but rather a very specific Ghost—the Arabian Desert.

She survived by her motto: haunt the living. She always excelled at her job and was always ready to ply her trade. That day was no different. Other Ghosts had names and countless victims. I had already met Sahara, Arctic, Mojave, Sonoran, Puntland, and now Arabian.

I had formally met the Ghost ten years earlier. She'd revealed herself while I chased warlords through the vast Somali desert. She'd come with her full force and wrath just a few miles from Mogadishu, the Somali capital. Somehow, some way, and by some chance of fate, I had escaped her. Or maybe she had purposefully spared me and my crew—a perverted game of cat and mouse. I knew then she felt cheated. She would not miss another chance to exact her brand of vengeance.

This Ghost operated differently from the others. She didn't whisper a cold and unintelligible message into my ear. She didn't signal her presence with a shrill cry into the darkness. She wouldn't drag her chains across the floor or captain her haunted ship through an endless sea. Instead, she had real skills.

She appeared subtle but simultaneously ruthless. A sister of the wind and a cousin of the sands, she could, and had, literally changed the weather. She would obliterate light, kill the sun, and strangle the moon. That night, she'd perform at an elite level, using every tool in her deviant kit. She represented exactly what the desert night had long become to me—a merciless, cunning, laugh-in-your-face, no-quarter-given jackal—and tonight, she seemed determined to win.

I knew the Ghost followed me, looking for any chance to win. Winning creates so much friction and so many contradictions. The Ghost and I both worked in the business of winning. Perhaps, more accurately, we both worked in the vendetta business. She desired to settle a score for my unspecified crimes. I was here to fix a problem. No one calls for Marine attack helicopters when things are going well. The Marine Corps and the president had tasked me with this mission. Maybe we were there to right a wrong, like a fixer.

That mission implied simpler tasks like to fly, to fight, and to protect our brothers and sisters preparing to cross into the unknown. Foremost, I considered myself a servant—a loyal servant. Maybe a fixer was too cordial. Maybe I was less a fixer and more like a debt collector. Regardless of how I classified myself, that mission required prototypical Marine expeditionary operations. The nation called, and we responded. I simply needed to execute the same way I had for the last fifteen years. The Ghost presented just another target. Just another obstacle, right?

My version of winning lay directly in front of me as we flew over the Kuwaiti desert at nearly 120 knots. I couldn't see anything out of the ordinary. In fact, I couldn't see much of anything at all. I couldn't smell anything out of the ordinary, and I couldn't hear anything out of the ordinary, but that voice in my head wouldn't accept it. I did the math, but how could one plus one plus one equal twenty? All my senses recognized the calm before the storm. Something was about to happen—something I couldn't predict with any certainty and something only the Ghost knew.

Am I the only one who knows she's here?

My copilot, Captain Matt Ziegler, sat two feet in front of me, saying little other than the idle chatter of a crew. He hadn't yet earned his callsign, so I simply called him Matt.

"Matt, tell lead we are on board," I requested.

"Sir, copy. Marjo 41, you've got Marjo 43 and 44 with you on the right," Matt replied.

I added a slight touch of power and pushed my flight of two Cobra helicopters closer to the two Cobras flying just two hundred feet in front of us.

Doesn't Matt see the Ghost too? We are in the same aircraft, so why can't he feel her leering at us?

I couldn't see her, but I knew she was watching us. Perhaps she was as iconic a Ghost as I suspected, wearing her white, blood-soaked dress, appearing in areas across history fraught with tragedy. Perhaps she was doomed to wander forever in torment. Or was she the tormentor? I didn't know, and I sure as hell didn't want to find out.

All five of my senses peaked. I felt the vibrations of the engines running through the stick and throttles, into my hands, and up both arms. I felt more vibrations coming through the control pedals into my feet, through my knees. I needed to breathe, slow and controlled.

I sucked in a full gulp of air, then expelled it with a deep exhale. I could now smell the familiar scent of the cockpit. That always had a calming effect for me. I didn't need to close my eyes to hear my heartbeat. It pumped hard. Time began to accelerate.

I saw the outline of Matt's desert camouflage helmet in the front seat, but he otherwise vanished in the darkness. He sat directly in front of me but might as well have been a hundred miles away.

It was dark, and I needed answers. "Matt, can you see the lead? I lost him."

He quickly countered, "I can't see anything. I am trying to find him. We are two minutes from the target."

Matt knew where we were, and the pause in his voice let me know he had been looking into the targeting sensor.

He keyed the radio. "Got lead in sight. I see the target. I am going to open up with the 20mm rounds once I see your rockets impact the target!"

I still couldn't see anything. I knew we were close.

Where the hell are they?

Both the Ghost and the Iraqis recognized our presence. I felt like I'd just sunk deeper into my seat. An oppressive pressure grew on my chest. It weighed more than my body armor, radios, pistol, and ammunition combined. I forced myself to breathe. These were shallow little sips of air. I felt trapped. Restricted to this cockpit. No way out now.

The Ghost never felt trapped. She held an enviable level of freedom. I wished I had her freedom. The Ghost enjoyed unlimited privileges and answered to no one—or, at least, no one I wanted to imagine. If I only had her freedom. Her clarity. Not that night. On that evening, I needed to be the absolute best version of myself. That night, I needed to use whatever tools I had available to me to outthink, outmaneuver, and outwit not only the Ghost but an enemy—an enemy who, by now, had certainly heard and could likely see us.

Matt pressed the foot switch on the floor of the front seat. "Sir, one minute out from the target. I am not seeing it yet."

I double clicked the intercom.

Click. Click.

It sounded like two bursts of static but meant I'd both heard and understood him. Otherwise, I couldn't muster a reply.

Matt continued. "Heading 355 degrees. We are at three hundred feet and 120 knots."

I confirmed, "Got it, Matt. Master arm is going to arm. Call the target."

There we sat, strapped into the cockpit of a Marine attack helicopter, accelerating to 130 knots into the darkness and trying to remember why the Ghost wanted to destroy us.

CHAPTER 2

Location: Persian Gulf, 27 Miles from the Iraqi Border, Amphibious Task Force East
Date: 15MAR03
Time: UNKNOWN

The United States Navy commissioned the USS *Saipan* (LHA-2) in 1977 as the second ship in the Tarawa class of amphibious assault ships and the second ship in the Navy to bear that name. She ran 833 feet long from bow to stern and 106 feet wide. My four-thousand-ton home that functioned like a small city included a crew of 950 officers and sailors plus the nearly two thousand embarked Marines. Armed with two Rolling Airframe Missile (RAM) systems, four 25mm Mk 38 gun mounts, two Phalanx CIWSes, and five .50 caliber mounts, she epitomized a capital ship.

Saipan's commanding officer (CO), Captain Norma "Lee" Hackney, had spent her entire career preparing for that command and that moment. She would serve as the first woman to command an amphibious ship in combat and would remain a fan favorite of the embarked Marines. We found her so popular, we referred to her as "Mom." Her understanding of *Saipan*'s mission and the mission of her embarked Marines would prove invaluable in the weeks and months that lay ahead.

Saipan represented not only one of the three capital ships that sailed from North Carolina but also another famous amphibious operation of the Second World War. The other two large deck amphibious ships were the USS *Bataan* and the USS *Kearsarge*. These mighty vessels, along with several smaller amphibious assault ships, made up the seven-thousand-strong 2nd Marine Expeditionary Brigade.

Once ashore, the brigade would lose its aviation assets and therefore no longer be a task-organized brigade. At that point, the remaining units would form and operate as Task Force Tarawa. They'd chosen the name Tarawa in honor of the 2nd Marine Division and their historical performance on Tarawa during the Second World War. We would also carry the label of Amphibious Task Force-East, with nearly every unit belonging to II Marine Expeditionary Force (MEF), the Corps level Marine force headquartered at Camp Lejeune, North Carolina.

Captain Hackney's understanding of our mission wasn't lip service; she was as committed to "her" Marines as she was to her own crew. This was evident in everything she said and did. She backed up her words with action by refusing to go "off station" or into a port while Marines were ashore. Being "on station" meant *Saipan* didn't stray far from the Iraqi coast during all of *Operation Iraqi Freedom*.

It was our collective opinion that no other ship was as available, or as reliable, as *Saipan*. The ship also carried critical aviation tooling systems, supplies, and naval aviation experts, along with both heavy and specialized aviation equipment. Our squadron's plan was to leave two or three helicopters on board and keep a small maintenance detachment there to make sure those helicopters were always ready. We didn't know it then, but the ability to rotate battle-damaged helicopters and complete heavy maintenance aboard the ship, versus in the desert, was critical to generating combat sorties. It would not be until much later that we'd realize how important *Saipan* was to our squadron's ability to generate combat power for "her" Marines fighting ashore.

The Marine Corps had three MEFs. One or I MEF was located at Camp Pendleton, California, which had three primary subordinate commands all working together to build a combined arms team. In January of 2003, I MEF's subordinate commands were the 3rd Marine Aircraft Wing (3rd MAW) commanded by Major General Jim "Tamer" Amos, the 1st Marine Division (1st MARDIV) commanded by Major General James "Chaos" Mattis, and the 1st

Force Service Support Group (1st FSSG) commanded by Brigadier General Edward Usher.

The I MEF commander, with some oversight from both the senior Marine and the US Central Command's four-star commander, had the responsibility and authority for all things Marine in theater. This also included the 2nd Marines Expeditionary Brigade/Task Force Tarawa/ATF-East.

Both II MEF and III MEF were smaller than I MEF but were similarly organized. Understandably, and for several practical reasons, the Marine Corps gave I MEF the nod to lead the fight into Iraq. Besides the size of I MEF, their training and planning focuses were on the Middle East, while II MEF's were oriented toward Europe and Africa and III MEF's were oriented toward both the Pacific and our regional allies.

We sailed from North Carolina as a separate unit, not yet under the command of I MEF. As 2nd Marine Expeditionary Brigade, we represented only a portion of II MEF's full combat power. The MEF planners had carved out what they believed were critical warfighting elements and leadership components of II MEF for this deployment. We were considered a brigade-sized force, which meant a smaller command element and smaller everything. From my vantage point, the brigade brought more combat power than support and logistical power. What we lacked in a logistical tail would be made up once we were in theater.

Brigadier General Richard Natonski commanded the brigade. We had served together in Somalia ten years earlier when he'd commanded the 1st Battalion of the 2nd Marine Regiment during *Operation Restore Hope*. That deployment had had his battalion and the entire 24th Marine Expeditionary Unit (MEU) doing what Marines do best. Throughout Somalia, with a much younger Captain Buer flying overhead and a younger Lieutenant Colonel Natonski commanding the battalion, we chased smugglers, fed the hungry, protected the weak, and attempted to catch warlords across the vast Somali coast and desert. No doubt the Ghost watched, listened, and learned from us.

The brigade-sized unit assembled here, on this clear day in March, was about to be chopped into smaller units and assigned to the MEF. Both Brigadier General Natonski and the remnants of his brigade had offloaded in Kuwait in January for training in the Kuwaiti desert and would be renamed Task Force Tarawa. It left only Marine Aircraft Group 29 (MAG 29) aboard *Saipan.* Additionally, MAG 29 was now under the operational control of the 3rd MAW, but in the weeks and months ahead, the aircrews of MAG 29 would not stray too far from the east coast counterparts. This was a gift for MAG 29, an open flight deck and unlimited opportunities to train. MAG 29 continued to fly and train, as did the other MAG 29 units married to the three other amphibious ships.

As the regiment and all its components departed, we could almost feel the apprehension and tension build. Something was off; something was not right. Those units left but not to simply train for a war; they had gone ashore to prepare for a very specific war. A war in the desert was coming. The problem was we didn't know when—or where or how—but we knew it was inevitable.

Colonel Ron Bailey, a native Floridian and distinguished graduate of Austin Peay State University, commanded the 2nd Marines, which made up the heart of Task Force Tarawa. An infantry regiment, 2nd Marines consisted of three infantry battalions: 1st Battalion 2nd Marines, or 1/2; 3rd Battalion 2nd Marines, or 3/2; and 2nd Battalion 8th Marines, or 2/8. With the regiment's 2nd Battalion 2nd Marines already deployed with the 24th MEU, the division added 2nd Battalion 8th Marines.

Task Force Tarawa also had 1st Battalion 10th Marines, or 1/10, assigned to them. This was an artillery battalion, and their 155mm towed howitzer cannons brought significant firepower to the brigade. Lastly, company-sized units were added to provide additional firepower and capabilities. These included companies from 2nd Tank Battalion, 2nd Light Armored Reconnaissance (LAR) Battalion, 2nd Amphibious Assault Battalion, and 2nd Combat Engineer Battalion, as well as a series of other combat and combat support units, both active duty and reserve.

The Marine Corps had assembled the MEF under one Marine commander once we had arrived in theater in January. Decisions well above my pay grade had deemed that every Marine would fight under the overall command of the larger I MEF based at Camp Pendleton, California. You do not need to be a historian or military expert to know the value of a single chain of command. History is littered with failed campaigns designed with multiple, confusing, or competing chains of command. Lieutenant General James Conway, the commanding general of I MEF, would serve as the single Marine commander. I didn't know the Walnut Ridge, Arkansas, native and it didn't matter to any of us who commanded the MEF. All we knew was that we needed to fly and train and that the departure of Task Force Tarawa meant we were running out of time.

CHAPTER 3

Location: Atlantic Coast, 18 Miles from Jacksonville, North Carolina
Date: 03JAN03
Time: 0940L

The USS *Saipan* had sailed from Norfolk in late December, giving her crews and commander only a few days to celebrate the holidays. She cruised off the coast of North Carolina as Marine units embarked. That included 2/8 and their nine hundred Marines and sailors, along with associated supplies, weapons systems, and specialized equipment.

Saipan normally carried the twenty-three helicopters of a MEU plus the Marine maintenance crews and pilots, along with a Marine battalion and associated combat equipment. It also carried two US Navy MH-60S helicopters and another six Marine AV-8B Harriers. On an air-capable amphibious assault ship like *Saipan,* as well as larger conventional aircraft carriers, squadron personnel had to undertake the herculean effort of moving all their equipment, aircraft parts, personal gear, and themselves from their shore-based home station to the ship. Once on board, they were joined by their aircraft and aircrews.

On that occasion, we had two squadrons and 2/8 embarked with all three units commanded by a lieutenant colonel. In the case of 2/8, the lieutenant colonel commanding the battalion was Royal Mortenson. The Chicago-area native and University of Wisconsin graduate had spent the past twenty years leading Marines. He was complemented by another career infantry officer, Major Dale Alford. Alford, a Georgia native, served as Mortenson's executive officer

(XO) and was already a seasoned combat veteran. The two officers would make a formidable leadership team.

On board *Saipan,* we also had the higher aviation headquarters CO and his staff embarked. Colonel Robert "Boomer" Milstead commanded MAG 29 from Marine Corps Air Station New River, North Carolina. MAG 29 would be one of the eight flying and supporting air groups eventually assembling in the theater, all supporting the initial invasion or *Operation Iraqi Freedom.* They would arrive by military airlift, commercially contracted airplanes, combat ships, and commercial ships from bases and stations located throughout the Navy and Marine Corps.

I had known Colonel Milstead, or Boomer, since my days as a 2nd lieutenant while a student at The Basic School in Quantico, Virginia. He counted as one of many memorable instructors at The Basic School, the Marine Corps' six-month course that every Marine officer must complete. The experience grounds each officer in the importance of leadership, critical thinking, and tactical skills and instills in them a deep appreciation of our Corps values as well as the immense responsibility of leading Marines.

A native Texan, Boomer had grown up in a military family steeped in traditions and service. I found him approachable, practical, and disarmingly calm. He was a no-nonsense leader who was singularly focused on employing his MAG to best support Marines on the ground. It may sound a bit cliché, but it was the truth. He had spent the past twenty-eight years flying Cobras, had previously commanded a squadron as a lieutenant colonel, and saw no better way to end a career than commanding an air group in combat.

The aircraft and aircrew flying the opening mission from *Saipan* were all assigned to MAG 29. We had sailed together across the Atlantic, through the Suez Canal, and into the Persian Gulf. Many of the aircrew and Marines assigned to both squadrons had known each other from previous deployments.

Eighteen AH-1W Super Cobra attack helicopters and nine UH-1N Iroquois utility helicopters established the backbone of Marine Light Attack Helicopter (HMLA) 269, rightfully called the "Gunrunners." The twelve CH-46E Sea Knights, or Phrogs, were assigned to the "Golden Eagles" of Marine Medium Helicopter Squadron (HMM) 162. As a second tour pilot, I knew most of the pilots from both squadrons, including both their COs.

Lieutenant Colonel Robert "Fuzzy" Hedelund commanded HMM 162. A native Floridian, Fuzzy had served as a flight instructor of mine in Pensacola some thirteen years prior during my initial flight training. He had been my flight lead at Helicopter Training Squadron 18 at Naval Air Station Whiting Field, Florida. We had also deployed in the mid-1990s as members of the world-famous "Blue Knights" of HMM 365.

In 1994, I had the great fortune of working for Fuzzy in the tactics department of 365, where we both served as captains. Although equal in rank at that time, I had no illusion that we were peers or buddies. In the military, there exists both a quantifiable and qualifiable difference between a two-year and a six-year captain. Fuzzy, as a former Marine Corps Aviation Weapons School (MAWTS-1) instructor pilot, brought significant tactical and technical expertise. With an aggressive and daring nature, he led from the front. The squadron would soon reflect his personality, resulting in their exceptional performances to unfold over the next several months.

Prior to rejoining 269 in the summer of 2002, I had spent 2001 assigned as a Deputy G-1 at the 2nd MAW headquarters. The G-1 is the administrative and manpower lead for the commanding general. In this loveless and thankless role, I begrudgingly made the hour drive from my house in Jacksonville to the 2nd MAW headquarters. These are not sexy jobs that easily make the jump into a Hollywood script, but they are vital to the success of so many units. In hindsight, I learned more than I thought possible.

I was on the inside seeing how commanders like Boomer and Fuzzy competed for talented inbound officers and senior non-commissioned officers (NCOs) and how deploying units were given priorities for both personnel and critical assets. Most importantly, the job allowed me to observe, from a seat one removed from the "big table," the discussions between the commanding general and their group and squadron commanders.

The 2nd MAW encompasses four flying air groups, one support group, and one communications and air defense group from their headquarters at Marine Corps Air Station Cherry Point in Havelock, North Carolina. After having spent 1999 to 2000 as a student at the Command and Staff College in Quantico, Virginia, and another year at the headquarters, I was desperate to get back into the cockpit full time. As I completed my year at 2nd MAW, the commanding general rewarded me with a school seat at the aviation maintenance officer's course in Pensacola, Florida. By the time I checked back into 269, I was in position to serve both as the maintenance officer and a flight lead.

Like nearly all the majors serving as department heads, we had graduated from the MAWTS-1. We were all expected to execute our "ground jobs" and serve as flight leads and instructor pilots. As a major, I would serve in a senior leadership position outside of the cockpit. Majors served as the command's logistics, operations, safety, maintenance, administrative, executive, and tactics officers while also leading daily training and combat missions. Thankfully, in my case, we had exceptional NCOs and warrant officers to do the real heavy lifting of that maintenance department. That let me concentrate on developing a plan to support our CO's vision of how we would operate from *Saipan* and, eventually, in the Iraqi desert.

The maintenance of twenty-seven attack and utility helicopters was something to behold. With the squadron size nearly two times the size of the average Marine squadron, we counted on the more than three hundred Marines, NCOs, staff NCOs, warrant officers, and limited duty officers (LDOs) to maintain and sustain these aircraft. Our CO had also graduated from the weapons school, and the Marine Corps expected him to lead from the front. There were no empty cockpits in an HMLA, so even the CO lived out an ethos to fly, fight, and lead.

When remembering the HMLA 269 CO, words often escape me, and when I do find them, they fall well short of the mark, but here's a snapshot. Lieutenant Colonel Jeff "Huey" Hewlett represented the typical New Yorker with a quick wit, sharp tongue, and wry sense of humor. He was consistently in the middle of anything and everything. Whether at the officer's club over a few bourbons or in the ready room debating tactics, weapons, or the next war, he was there, and he was engaged. We found him to be a good fit for the squadron because he let leaders lead, and he trusted his officers and NCOs.

While we all respected the CO and his position, most of the officers had not served with him, and that included me. The few interactions I'd had with him over the years were less collegial and more competitive. The HMLA community was small with only six active squadrons. So, your professional reputation was pretty much cemented by the time you were a major. He had a reputation as being aggressive and outspoken but also a recognized expert of ordnance systems and weapons performance.

Ironically, once in the air or during mission briefs, where rank generally is replaced by competence and flight leadership abilities, we talked candidly. Like most, I much preferred candid discussions over listening to someone's biased opinions based on personal experiences. The CO's opinions were his own, and he and our XO sought out contrary opinions and positions. It certainly kept our discussions lively. One of my most important jobs was to challenge decisions about how the squadron would fly, what we expected from our flight leaders, and how we could improve our young majors and captains.

No CO wants to be managed, but there was only so much time I had to talk about details, especially aboard ship. There was nothing but time on the ship. I had a responsibility to make the CO aware of important events related to the safety, accountability, and welfare of the Marines and aircraft status, but giving any commander too much information was a slippery slope. This may sound more nefarious than it was. Trust me, his insights into our maintenance practices, parts status, and aircraft capability status were in 99th percentile.

Some of my choices were easy, while others required additional contemplation. For example, if we had two maintenance Marines constantly at odds, even to the point of fist fighting, that was a problem solved by the sergeant. If it happened again, it was time to engage both the officer in charge and the senior NCO. If it was an issue that was created by or impacted the entire squadron or involved

Marines serving in another department, then the CO and XO were brought in. Otherwise, it was handled "in house."

Some COs wanted to know about every issue and then provide their own solutions. Not here, and not now—that was my job. We were not back at New River in an administrative setting. We were on a war footing.

Our maintenance department was just like any unit of three hundred plus Marines. There were the newly minted nineteen-year-old privates on their first deployment, and there were the salty twenty-year gunnery sergeants on their sixth or seventh. Some joined the Marine Corps to escape the fate often found in big cities or small country towns. They came from southern California to Maine, from Michigan to Texas, from Florida to Washington, and still others from across the globe. This incredibly diverse and talented group was not without its faults.

There remain inexplicable acts of God that occur on a ship at sea. These, more often than I ever wanted, had me walking to the CO's stateroom, typically asking myself how I was going to explain the unexplainable. While I tried to insulate our Marines from more of the mundane screwups, there were some that needed the entire command's attention.

Such an incident occurred when not one but two sets of night vision goggles (NVGs) were lost over the side of the ship on the same night. I interviewed both potential felons, one Huey crew chief and one pilot. Neither had a good excuse, but both had been following a trend of removing the small strings that attached the NVGs to the helmet if they came off the mount. With the cost in the tens of thousands of dollars, I knew I was going to hear a litany of F-bombs, what the hells, and you better unscrew those Marines…but it got worse.

This was followed by a piece of encryption gear suffering the same fate the very same week. Yup, a very limited and classified piece of equipment took a dive over the side of *Saipan*. These specific devices were required to upload the technology into our radios that made them secure. Secure meant our radio transmission could only be heard by other aircraft with the same technology uploaded. If the Iraqis were on the same frequency, they would only hear heavy static. There were rarely new mistakes, just old ones we forgot about or procedures we became complacent about executing. These were easy fixes.

After hearing the watery fate of the third piece of irreplaceable gear, I enlisted the help of the maintenance department's senior ground officer, Monty Campbell. "Monty, please ensure everything, within reason, is dummy corded to a maintainer, and I'll handle the pilots."

"Sir, I got this. I'll ensure the message is heard." There was no doubt the twenty-six-year veteran of maintenance would ensure nothing else found its way into the Atlantic Ocean, Mediterranean Sea, Suez Canal, Red Sea, or Persian Gulf.

Dummy cording is the ancient art of tying a valuable piece of gear to a Marine, so if it's dropped or the maintainer trips while working close to the deck edge of the ship, we don't lose the piece of gear. Unless the Marine goes over with it, but that's another thing entirely.

Commanding any unit carried with it degrees of risk and a nearly incalculable number of challenges. Commanding a unit in combat presented a daunting task and commanding a unit of that size required extensive training and trust, lessons that I would be putting into practice much sooner than I could have anticipated. The CO couldn't sit in every cockpit, watch over every flight, or be involved in split-second decisions. Compound that with planning for a complex opening night and anticipated follow-on operations the following day.

The first night of combat operations would be followed by the first of an unknown number of days. It's sometimes hard to get past the first day, kind of like anticipating the first punch in a fight. On the first day of operations, our CO's Cobras and Hueys would engage the enemy with literally thousands of rounds of light and heavy machine gun fire, cannon and rocket fire, and missile fire. The trust in his flight leaders and the trust in his NCOs provided the tools that made any of that possible. His entire command of machines and Marines prepared to step over the side of the USS *Saipan* and into history.

When our CO signed the flight schedule on the evening of the 18th of March, a new normal had begun. The first day of many. Though we had no teenaged pilots, we certainly had a few that acted like ones from time to time. I am not throwing stones since I would have likely made the list. In those moments, as the CO planned to fly ashore, I wondered if he realized he had just signed a check giving the remaining twenty-six helicopters to more than a few loose cannons. I suspect the only thing he could do was watch us fly away and pray that the nearly three hundred million dollars' worth of helicopters and his crews were up to the challenge.

Aboard *Saipan*, on the afternoon of the 18th of March, we prepared the flight deck for operations and got ready to send two waves of helicopters into a small airfield that had been recently constructed in northern Kuwaiti desert. The Marine crews and US Navy deck crews worked in harmony to ready the flight deck. It was soon lined with Cobras and Hueys, rotors spinning, armed, fueled, and awaiting clearance to launch to the beach.

Howdy 's voice chirped on the radio. "Marjo flight check."

Each Cobra checked in with a curt: "42"; "43"; "44."

A good sign that all four had checked in and all without any maintenance or ordnance issues.

The staff of MAG 29, squadron planners, and the flight leads had planned and trained for weeks for the initial mission into Iraq. We'd had day-long rehearsals in Kuwait. We'd used buildings to replicate our initial target of Safwan Hill with the focus on timing and communications. Unfortunately, we had only done a few nighttime desert landings. It was more crucial for the transport helicopters since they were the ones who were going to land on Safwan Hill. Even they had been unable to practice at night based on a host of constraints associated with airspace, deck cycles, and other training requirements.

We were all getting comfortable with being uncomfortable, a graduate level ability. Being able to fly with both anxiety and an awkward nervousness had begun to dominate my senses. I lacked control over the situation, the weather, the mission, and the anticipated enemy.

As a planner, you must make assumptions when you don't have facts, and we found it difficult to know what we'd face on Safwan. So, we worked on the things we could, such as NVG flying, formation flying at night, night weapons firing, and a few other building blocks. Although we were in uncharted and untested waters, the Marine Corps had given us our mission, and like it or not, it was the only mission that mattered right now.

Boomer, Fuzzy, and Jeff Hewlett all had ideas of what they were asking from their aircrews, but no one had a crystal ball, and no one could have predicted the chaos. With eight Cobras and two Hueys going ashore, the CO also flew off to lead a section during opening night operations. Boomer and Fuzzy stayed on board to plan for the next days and weeks ahead and would also track the mission from the operations center aboard the USS *Saipan*. They could only cross their fingers and hope all the planning and training over the past year had prepared the aircrews for the unprecedented, the unanticipated, and the unimaginable.

In our case, the time had come for us to leave the comforts of the ship behind. The Air Boss and his entire flight deck crew worked hard under the punishing Arabian sun while each colored jersey fulfilled their designed role. Purple shirts fueled the aircraft, red shirts armed the ordnance, green and white shirts made their final inspections, blue shirts removed chocks and tie-down chains, and then yellow shirts directed the helicopters to flight. All worked in harmony from a plan designed and executed by the Air Boss.

I watched as the first two Cobras in front of me were armed. They already had their chains removed. I saw the deck crew jog toward us, and I raised my hands to show I didn't have them in a position to fire any weapons.

I let my copilot get ready. "Matt, chain crew and ordies are coming."

"Copy. I see them. I'm checklist complete," he countered.

We had executed our own arming checklist as the ordies, short for ordnance-trained Marines, waited to walk under the rotor arch and armed the cannon, rocket pods, missiles, and flare pods. Each helicopter carried 120 flares or chaff designed to trick enemy heat-seeking or radar-guided surface-to-air missiles (SAMs). The verdict was still out on how effectively either would perform against the more sophisticated Soviet systems the Iraqi military operated.

Matt gave the signal to remove our chains, a wiping motion from elbow to wrist. Two sailors wearing blue shirts sprinted under the rotor arch and removed the chains that held our Cobra to the flight deck. The third sailor and team leader counted the chains and gave us a thumbs up. We responded in kind.

The team of three ordies confidently walked under the rotor arch and armed all of our systems. Once back out from under the Cobra, the team leader stood tall and saluted. Matt returned the salute and gave a thumbs up. I could feel my pulse quicken and blew out a deep breath. We had armed all the systems.

I knew he was but asked anyway. "Matt, you ready?"

Click. Click.

With the chains off and systems armed, we looked and saw the deck lights that were positioned near the Air Boss's perch had turned green. That was our signal to launch.

I heard Howdy a second later. "Tower, Marjo flight is ready for takeoff."

Up in *Saipan*'s tower, the Air Boss wanted us off the deck and wanted to get the other helicopters ready or spotted for takeoff.

Tower frequency crackled. "Marjo 41, 42, 43, 44, spots two, four, five, and six, winds are twelve knots off the bow. Cleared for takeoff."

We sat on spot five midway down the ship. I watched Howdy and then his wingman, Flash, lift off. Each saluted the lineman, then pulled into hover, checked power, slid to the left clear of the deck, and accelerated forward. The deck was clear, and I asked for a deck run. Deck runs from spot five use roughly the three hundred remaining feet of deck to make takeoffs easier under heavy weight.

Though we were not that heavy, it also offered a mini flyby to the Marines on the flight deck.

What's wrong with a little flair on the way out? I pulled in full power, and the Cobra accelerated quickly to seventy knots by the deck's edge. Clearing that, I began a turn to the left to rendezvous with 41 and 42. Buss flew right behind me.

Howdy called out, "Heading 340, three hundred feet, and 120 knots…call on board."

The Air Boss cleared us left to join, and outside of five miles, we switched to Green Crown—the name of the command-and-control ship tracking all air assets. That provided our first test to ensure that our Identification Friend or Foe (IFF) worked, a big deal since they also controlled the air-to-surface fires.

Four Cobras in formation, fully armed. No clouds, an easy afternoon sun to the southwest, a perfect day for flying.

Howdy checked the flight in. "Green Crown, Marjo 41, flight of four, cherubs three going feet dry."

That meant we flew at three hundred feet above the water and were about to cross into the desert north of Kuwait City.

Green Crown granted our wish. "Marjo 41, frequency change approved. Happy hunting."

That was it. No more formalized command and control for a while. We passed Kuwait City off to our left and followed the global positioning system (GPS) to Tactical Assembly Area (TAA) Coyote. Ahead was only desert and our thoughts. Our destination was a grid coordinate, and no one would know or could predict what was waiting for us.

CHAPTER 4

Location: TAA Coyote, Iraqi Border
Date: 18MAR03
Time: 1425L

We had arrived midafternoon to a no-name patch of land on the Iraqi border. Actually, we named it TAA Coyote and would soon rename it Joe Foss Field.

Marines from the supporting Marine Wing Support Squadron 272 had built the field. This squadron of exceptional Marines made up of engineers, logisticians, supply experts, and mechanics created a grated runway and some plywood shelters built by both the Marines and a handful of talented US Navy Seabees. They were thoughtful enough to bring several pallets of water and meals ready to eat (MREs). These are plastic-packaged meals that can survive decades inside their industrial plastic covers.

Blowing sand and endless miles of lifeless open desert became our reward for getting our unit halfway around the globe. I could tell the Ghost knew we were there. We had just repositioned eight Cobras, three Phrogs, and two Hueys from the USS *Saipan* to our temporary home.

We knew our mission and now prepared for the opening night of combat operations against Saddam Hussein's southernmost forces. Our mission appeared to be simple enough. We were to engage Iraqi reconnaissance units and positions located on Safwan Hill. We'd accomplish that mission, or at least attempt to, with the three Phrogs, the four Cobras, and a single command-and-control Huey.

We also had two additional sections of two Cobras with us at Joe Foss. Those two sections would strike Iraqi border posts—an amazing feat. Those helicopters, aircrew, and mechanics, only recently in North Carolina, were repositioned, fully fueled, armed, and ready for combat at Joe Foss Field. Not to mention we also had several large KC-130 Hercules aircraft positioned on Joe Foss. The detachment of KC-130s was a combination of active duty and reserve crews of the "Yankees" of Marine Aerial Refueler Transport Squadron 452 (VMGR 452), one of two Marine KC-130 squadrons assigned to the Marine Corps 4th MAW. At the time, we didn't truly understand why they'd landed there, but we would learn and appreciate their mission soon enough.

Though my focus remained on this mission, I also considered the achievement that was the twenty-seven attack and utility helicopters and our three hundred Marines brought halfway around the world on *Saipan*. But we now lived in another place, altogether different from the comfortable passageways, staterooms, gyms, and wardrooms of *Saipan*. We had little time for patting ourselves on the back or for reflection because the time had come for us to earn our place alongside the Marines from generations past.

We had moved Marines and machines ashore only a few short miles from the Iraqi border. Our opening night's missions brief called for two flights of HMLA 269 Cobras to hit key Iraqi border posts. We would follow that up with the five of our aircraft supporting the insertion of forces onto Safwan Hill. Other things were also happening outside of my view. These were plans and decisions made by colonels and generals. We—more accurately, Boomer and MAG 29—had been "chopped," an acronym meaning change of operational control, from the 2nd Marine Expeditionary Brigade to the 3rd MAW. The entire Marine force was being realigned.

That meant the Marine Corps had husbanded, or consolidated, all aviation assets under the 3rd MAW. This also allowed a single commander to be held both responsible and accountable for everything the Marine aviation did or failed to do. This was likely the intent of the I MEF commander. It simplified his chain of command

and removed potential friction points for his staff and planners. This was the epitome of unity of command.

At the Command and Staff College, we had read and discussed many of the great military failures in history. We'd also analyzed and dissected more modern military failures, such as Desert One, the failed rescue attempt of US hostages in Iran. The chaotic and ever-changing character of warfare often pits political short-sightedness and seemingly modern agendas against enduring realities. Many of those failures were often linked to dysfunctional command structures, where subordinate commanders had confusing or multilayered reporting chains and commanders. Not so here. From my perspective, we were purpose built, and we would succeed or fail as I MEF.

Back aboard *Saipan,* we had the remainder of the squadron preparing to support the MEF. We positioned our Huey utility helicopters to support the command-and-control missions of each infantry regiment, along with both Cobra and Huey crews briefing the close air support (CAS) mission, the reconnaissance mission, and the forward air controller (FAC) mission and gaming other scenarios to best support the ground commanders. This macro mission would begin on the morning of the 21st, when I MEF's ground combat element, consisting of the 1st MARDIV, the United Kingdom's 7th Armored Brigade, and Task Force Tarawa, would pour across the Iraqi border.

M1A1 Abrams' main battle tanks, armored Amphibious Assault Vehicles (AAVs), LAR units, 155mm howitzer cannons, and thousands of support vehicles would roll through those initial holes, or breech lanes, punched into the Iraqi border. Those units would have hundreds of Marine and coalition aircraft flying overhead. They would also have, as mentioned, one HMLA 269 Huey assigned to one or several ground combat units. I MEF had a total of four infantry regiments, all reinforced with armor, artillery, and other specialized units.

Our Hueys resembled a Swiss Army knife, capable of firing fourteen 2.75-inch rockets, and they carried one 7.62mm minigun as well as one .50 caliber heavy machine gun. Many of our pilots were also qualified as forward air controllers airborne (FAC[A]s).

That capability gave us yet another competitive advantage. It allowed our aircrews to become, when needed, an extension of the ground commander. We were trained to control fighter/attack aircraft, artillery, mortars, rockets, US Air Force (USAF) AC-130 Spectre gunships, and just about anything else that went boom!

The 7.62mm minigun was anything but a miniature gun. It was a six-barrel electric machine gun that fired up to six thousand rounds of 7.62mm or .308 rounds per minute. Originally designed by General Electric, they called it mini due to the larger variant, like my own M-197 20mm cannon, firing larger rounds. It was the first choice for our Huey crews for the close fight. Not so amazing was that the minigun was normally manned and fired by a young NCO. There is something so refreshing and yet so amazing that a nineteen- or twenty-year-old Marine crew chief could deliver US foreign policy with such volume and violence.

On the other side of the Huey, there was another weapons system, a living legend. This was the venerable .50 caliber M-2, a heavy machine gun. It was commonly referred to as the Ma Deuce, and I had experience with it as a 2nd lieutenant on the ranges of Quantico. Every Marine lieutenant could adjust the "headspace and timing," ensuring we could not only deploy but also employ the sixty-pound relic. In service since the end of the First World War, it was almost a throwback to black powder and muskets. It had earned its place in history from World War II, fighting effectively in every conflict. It was a .50 caliber round, and by 2003, it had rounds manufactured with a variety of warheads to include high explosives (HEs). In the hands of an experienced crew chief, the Huey could "reach out and touch someone" effectively at ranges of two thousand meters and could "spray and pray" out to ranges beyond three thousand meters.

We also had trained FAC(A)s, not just embedded in the Huey crews but embedded in every flight. We valued this capability as much or more than any other. We complemented the ground commander and their own FACs. Since nearly all ground maneuver units also had an embedded aviator or flight officer who served as a FAC, we could all speak the same aviation language.

That officer had specific training to control both helicopter and jet attack aircraft. The embedded ground FAC, with the support of motor, artillery, and rocket fire, would soon prove critical for the ground commander's aggressive and fast-moving maneuver warfare plans. It also meant that the ground FAC could, if the situation demanded, pass control of those assets to FAC(A)s, letting us best support the ground forces.

By the afternoon of the 20th, we had completed dozens of briefs, updates, and mission rehearsals prior to flying off *Saipan* and once ashore at Joe Foss. The constant threat and potential effects of Iraqi missiles became quite distracting and somewhat annoying. We had been fired upon about a dozen times, and it became tiresome. The Iraqis had likely fired the missiles ballistically, or without a radar or other tracking system. They fired them blindly in the direction of the MEF massed in Kuwait or in the direction of the Persian Gulf in hopes of inflicting casualties on one of the growing number of warships.

Every time the Iraqis fired a missile, a siren would warn us, and we would sprint into designated bomb shelters. In nearly all cases, US Army Patriot missile sites effectively engaged and destroyed the missiles. These Iraqi missiles were found later to have HE warheads, but we had been briefed they could be loaded with chemical payloads, not a good thing for morale.

The shelters were large cement pipes—drainage pipes—and by the afternoon of the 20th, we became sick of the drills. In hindsight, it seemed almost comical. The siren would wail. Marines would run to the shelters while trying to pull out their gas masks. The trail behind us was a yard sale of atropine packets, mask filters, lenses, and whatever else was in a gas mask case.

After several of these panic-infused sprints, we noticed a group of five or six already there and asleep as we ran in. After one of the events, once the "all clear" had sounded, I tapped one of the guys on the shoulder to see what they were doing. With a slight grin, he explained that for him and his buddies, they found it easier to simply sleep with the masks on in the bunker. Navy SEALs are certainly different.

The afternoon of the 20th was exactly the day we all hated. Blowing sands, a slow-setting sun, and no moon. Based on the lunar cycle, the moon would never rise, something we had planned for. We were all experienced night fighters, and the MEF had purposefully chosen dates with no moon. It created what was already predictably becoming a memorable night.

As I mentioned, besides the mission on Safwan Hill, the other two flights of Cobras planned to strike Iraqi border posts. We considered those missions equally important and equally challenging. So important were the targets that our squadron commander and another experienced flight lead planned to lead those two flights.

Two Cobras or any two aircraft flying together were called sections, and we called flights of four a division. We didn't normally fly as a single aircraft, minus our direct support Hueys. Our doctrine called for a minimum of two aircraft to conduct CAS and other HMLA missions. Having a wingman or having the mutual support of a lead and wingman made both aircraft more capable and more survivable. The two aircraft section composed our squadron's preferred formation and deployment scheme of choice.

Two aircraft can cover each other's backs when engaging targets, and that also allowed one cockpit to essentially navigate and communicate while the other could coordinate with artillery, other attack platforms, and the ground commander. Operating with four aircraft, or a division, could prove cumbersome, and with only eighteen Cobras and nine Hueys in the squadron, we could cover more ground units as sections. That didn't mean we didn't join up with other sections and operate as flights of four or more, but we specifically wrote the schedules for flights of two.

We were not the only game in town, and the larger plan called for Cobras from the other two HMLAs in the theater to strike similar border posts on the night of the 20th. Those squadrons, like others, had their crews staring into the same blank and lifeless face of a desert that we saw but from their base further south in Kuwait. No one knew how close we would come to meeting those same crews tonight.

CHAPTER 5

Location: Joe Foss Field, Kuwait
Date: 20MAR03
Time: 1700L

An almost unlimited number of considerations existed for this and any other combat mission. We often looked at problems based on their size, their scope, and their complexity, and this had them all. In addition, we had significant technical, physiological, and atmospheric concerns, along with mental and physical demands on the aircrew. NVGs and forward-looking infrared cameras (FLIRs), all of which we found essential to any night operation, particularly with reduced visibility, replaced our eyes at night.

NVGs and FLIRs buy the pilots and aircrew a slew of advantages, including situational awareness and targeting abilities, but they can't replace decision-making and flying skills. Imagine yourself trail running or biking as fast as you can. Now imagine doing that at night. This technology would allow you to not only see your route but also anticipate turns, obstacles, climbs, and descents. Now add a FLIR that can also see heat signatures. Your run could avoid both rocks and ledges but also avoid predators lurking in the cover of darkness or maybe identify a friendly armored vehicle.

Those same advanced technological capabilities in our helicopters were critical for takeoffs, seeing obstacles in flight, targeting, and landings. They were particularly important for Cobras and any aircraft tasked with an attack mission. We had spent hundreds of hours analyzing and identifying enemy and friendly armor, artillery, and fighting vehicles. This allowed us to, in a matter of seconds, quickly recognize and classify the target as friend or foe using FLIR.

It also ensured we employed the correct weapon for the appropriate target. We didn't want to use a Hellfire missile on a small truck or try to destroy a main battle tank with a single rocket.

Each of our flight leaders for this mission was capable, qualified, and vetted by the squadron commanders and then briefed to Boomer at MAG 29. Though no two leaders are the same, each flight lead and nearly every aircraft commander launching tonight had been through the Marine Corps' graduate-level aviation weapons course in Yuma, Arizona.

The Marine Aviation Weapons and Tactics Squadron One at Yuma, Arizona, hosted the seven-week-long Weapons and Tactics Instructor (WTI) course. This incorporated Marine Corps planning and implementation of advanced air and ground tactics to produce certified WTIs. Many often compared this to the US Navy's Strike Fighter Tactics Instructor program (TOPGUN) and the USAF Weapons School, which had many of the same goals. These goals included creating agile and creative thinkers, honing flight skills, improving flight leadership skills, and making those chosen few weapons experts.

Pilots don't limit their weapons expertise to a particular airframe, but that's where they'd start. The WTI also provided the squadron commander an expert on enemy weapons and tactics, which included their fixed-wing and rotary-wing capabilities, missile defense, electronic warfare, surface-to-air threats, and other communication and command-and-control capabilities. I had completed that course nearly ten years prior, but it fueled a lifelong learning process. The course gave us the basics, but we had the responsibility to study new threat weapons and tactics as well as refine how we lead and teach in the air.

Not much of that mattered that night because I remained focused on the present, doing it right, and doing as best I could in the moment. Whatever you want to call it, it was here. It was game day. Time for the rubber to meet the road. Prep time was over. Bottom line, there was no going back. With a slowly setting sun, we had gotten the call to launch early. It was not an ideal time, but we all made the short walk to our recently created flight line and to our helicopters, greeted, as always, by our crew chiefs and plane captains.

Plane captains and flight line mechanics are the lifeblood of any squadron. These are nineteen- and twenty-year-olds just out of high school and recently out of training. Unlike other services or fighter/attack jet squadrons, there are no pilot names painted on the side of our helicopter. Only the plane captain gets that honor.

They quickly opened doors and panels and removed tie-downs from our rotor blades. No one really talked, but we listened to our plane captains. They would tell us of anything they had seen or recently fixed, removed, tightened, or adjusted. Otherwise, we studied the weather, staring into the late afternoon sky. I wondered how we would execute an attached escort mission followed by a CAS mission. With the visibility maybe a quarter mile in blowing sand, there was no recognizable difference between the ground and the sky, absolutely no visible horizon.

I tried not to think too much about it as I put on my body armor, checked my pistol into my holster, secured my M4 carbine inside the rear cockpit, and found space for my gas mask. Yes, a gas mask. Some were even issued special gloves. Iraqi use of gas, not unprecedented, posed a real threat. I honestly was not sure how we would react to an Iraqi chemical or biological attack, but we had masks.

In hindsight, a chemical or biological strike on helicopters would have been devastating, catching us all unprepared. We were unlikely to be able to respond while flying. If the Iraqis fired chemical or biological rounds, it would kill us just as quickly and efficiently as any Marine on the ground. In our case, it would do so more expeditiously. This included more primitive choking agents. Since we couldn't simply take a knee to let the irritants' effects pass, we would be trapped in the cockpit with no way to get clean. It was a horrifying thought.

We completed the preflight as I ran through my mental checklist. We had completed a brief for the division, and I had briefed my section. *Had I briefed our flight in enough detail? Did we cover every logical branch or sequel? Would we have enough time, fuel, awareness, and luck to pull this off?* The time to second-guess had passed. It was time to put on a smile and time to climb in the cockpit, so I went in.

CHAPTER 6

Location: Joe Foss Field, Kuwait
Date: 20MAR03
Time: 1710L

I considered the cockpit of the Bell AH-1W Super Cobra my home, my office, and my dirty little pleasure. It was fifteen thousand pounds of rotor blades, radios, armor, engines, weapons, jet fuel, and that engineering "magic dust" that makes any helicopter fly. I find it almost hard to describe how comfortable I became in that machine. I recognized every sound and knew where every button, dial, switch, grip, trigger, push, pull, or twist knob and circuit breaker was located. It felt like my security blanket.

I sensed that no matter how desperate things became that night or in the hundreds of nights to follow, I sat with an old friend. An old friend who knew me, knew I was sometimes too confident, too arrogant, too stupid, or too scared to reason with but always believed in me. It's strange to say that someone loves a machine, but I loved that machine. I believed that if she carried me through just one more day, just one more night, just one more mission, I would simply be better. A better pilot, better leader, better thinker—just better.

I didn't need to spend time reminiscing or thinking about anything except getting Marines onto Safwan Hill and hitting our targets. That night had so many sharp angles and odd aspects that we could never have been expected to see the unforeseen. We counted on standard operating procedures (SOPs) and checklists that made certain we didn't miss any small detail that could potentially impact the mission. We had so many details to consider that we couldn't allow our brains to wander too far, and even during the debriefs that would ultimately follow from the missions, we'd have to strain to remember. It would all become a blur.

I focused on the little things in my own space while Matt did the same in the front. I started the checklist in my head as I strapped into my seat. I had run through the Cobra checklist so many times that the routine was now both calming and reassuring.

I started my mental checklist of helmets on, batteries, intercom system (ICS), anti-collision lights on, area's clear… What's the date? The 20th. Okay, starting the number two engine. Now I was ready.

I finally initiated the actual checklist by turning the batteries on. "Matt, ICS check?"

"Loud and clear," he quickly snapped.

I continued. "Helmets on, batteries on. Area's clear. Starting the number two engine."

Again, with the tandem seated attack helicopters, we only had voice inflection to show concern or pause. There were no nonverbals, no waving hands or eye contact. We each had our own tasks to complete, and we'd talk only when we hit portions of our checklists that needed a two-way confirmation. Or when he would read a "challenge" question, in which case I would either look, flip, or turn a switch to give the correct "response."

Any pause by me or Matt meant we were looking at something inside the cockpit, and it also meant "give me a second." Normally a second to look at a gauge or to wait for a pressure to register or a radio to come on. I had literally done thousands of engine starts and slowly got that comfortable or cocooning feeling you get once you finally close the canopy.

I picked my head up to see our plane captain, Lance Corporal Blanchard, signaling the number two engine was running as advertised. I continued to look outside past Lance Corporal Blanchard. As I gazed into a swirling dust cloud, I felt that familiar cramp in my stomach. A cramp telling me I was absorbing the enormity of the situation and, of course, the complete lack of a horizon.

The sun, while just a western hue, hung near the horizon but would soon set. We had all heard during our briefing that no moonlight would replace the sun because we had opted to attack in zero moon conditions to give our night vision the best advantage. I pulled my canopy shut and locked it. The sunlight seemed to dim slightly, and the sands and dust blew just a bit heavier.

"Matt, I'm going hot on the number one engine," I warned.

Matt had his head down. He was already activating the radios, navigation, and weapons systems. One of the many amazing things about flying Cobras is the sound of the engines and rotor system. The high-pitched whine of two 1,690 horsepower turbine engines is unique. Both the engines were sitting only a foot from my head, so I knew the sound well.

I glanced to my right to see Lance Corporal Blanchard looking at me, and I gave him the signal that I was starting the number one engine. First, I heard the turbines spin. Then, the igniters clicked as I twisted the throttles. The nozzles inside the engine's combustion chamber sprayed in fuel, and then I heard the baritone sound of fuel catching the spark of the igniters as the jet engine slowly came to life. It was a sweet sound. I watched the engine temperatures and oil pressures rise, and I continued to run the throttles up to full, where they would remain for the next few hours.

Almost as fast as the first engine started, the blades began to spin. I found comfort in the unmistakable sound of the massive main rotor blades. I looked up and saw them slowly, begrudgingly move and gradually increase in speed as I listened.

Thump. Thump. Thump.

The sound is a bit more nuanced but only to those who have been around Cobras for a while. The first pass of the main rotor sounds like someone swinging a broom too close to your ear, more of a whoosh. It graduates to the deeper sound—perhaps of a big truck passing you on the highway. At that moment, I could almost feel the enormous down forces created by the rotors. As I ran the throttles of both motors to full, the main rotors were at 100 percent, and they settled into a nice, steady two-per-full-revolution beat. A truly magical sound.

That sound would only get stronger and healthier once we took to the sky. It wasn't until the Cobras were under the stress of a full load of fuel, weapons, and the crew with me "pulling" every ounce of the engine's power that one could really appreciate the authority and dominance it represented. It is an unmistakably delicious sound, a favorite dish best served flying low at 140 knots.

Whooop. Whooop. Whooop.

It is both a fantastic and a terrifying sound. It would become music to any Marine's ear while simultaneously chiming the opening note to a death ballad for our enemies, its first, often faint, note announcing impending death and their inevitable fade to black.

To hear both engines, watch the turning rotor blades, and see a thumbs up from Blanchard made me happy. Maybe too simple an emotion, but simple and predictable is what I needed. The aircraft was operating as advertised. It was fully mission capable. The plane captains and all the ground crews had worked to make it perfect. No excuses now. The forty-eight feet of rotor blades continued to spit dust and grit into everyone around the Cobra, including our plane captain, who maintained his thumbs up.

Next up, the ordnance teams. Matt and I raised our hands to show we didn't have our fingers on anything. A promise to not pull a trigger or accidentally launch a missile. Ordnance ran under the rotor arc and went to work.

In that particular case, they attached the electrical plug or wire to provide electricity for the 20mm cannon; removed safety pins from our rocket pods; armed both the tube-launched, optically tracked, wire-guided (TOW) and Hellfire missiles; and did the same to our defensive flares and chaff. The science behind all of it made sense. I had programmed my flare and chaff dispenser myself, but of all the systems on the Cobra, that is the one where we simply pressed the "I believe" button.

Before long, the ordnance teams climbed out from underneath our Cobra, then moved quickly over to Buss and did the same for him and Rosie. We'd soon launch.

CHAPTER 7

Location: Joe Foss Field
Date: 20MAR03
Time: 1745L

The Marines built TAA Coyote and quickly named it after famed World War II Marine Corps aviator Joe Foss. Captain Joe Foss, who had downed twenty-six Japanese aircraft in the Pacific, had received the Medal of Honor for his heroic flying at Guadalcanal. He had died just a month earlier in January. Another legend lost but not forgotten.

We lifted out of Joe Foss Field in the most non-standard aviation takeoff and rendezvous I could recall. We had executed a maximum performance takeoff where every helicopter strained to get airborne. Pilots used every single bit of their skills while pushing their aircraft to their performance limits. It was similar to a carrier launch, but instead of a jet aircraft catapulting down a flight deck, we flew straight up, hoping to climb out of the dust—much less preferred to a standard "running takeoff" we'd normally use if we had a runway or additional space or clear visibility.

As for my aircraft, tactical callsign Marjo 43, things were far from simple and anything but calm. I had been hellbent on getting airborne and getting these pregame jitters flushed out of my system, but the Ghost had other ideas. As each aircraft had lifted off ahead of me, it had added more sand and debris into the air. I had assumed the weather would improve once we got out of Joe Foss Field, but the winds created a thick brown haze that was getting progressively denser. It was packed with more debris along with thousands of pounds of sand.

A running takeoff allowed the helicopter to use the rotors to create lift as a cushion of air formed underneath the rotor blades similar to the way a plane uses a wing and forward motion on takeoff. That cushion formed and allowed the helicopter to gain airspeed, all reducing the amount of power needed. A nearly straight-up liftoff increased the need for power and could put the crews in danger should they lose one of the two engines.

Lastly, we executed an instrument takeoff. This meant I had to rely on my instruments, and Matt, to tell me our altitude, heading, and speed while he saw nothing except the sand outside. That's the nature of the Ghost. She didn't wait for a specific opportunity; she used every opportunity. She fought against us simply trying to take off.

I kept adding power and listened as Matt called out headings and altitudes. He had picked out a few outside references through his FLIR. The top of our manmade tsunami of dust and debris reached about seventy feet, and above that rested a run-of-the-mill sandstorm.

Chatter filled the radio frequencies as each helicopter called out headings and altitudes and each crew searched for their lead or wingman. As soon as we emerged from the "brownout" of the takeoff, I noticed another Bell AH-1W Cobra about two hundred meters in front of me.

I keyed the radio. "Marjo 42, call altitude and heading?"

Marjo 42, AH-1W Cobra, was flown by Captain Mike "Flash" Richman. He piloted the number two helicopter, or dash two of the flight of four. Marjo was an odd callsign, but every aircraft flight in the theater was assigned a specific one that changed daily. We had been assigned "Marjo" as the mission tactical callsign. So, our four Cobras were Marjo 41, Marjo 42, Marjo 43 (me and Matt), and Marjo 44.

Flash responded curtly. "We are three hundred feet, 120 knots, headed 340."

"Four-three copies." That was all I needed to say.

"I got 41 and 42 left at eleven o'clock, level," Matt said.

Matt and I used an ICS and didn't need to press any switch to talk to each other. Our ICS was voice activated, so once I began to speak, he would hear me. The ICS would also transmit coughs, "oh shits," and anything mumbled, shouted, or muttered.

Matt's call that 41 and 42 were in sight was a good start. It provided me with some relief. My focus immediately turned to my wingman. As I looked over my right shoulder, I spotted him. And damned if my wingman, Buss, wasn't tucked into what we call the parade position.

How the hell did he get there so fast?

I quickly made a mental note to ask him later—if we survived for a later. He flew about fifty feet away and mimicked all my moves by using physical checkpoints on my helicopter, such as the pylons that held our rockets and missiles, to keep him at a safe distance and altitude.

We hadn't exactly executed what we had briefed and rehearsed over the past weeks. Whether we had audibled, flexed, improvised, or adapted, it only contributed to overall confusion or fog of war.

Circa 2001, the Marine Corps had invested quite a bit of time and effort to educate me at the Command and Staff College in Quantico, Virginia. Professors such as Dr. Jack "Blackjack" Matthews, lieutenant colonel, USMC (ret.), had assigned the readings of some of the world's greatest military minds. They included Carl von Clausewitz, Sun Tzu, Thucydides, T.E. Lawrence, and Antoine-Henri Jomini, among others.

Blackjack was a good Catholic from his hometown of Troy, New York. With a twisted sense of humor, an infectious laugh, and a legendary past, he always gave more than he took. A two-sport athlete at the University of Notre Dame, he was commissioned a lieutenant in the Marine Corps in the 1960s. He served remarkably throughout the next two decades. As a young lieutenant platoon commander, he was severely wounded in Vietnam and later commanded a battalion of the 2nd Marine Division in Beirut.

Blackjack was unapologetic and demanding yet empathetic. He was the single most influential educator I ever had, a title he likely didn't recognize or accept. He not only forced us all to read, think, and write critically, but he also implored us, demanded of us, to lead and care for Marines with a sense of purpose.

Even with Blackjack's influence, I had read or, more accurately, skimmed the writings of the mystical Sun Tzu and remembered he had said something like, "Let your plans be dark and impenetrable as the night." Well, we got that right. He continued with, "Fall like a thunderbolt," which was a fitting possibility during that flight. I thought about adding our own addendum to *The Art of War*: "Enter like the lightning and exit like the carnival" or "blow in with the strength of the western wind and then let chaos push you to find any exit you can." Just a thought.

I knew our plan well and knew that, within minutes, we'd cross over the Iraqi border. We had designed a simple escort scheme of the transports followed by engagement of a preplanned target and then a switch of roles into CAS. The CAS role to our 1st Force Reconnaissance, or simply Force Recon, Marines had more than a few critical aspects to keep in mind; execution would be everything. However, no one involved in the planning had anticipated the weather.

We had excellent flight leadership and well-trained crews, but the low visibility challenged the most experienced among us. An abyss does not adequately describe that night. The Ghost had created a black hole that threatened to swallow us as we accelerated into its depth at 120 knots and four hundred feet above the desert floor.

As each of the four Cobras slowly ascended into the darkness, we found no horizon, and the fun had only begun. I strained to see everything and anything in front of me.

How is it still daytime?

The visibility had decreased and was best guessed at less than a quarter mile in the blowing sand with no difference between the desert floor and the sky. That quarter mile gave little comfort at the speed we traveled. To the credit of the flight leads and the aircrew, all seven helicopters, plus the additional command-and-control Huey, had taken off one at a time. That Huey had turned to the north and would eventually establish an orbit near the Kuwaiti-Iraqi border.

The Huey crew was led by the aircraft commander, Captain Andy Dyer, and his copilot, Captain Len Walker. Inside the Huey was the mission commander, Lieutenant Colonel Darrell Thacker, one of Boomer's several talented bench players, and two crew chiefs.

"Marjo flight, check in," came through on my number one radio.

That call required us to reply, in order, with our status. I waited my turn as the number three. I was ready to call Marjo 43 "up." After I chimed in, Buss, Marjo 44, would do the same. Buss held the number four spot of the flight of four Cobras.

Marjo 41 was tonight's flight leader, Major Brian "Howdy" Kennedy. He led our Cobra flight while Flash, Marjo 42, served as his wingman.

I keyed my radio. "Four-three's up."

Immediately after, Buss spoke. "Four-four's up."

As we finally maneuvered into position, the formation accelerated toward the Iraqi border only three minutes after launch. The radio chatter had quieted, and the helicopters flew in formation, offering the illusion of calm.

The Cobra, fully loaded with fuel and ordnance, weighed about fifteen thousand pounds. Bell Helicopter had built an amazingly capable attack helicopter. The AH-1W Super Cobra, its official name, had served the Marine Corps since the mid-1980s. Over the past several decades, designers had installed numerous upgrades to enhance its ability to fight at night.

That night, it carried four TOW missiles, four Hellfire laser-guided missiles, a three-barrel 20mm cannon with six hundred rounds of ammunition, and thirty-eight unguided rockets. We carried the ability, on cue, to unleash our version of hell.

The Cobra furnished quite a bit of maneuverability. That maneuverability came at a cost—an unstable platform. A stable platform would be important for reducing our workload, particularly during critical phases of flight such as taking off and landing and, in some cases, when firing on target from a one-hundred-foot or two-hundred-foot hover.

Some other attack helicopters had a more advanced stability control system, which allowed near hands-off hovering. Not in the Cobra. You could *try* hands-off hovering in a Cobra—good luck with that. Stability aside, I relished its speed, loved its reliability, and, most importantly, it was mine. We had no ejection seats, no parachutes, no autopilot or automated systems to improve stability. It was only as stable and capable as the crew flying it.

The Cobra required a crew of two, both qualified pilots, with the pilot in the rear seat doing most of the flying and talking while the front seat's copilot did more of the shooting and navigating. I would spend most of my time in the back seat. I believed it gave me the most situational awareness and, therefore, left me better positioned to make decisions for the flight. Plus, I trusted Matt with identifying and engaging targets, something not all aircraft commanders did.

The two General Electric turbine engines produced 1,690 shaft horsepower each. That's more than enough horsepower to hurl the Cobra to speeds of nearly 160 knots, but the transmission limited that effectiveness. The transmission could only handle about half of the engine's power or torque. So, 100 percent power meant the transmission operated at its maximum performance, and adding more or pulling more power would over-torque the transmission. This not only sounds bad—it *is* bad.

Although airborne and anything but pretty, we had at least made it up and were flying. I strained to view Buss but could see Flash flying the second Cobra, which served as my primary reference point in the formation.

I considered my wingman, Buss, an unexpected gift. A Boston native and an avid rugby player, Captain John "Buss" Barranco had graduated from Annapolis with a degree in history but possessed the insights of an engineer. He had proudly graduated from the academy fifth in his class….in demerits. Buss flew as one of several aircrew on loan from the Marines Corps' aviation weapons school. The loaned instructor pilots and aircrew had all joined us after we had arrived in theater, and we'd sprinkled them throughout the unit.

Buss brought experience, expertise, the latest tactics and techniques, and, most importantly, an unbreakable and positive attitude. His disposition and problem-solving mindset would serve our flight well over the next several weeks and through some of the most challenging days and nights that lay ahead.

As Buss flew onto my wing, a position about fifty feet to my right side and about ten feet above my rotors, I still struggled to keep the lead section of Cobras in focus and at the proper distance. In front of them, somewhere in the dust and dark, flew the three Boeing CH-46E Sea Knights. As I mentioned previously, these are sometimes nicknamed Phrogs. Don't ask me why. It's only known to the secret society of Frog or Phrog crews. The military loves their nicknames and their secrets, and the equipment of war holds that same lore. Those helicopters had served as the backbone of Marine aviation for the past forty years with the mission of the venerable transport helicopter. They carried everything the Marine Corps asked them to, which included the most valued commodity of all—United States Marines.

In service since the 1960s, they had served in Vietnam, Grenada, Desert Storm, Somalia, and every place where Marines operated. The Phrogs required a crew of two pilots and two crew chiefs and carried two defensive .50 caliber heavy machine guns. Their storied history and legacy were going to be put to the test tonight. Carrying a squad of combat-laden Marines, they were charged with inserting the "eyes and ears" of I MEF—or so they thought.

CHAPTER 8

Location: 8 Miles from Safwan Hill, Iraq
Date: 20MAR03
Time: 1750L

You hear about the fog of war. The friction and chaos that define it. But sometimes it's only a series of events that, when linked together, create a situation ripe for tragedy or failure. We had analyzed the situation, seen the risks, recognized the obvious dangers, and then ignored them all as we flew off into a moonless, ruthless, and unforgiving sky. Our nation depended upon it. Our jobs demanded it.

We had launched into a fifty-year sandstorm at the absolute worst time—as if there were a good time. We had little visibility in the period before sunset, but that really didn't matter since we had no sun either. Twenty-mile-per-hour winds create their own weather, and the sun was blocked by dust and debris that had been thrown into the air. Yet it remained too bright for night vision to aid us. As the sun set and no moon rose, we saw no city lights and no roads and had no options. The only thing we did have was a time on target.

Eight crews had all scrambled to their aircraft. Eight crews all prepared to fly into the unknown. Eight helicopters that included three Phrogs to transport boots on the ground, four Cobra attack helicopters that would act as both the armed escort and CAS, and a single Huey utility helicopter serving as the command-and-control aircraft.

The first two transport helicopters carried Marines but not just any Marines. They were all hand-picked from the elite 1st Force Reconnaissance Company. They carried the burden of being the

I MEF commander's "eyes and ears" for all Marine forces moving toward the Iraqi border as well as some of the first US forces into Iraq.

The third CH-46E transport helicopter would provide casualty evacuation (CASEVAC) should we need it. The CASEVAC mission was designed to get injured or wounded Marines to medical help as quickly as possible. This would be crucial in the months ahead. Getting wounded Marines to care—and fast—was not only an imperative but an unwritten covenant between those that fly and those whom we support. The ground combat units all knew that we would do everything possible to ensure their survival, and CASEVAC was one of those lifelines.

Having a single CASEVAC was a nice gesture; having more would have been too risky based on the weather and number of helicopters already flying. I thought about whether we needed it. Should we need it? If we did, that single CH-46E helicopter would be totally inadequate for the mission. If we had a midair collision or one of us flew into the desert, one helicopter wouldn't be able to answer the call. We would need a couple of garbage trucks and half a dozen helicopters to pick up the pieces. That helicopter really served to assist should one aircraft have a mechanical issue or if our 1st Force Recon Marines became injured or wounded.

While both of those realistic possibilities could happen, the most likely event we considered involved one or more of us either flying into each other or into the ground. Both scenarios would create a catastrophic event, and our CASEVAC CH-46E or Phrog would do little more than record and recall our tragic demise, then pass those observations to investigators. The actual mission concerned me more than those potential circumstances.

Once airborne, I stared outside of my canopy and looked directly at the reality of the weather, considered the complexity, and finally gave the yet unseen enemy a mild consideration. When does confidence become cockiness? When does cockiness combined with some luck become arrogance? All are the seeds of destruction. They eventually write their own epitaphs. Epitaphs written on the grave of the countless.

Why was my mind seeing this as a potential mission impossible?

My brain quickly snapped back to the present. I talked into my mic. "Matt, where are the 46s?"

"No clue. I'm trying to find Howdy and Flash on the FLIR." Matt peered into the FLIR, again asking technology to help pilots see things the naked eye couldn't.

The FLIR sees heat. If it's warm, it shows a lifelike scene with everything warm in white and the cold background in black. It sees the friction of warm wheels. It sees hot barrels from a tank or the cold barrel of an unmanned artillery piece and can tell if the AK-47 in a person's hands is hot from being fired. It's one of the great advantages of night flying. Matt was now searching the horizon for the Phrogs and their distinct heat signature—without luck.

That concerned me. I wanted to link up with the two lead Cobras, find the Phrogs, and turn to the target. The more we remained scattered, the more we created uncertainty in our position—uncertainty that might affect mission success or cause a collision.

I conducted a visual scan of the cockpit, looking at every engine, oil, hydraulics, and electrical readout. My eyes darted rapidly from one gauge to another. I supported my primary scan through my heads-up display (HUD), a useful device that helped pilots keep their head looking up and forward. I saw that we maintained the right heading. Going in the right direction seemed the most basic task, but we had to start somewhere.

I knew my impatience was beginning to wear on me. I was tired. Everyone was. The Ghost fatigued me as well, but I had mostly put her behind me. That didn't mean she had gone away, rather that she hid in the shadows for a moment. Focus. I simply had to focus. I needed to compartmentalize and only think about the task at hand. Easy, right?

My HUD showed eight nautical miles to the next checkpoint. Or was that to the target?

"Matt, what's the next checkpoint?" I queried.

"It's the holding point," he replied.

"Copy."

Had I just said eight miles? Had I been humming that part of the Eminem song "Lose Yourself"? "If you had one shot, or one opportunity, to seize everything you ever wanted?"

I could see nothing in front of me except the faint silhouette of the number two Cobra flown by Flash and his copilot Captain Sam "Country" Meyer.

I am so tired of this shit, and we have just started.

We flew at three hundred feet. We couldn't see more than a quarter of a mile in front of us, we could barely see the desert floor, and we certainly couldn't see the sky or horizon.

CHAPTER 9

Location: Holding Pattern South of the Iraqi Border
Date: 20MAR03
Time: 1810L

"Marjo 41's turning left at 120 knots and three hundred feet. I have eyes on both of them," Matt said.

Fortune put Captain Matt Ziegler, a Penn State graduate, as my front seat pilot. He had come to the squadron a few years earlier, with *Operation Iraqi Freedom* being his first deployment. We had been crewed together since sailing from North Carolina. We called that practice combat crews and combat sections. The crews and sections didn't change, and you flew with the same pilot or copilot and same wingman or lead for the entire deployment. That concept fostered teamwork and camaraderie while matching strengths and weaknesses. The intent was to build and refine a more combat-effective cockpit and section. In our case, it worked better than any of us could have imagined.

Matt was dialed in mentally and focused on our mission. He worked hard looking through both his NVGs and the FLIR. He also tracked our movement via the GPS and compared it with the thirty-year-old maps we had been issued.

Matt moved the FLIR camera with an actuator, more like a metal joystick, with his right hand. He used a toggle switch, located on a pistol type grip for his left hand, to increase or decrease magnification of the camera. That same pistol grip had a trigger for firing the laser, the 20mm cannon, and the TOW and Hellfire missiles. Tonight, the FLIR let him scan the desert for the enemy and obstacles. He would routinely lock the camera onto one of the two Cobras in front of us. It would impose a symbol in my HUD to orient me to their location. It not only provided a good way to maintain awareness but, more importantly, it helped to prevent a midair collision. Our strict attention plus constant discussion with Matt and Buss were required to stay oriented and remain one step ahead of the Ghost. Even though six other helicopters surrounded us, and we had more than enough radio chatter, we seemed alone.

But misery does love company, and fortunately, we had plenty of that. Just ahead, maybe seventy-five yards in front of Howdy, flew those three Phrogs. They intended to add another notch to their war chest or stick or whatever. These Phrogs and their crews were, once again, carrying Marines into battle. The 1st Force Reconnaissance Marines would be some of the first ground forces to cross the border. The high-pitched sound of the Phrog engines combined with the low guttural thuds of the Cobras' main rotor blades would announce their arrival. And not only the arrival of their unit but also the sixty thousand Marines assigned to I MEF who had arrived in the Kuwaiti desert from camps, bases, and stations across the globe.

The 1st MARDIV commander had assigned Force Recon the mission on Safwan Hill. That hill, at about 450 feet high, was the tallest terrain feature in southern Iraq and was the location where Iraqi forces had surrendered to the coalition following Desert Storm in 1991. The 1st MARDIV planners believed the Force Recon Marines would provide critical eyes and ears for the commanders of the entire attacking MEF as well as report on the movements and intent of the Iraqi Army. More critical was ensuring Marine forces could identify and engage Iraqi artillery. If any of the Marine units became trapped in the breach lanes and were spotted, enemy artillery could be devastating.

Force Recon Marines need no introduction. Their storied history and combat accomplishments are those of legend. They are not normal Marines—not to say that any of us are normal, but they are not the spit shine, starched blouse, polished brass, "Yes, sir. No, sir. Three bags full, sir" type. Instead, they prefer to work under the radar, keeping to themselves. They operate at their best when told what to do but not how to do it—mission type orders. Recon, short for reconnaissance, describes a typical mission for them. Yet, many times, they are called for deep reconnaissance and less conventional operations. They are dropped from aircraft to parachute behind enemy lines or told to swim behind enemy lines to execute their mission. This also implies the type of work where they must be prepared to fight their way back out. Their training includes airborne, dive, sniper, explosives, observation, and other specialized skills that I could only guess at. I generally avoided them.

There we hovered in time. Holding and waiting. Waiting and holding. We had decided to keep the FLIR locked on Flash, and I would keep a steady platform for Buss. The darkness remained, the wind never let up, and the sand kept blowing away any chance for a visible horizon. Yet we were prepared to execute this mission. We didn't know it then, but we had already learned to adapt. We had already found a new normal in this strangest of situations.

We slowly settled into a rhythm—or were at least able to maintain our formation. We considered that formation a "loose cruise" with an established holding pattern and a distance between aircraft of 150 to two hundred feet. I had begun to appreciate the relative calm and simple act of flying straight and level. Holding in nice lazy left-hand turns soon gave way to thinking about other things. I had enough time to think about my situation and my abject loathing of that desert. I couldn't see the ground and couldn't recognize the sky. I just had to visualize both.

Occasionally, the blue strip lights, which were actually green, could be seen on the side of Flash's Cobra. Aviation engineers had designed these two-foot-long strips of lights drilled into several places on every Marine helicopter so that aircrew, using NVGs, could see them. They were also called NVG compatible lighting, meaning you couldn't see them with the naked eye but could see them wearing NVGs. Genius! They mainly installed them to help prevent midair collisions. During "normal" night operations, the lights helped orient other pilots to their lead or wingman's heading and altitude. Unfortunately, we weren't wearing NVGs yet. The sun had dipped below the horizon but had not yet fully set. Technically, we were still flying in the daytime.

Aircraft lighting was very important, but right now, it was nearly useless. The lights provided little value until you were nearly on top of the other aircraft. In front of me, I would catch a slight glimpse of the blue lights or the outline of another helicopter. In several turns, we could see what looked like the shadows of the Phrogs just outside of our periphery. The blue lights would provide an occasional silhouette of a helicopter or an otherwise translucent shape. Eerie.

Ghosts terrorize the living. It's what they do; it's why they exist. My brain began to conflate the two shapes. A barely visible aberration once again put a feeling of dread deep into my head. A fear, a debilitating sense of anxiety, was building again.

I had seen those Ghosts before and had tried, like any ten-year-old, to hide beneath my covers, but not anymore. It was time to stare them down. Tonight was yet another test. My Ghosts had names like Mojave, Guban, Puntland, Sahara, and now Arabian. I knew this Ghost had the advantage and thought little of me or my capabilities. She respected no one, so tonight, I knew I needed to trick her. I had to.

I fought to keep my brain from wandering aimlessly and made myself continuously scan the instruments and HUD. One tries not to think too far ahead during a flight like this. I wasn't sure who I was kidding, since I had never flown a mission quite like this, but I tried to simplify the flight by focusing on each small task.

I glanced at Flash, and suddenly, the picture was all wrong. Why was his nose pitching up? I paused and wondered, *What the hell is happening to me?* I had never seen this picture before. No recognition of the situation. I sat there, suspended in disbelief.

Immediately, the ICS barked, snapping me back into reality. "Power, power, power!"

I felt Matt heave back on the stick. The nose of my Cobra pitched up from what was at least a 15-degree nose-down dive. Flash hadn't climbed. Our Cobra had dived down, and Matt had pulled us out of a dive. I pulled back on the stick with Matt, and we climbed back to three hundred feet. I said nothing because there was nothing to say.

My internal monologue simplified our situation. *Don't fly into Flash or Howdy, be a better lead for Buss, and stop trying to fly ourselves into the desert.* I had to make keeping the Cobra safely airborne priority number one.

Battling the debilitating effects of spatial disorientation was closely tied to priority number one. Pilots commonly experience spatial disorientation, much like vertigo, when first learning to fly. It's especially dangerous in bad weather or at night when only using instruments to fly. We call that type of disorientation "the leans" because those in the aircraft feel like they're leaning or spinning while attempting to fly. The best remedy to overcome that requires focus on the aircraft instruments, such as looking at the HUD and believing what the instruments are indicating. Good luck with that.

"Marjo, flight goggle," came the call from Howdy.

That instructed us all to now make the switch to fly with night vision. I was happy to try something new but continued fighting disorientation.

"Matt, I'm goggled, but it's not much better." I paused long enough for a response that never came.

Within a few seconds, the entire flight had put on their NVGs. They were attached to the helmet by a mount on the front of our flight helmets and then rotated down. The NVGs sat about an inch in front of our eyes. I had been putting them up and down for a half hour, convinced that my NVGs had run low on battery power or I'd simply drawn a bad pair. I had logged hundreds of hours flying on NVGs and hundreds more flying solely on my instruments. All of that experience was somehow failing to translate when I needed it most.

I remembered Boomer, our air group commander, asking me what we needed as we flew off *Saipan*. Man, did I ever have an answer now. Yeah, I knew exactly what I should have said. "Hey, sir, can you get me a full can of situational awareness, one case of pull my head out of my ass, a double order of basic air work, and three packages of shit luck?"

After my recent attempt to kill us both, I didn't exactly need to confess my struggles to Matt. Since he worked hard on the map and the FLIR and was also fighting the environment, better that I suffer a bit longer in silence.

The always calm and collected Matt. He continued to work and talk as though nothing dramatic had happened. I was now refocused on my HUD, doing my best to keep Flash in sight and us out of the dirt. That near fatal nosedive resulted in the first real test for this combat crew and combat section and would make for our first notable team building exercise—but certainly not the last.

Location: Udari Range, Kuwait
Date: 16MAR03
Time: 2245L

The Cobra has the copilot or gunner in the front seat and the aircraft commander flying the mission from the rear seat. That's called a tandem seating arrangement. You can't see each other, and all communication happens via our ICS with tone and inflection often saying more than merely words. Effective communication in this cockpit configuration was critical.

We had begun to refine our teamwork during several tedious night flights into the Kuwaiti air-to-ground training ranges. It required two people, at times doing completely different tasks but still acting as a single crew. We had flown onto the range at night although we weren't familiar with it. Sounds about right.

"Matt, do you have any idea where we are?" I asked.

He countered, "No, sir. Do you?"

Matt had politely told me to stay in my lane. It was obvious he was navigating with both the map and GPS, and I was only as good as his ability to operate the GPS or orient to a map. On this night, we were shooting rockets and guns on a training range, a meat and potatoes mission. A mission designed to exercise both the aircraft systems and our ability to function as a crew.

After some discussion with Buss and Rosie, we found our way onto the range. "Matt, nice job getting us here."

Nothing from Matt except the *click, click* sound that came from his tapping on the ICS.

Another not-so-subtle dig. The double tap on the foot switch or ICS was a convenient way of telling the other pilot or wingman that you understand.

In this specific case, Matt's *click, click* likely said, "Piss off, Major."

This was followed by finding the old tank hulks and maneuvering the flight to engage them. After checking our run-in or final attack heading, I called, "Leads in hot, left pull."

Buss responded, "Two."

I pushed the master arm to arm and squeezed.

Whoosh.

The first rocket impacted two hundred meters long. I quickly adjusted and fired two more in rapid succession.

Whoosh. Whoosh.

One hundred meters short and then seventy-five meters short.

From the front seat came, "Sir, that's some excellent shooting."

Matt then opened up with the gun from four hundred meters. With the first rounds skipping off the tank, he held the trigger down as we started our pull-off to the left. Matt kept the trigger down as the gun fired nearly 90 degrees off the axis of the Cobra…fifty, seventy-five, one hundred, one hundred and fifty rounds, all sparking and skipping off the lone tank hulk.

I could only muster, "Damn, that was really good shooting."

I didn't say anything else. Matt knew he had just won this combat crew shooting match. It wouldn't be the last, but he knew from the tone in my voice the accolades were real.

Location: South of Safwan Hill, Iraq
Date: 20MAR03
Time: 1815L

"Matt, you good up there?" I asked, knowing full well he had just prevented a disaster. I could feel the same sense of dread building as fast as my confidence was running for the exits.

Matt responded with a double click on his foot switch. That simple act was a welcome sound. It meant that he was good, we were good, and he was focused.

That nonverbal was followed by, "I've got Flash back locked in on FLIR."

Just like that, we were back on our game. I continued to struggle to keep Flash in sight, but we kept up a continuous dialogue of what we observed and what we didn't.

At that moment, I truly didn't know how much Matt suspected of my struggles to keep Flash in sight. If he did notice, he didn't let it faze him—or, at least, didn't let me know that. His voice expressed a river of coolness, almost saying without saying, "Hey, Major, any problems back there? You good, Mr. Three-Thousand-Hour Weapons and Tactics Instructor?"

While he had the FLIR to help him maintain awareness, I had the HUD, and we both had NVGs. The HUD helped and provided key performance indicators of the Cobra that included speed, altitude, heading, and other communication, weapons, and navigation data. Even with that information, I struggled to process the data and keep an eye on both aircraft in front of me as well as my wingman.

We had just come out of another left-hand turn when the radio crackled with our final time on target (TOT). The TOT is the time we are expected to be on target and positioned to engage enemy positions. It's often the other actions occurring either simultaneously or in sequence that make TOTs so important. To the attack helicopter community, and frankly any attack aviation unit, being on time and then on target with your weapons is one of the marks of a well-led, well-trained, and professional unit.

Often, there would be suppressive fires coordinated to arrive just ahead of a TOT to protect attacking aircraft. There were also coordinated fires designed to cover our exit from the target. If you arrived too early at the target, that was bad. If you arrived too late to the target, that was bad too. Developing a reputation for not making TOTs could force ground controllers to have you attack without any suppression, and that was really bad.

The updated TOT from Howdy caused us to roll out of the turn, separate from the flight of Phrogs, and head into the target area.

The Phrog lead, callsign Scooter, announced, "We are coming left and going to establish an orbit."

Scooter kept in his left-hand turn to the south, and the four Cobras rolled out heading north.

We flew in a formation called echelon right, an uncommon formation. It put all our firepower facing toward the north or toward the enemy. It also allowed me to better see both Howdy and Flash while somehow feeling like I could see Buss's shadow off my right shoulder.

We expected two flights of Marine F/A-18 Hornets and AV-8B Harriers to drop bombs on top of Safwan Hill within the next five minutes. Mission planners considered them to be the symbolic battering ram, and we would flow in right behind them. I was beginning to wonder where our Hornets and Harriers were when a flash of movement caught my eye.

Right under Howdy's nose were two Cobras. Only they were one hundred feet below him and 180 degrees out—heading right toward us.

Where the hell are they coming from?

As I began to key the mic to ask Matt if he had the traffic in sight, I noticed off to our right, about a hundred feet below us, another flight of two Cobras and what looked like a Huey.

Matt quickly called the interlopers. "I got the three on the right. I don't see the others."

Son of a bitch. What the hell is going on?

I immediately sensed a midair collision at closing speeds in excess of three hundred miles per hour.

CHAPTER 10

Location: Holding 3 Miles South of the Iraqi Border
Date: 20MAR03
Time: 1822L

I spoke quickly. "Matt, where the hell did those Cobras come from?"

"No clue. They have to be west coast guys," he replied.

More specifically, why are they here on our route? I thought.

Things are tough enough without looking for more ways to kill ourselves. They presented a midair threat, a collision waiting to happen, friendly on friendly, any pilot's worst nightmare. It only added to the collective fog and friction.

We had seen them, only seconds apart, pass right underneath us. Were they that clueless? Didn't they get the brief? Why their flight path mimicked ours but 180 degrees in the opposite direction remained a mystery, but considering the weather, I suspected they were just happy to be off target and heading back south to their base in Kuwait.

I needed more clarity and called Howdy and Flash. "Four-one, you see those guys? Any clue who they are, and are there any more?"

Howdy and Flash remained as in the dark as me.

Marjo 41 came back. "Not sure, but we counted two flights of two or three. I think the 267 guys hitting border posts."

They couldn't be our other 269 Cobras since those crews had launched at nearly the same time as us. Or was it them? Did they get turned around by the weather and now looked for Joe Foss?

They could not have been our Cobras since we didn't hear them on any of our radio frequencies, but we still found the entire event unnerving. They most likely belonged to Colonel Rick "Shooter" Spencer, a former HMLA 269 CO and now the commander of MAG 39. MAG 39 was another Marine helicopter air group based out of Camp Pendleton, California, but now stationed in Kuwait. That must have been it, our "brothers from another mother," the west coast guys hitting their border posts. Not so unique.

However, their stateside locations made MAG 29 and MAG 39 uncommon in the Marine Corps. Both the North Carolina and the California-based air stations maintained a common proximity to their "customers" or infantry and other Marine units. Marine Corps Air Station New River sat just across the New River from Camp Lejeune, North Carolina, and Marine Corps Air Station Camp Pendleton was located inside the massive Camp Pendleton complex in southern California.

That may seem a trivial point, but many of the aircrew, infantry, logistics, and maintenance Marines lived in the same base housing areas or neighborhoods. That meant that a sergeant from 1st Battalion 2nd Marines, an infantry squad leader, could live next to a sergeant who served as Phrog or Huey crew chief. Those grassroots but important personal relationships helped Marines from private to three-star general understand each other and better understand their bigger mission as Marines.

We all understood that we had a mission, our solemn and sacred mission, to support infantry Marines. That mentality permeated every rank and every military specialty, but now more than ever, it gave us a collective sense of purpose. That was also true for the officers, many of whom lived next door to each other on Camp Lejeune, Twentynine Palms, or Camp Pendleton. That allowed personal relationships to easily turn into professional relationships, and both would prove essential over the coming weeks and months.

That said, and after removing the rose-colored glasses, cats and dogs living together is never easy. Living with and around the infantry community became both a blessing and a curse. Yes, I loved working out, but the infantry took workouts to another level. Yes, the job was physically demanding, but even within the Corps, there were clashes of culture. Just as I didn't appreciate the challenges and skills required to lead a company of two hundred Marines, that same captain may not recognize the skills and challenges of leading a flight of transport or attack helicopters. It was comparing apples to oranges, and leadership takes many forms.

There has always been a healthy, and sometimes unhealthy, rivalry between Marines serving in the infantry or any ground role and those in aviation. Jokes about flight pay and working half-days while "swinging with the Wing," referring to the air wing, were common. In reality, we knew that our mission remained dedicated to every Marine serving on the ground, and more importantly, they knew we would not ever let them down.

MAG 39 had arrived in theater about the same time we had arrived. Though the squadron and group commanders had been coordinating with both the Wing, division, and MEF commanding generals and their staff, the squadrons had not trained together, nor had they planned to integrate themselves in combat.

Shooter, also a career Cobra pilot and someone we all knew well, commanded MAG 39. Shooter was metered and calm. He was a no-nonsense North Carolinian who didn't need to say a lot to get his message delivered. Shooter had served off the coast of Beirut as a lieutenant and served during Desert Storm as a major. He then commanded HMLA 269 as a lieutenant colonel circa 1995 or 1996.

He allowed this overzealous, overconfident, and sometimes over-his-skis Cobra pilot to lead his Tactics and Training Department. He was both a mentor and coach to me, and Shooter never missed an opportunity to pass on living lessons of leadership and humility. Shooter, like many, saw something in me that I missed. He trusted me to not only fly his aircraft but to train and lead his young pilots. MAG 39 included two additional HMLA squadrons, along with an HMM of twelve Phrogs and a maintenance squadron. That meant another fifty-four Cobras and Hueys and another twelve Phrogs in the fight.

As those "lost" MAG 39 aircraft flew out of sight to the south, we made our final turn toward Safwan Hill. The sun was long gone, and without a moon, stars, or any ambient light from a road or town, the NVGs barely allowed me to keep the number two Cobra in sight. I began to wonder where the "shake and bake" was.

CHAPTER 11

Location: 5 Miles from Safwan Hill, Northern Border of Kuwait
Date: 20MAR03
Time: 1845L

We remained a flight of seven holding miles south of the target. Commanders assigned a new TOT over the mission common radio frequency—so we just waited. We waited for Marine F/A-18 Hornets to strike positions on Safwan Hill prior to our arrival. Dubbed "shake and bake," it would be the most overt and violent signal possible. The flight lead would drop MK-84 laser-guided two-thousand-pound bombs followed by the wingman dropping 750-pound incendiary bombs. It was going to be an amazing display of firepower.

I didn't know who would show up, when they would show up, or if they would show up. Planners initially briefed them as multiple flights of Marine F/A-18s followed by multiple flights of AV-8B Harriers from bases in Kuwait and off the carriers and amphibious ships, but we had no idea of who would actually appear. In fact, I really didn't care if they showed up at all. I just wanted to get it on and get it on now.

The fact we had remained airborne, oriented, and established in some type of formation demonstrated a veneer of success and normalcy. Days, weeks, and even years would pass before all aircrew would compare notes and experiences of this night. The NVGs simply couldn't provide the needed visibility. Every pilot and crew were left flying on instruments, using the NVGs as a distant secondary means to build awareness.

I finally established a rhythm, and the ability to fly straight and level with the ball centered helped.

"Matt, how is it going up there?" I asked every few minutes.

He'd give the same response. "Looking good, sir."

I still wanted to edge closer to see the helicopters in front of me.

Night vision devices are designed to take light from the stars, moon, or cultural lighting and amplify it. That magnified light essentially provided our eyes with a small television screen. That screen turned night into day, although "day" had a thick green hue and limited field of view. Imagine driving at night without lights on your car while having a pair of small binoculars to see through. It takes training, patience, and practice, but eventually, you adapt.

Tonight, we simply had to adapt. We were left no choice except to embrace the situation and use the occasional shape or light on the horizon. The Ghost had the advantage. The HUD helped us as we saw the Phrogs peel off to the south. The HUD was also going to play a key role in engaging our assigned targets. I rolled out and kept the flight of Cobras locked in my HUD and counted on Matt to maintain situational awareness while pushing me information on the time and distance to Safwan Hill.

Matt worked the FLIR and the embedded targeting camera. The camera with the FLIR and laser was simply called the night targeting system (NTS). It was nothing magical, but it did have some unique capabilities. The NTS sat in the nose of the Cobra and used the FLIR's infrared technology to find "hot or cold" targets. With the flick of a switch, the FLIR could be turned off, and the gunner could use the camera. Unfortunately, the camera was only good in the daytime and used magnification similar to a set of binoculars to locate targets. Lastly, the NTS had a laser for both determining the range and precise location of targets and for engaging those targets with laser-guided missiles and bombs.

The Cobra carried, among the long list of weapons, the laser-guided missiles known as Hellfire. The Hellfire missile, or, precisely, the AGM-114, could be trusted to hit ground targets from about five hundred meters to eight thousand meters away, depending on a myriad of tactical and environmental conditions. If we could see the enemy, we could destroy them, unless they saw us and shot first.

That night, we didn't plan to use the Hellfire, but we did plan to use a combination of unguided rockets and 20mm cannon fire to engage preplanned positions. The rockets came with several warhead options: white and red phosphorus for marking targets, HE for general purpose (GP) use, and flechette rockets for anti-personnel use. The 2.75-inch flechette rocket carried about twelve hundred small sixty-grain arrows or nails. We had nineteen 2.75-inch flechette rockets, seven HE rockets, three hundred rounds of 20mm cannon ammunition, four wire-guided TOW anti-tank missiles, and three Hellfire missiles on each Cobra.

We planned to strike positions suspected to hold Iraqi infantry and reconnaissance units with 2.75-inch flechette rockets and 20mm cannon fire. The rockets and their flechettes were designed for personnel, but they required the pilot to close within one thousand meters of the target to be effective. That meant a Cobra engaging a position at one thousand meters would need several seconds to detect, recognize, identify, and then engage targets. Traveling at 120 knots, or about sixty meters per second, meant every engagement had me or my wingman well inside the effective range of both machine gun and small arms fire.

The first two Cobras were led by Howdy, and he would position his two Cobras to strike similar targets on the west side of Safwan Hill. I would take my two Cobras to hit the eastern targets.

Howdy would come to symbolize the determination and unsung hero status of HMLA 269. He was an unpretentious Youngstown, Ohio, native with a contagious calm, a deep sense of service, and an even more fiercely competitive nature. His humble sheen hid the active and questioning mind of an engineer, which matched his degree in engineering from Ohio State University. We were friends, roommates, and sounding boards, and we went on to serve together over multiple combat deployments.

"Marjo flight, stand by," came from Howdy.

We had rolled out of the turn and were headed straight toward Safwan Hill as the plan came together. With Howdy leading his section to the northwest and me taking my section to the northeast, we would wait for Scooter and his Phrogs. Scooter would follow behind our clearing pass of rockets and guns. With his two Phrogs, he planned to insert the 1st Force Marines into the predetermined landing zone (LZ). Once in the zone, Howdy's flight would take up defensive positions to the northwest, and I would take up a similar position to the northeast.

We had designed those positions to isolate any Iraqi forces on Safwan Hill from being reinforced. Additionally, once the 1st Force Marines were inserted, both flights of Cobras would switch to a CAS and visual reconnaissance mission for the Marines.

I pushed the stick forward and took a deep breath. We rolled out of our final turn on course, on altitude, and less than two miles from the target. I didn't notice when, but it had gone stone cold quiet on the radios. Where were the F/A-18s, the Harriers, and the "shake and bake" we had been promised? I suspected the aircraft carriers, the land-based air stations and their associated fighters, and the other attack aircraft had likely encountered the same weather.

I investigated my HUD as much as I looked through it but found no answers in either place. I compared the barometric altimeter, or altitude above sea level, to the radar altimeter. In that case, the altitude showed about the same, but the radar altimeter told me about our actual height above the desert floor. The problem with any radar altimeter is that, by the time it detects rising terrain, it may already be too late. It simply tells me where I have been. The radar altimeter can't see in front of a Cobra like a ground following radar, so we had nothing protecting us from obstacles.

I had turned my attention back to finding the tail of Flash's Cobra flying in the number two position. I found him. There he was, one rotor, two pilots, and three minutes to our TOT. I tucked in a bit tighter to him, putting us no more than one hundred feet apart. I planned to orient off him until we fired on the first targets. My mind was drifting again. Still nothing on the radios.

No sooner had I looked down to my kneeboard, which held a paper list of frequencies, target coordinates, timelines, and notes all strapped to my right, when a blinding flash of light answered our prayers.

Two F/A-18D Hornets from Marine All-Weather Fighter Attack Squadron 121 (VMFA[AW]-121), the Green Knights, had delivered. I saw a plume of light followed by an explosion created by the lead pilot dropping MK-82 five-hundred-pound bombs. His wingman followed. There was only one opening act and a single encore. Our encore included two MK 77 750-pound incendiary bombs.

Based on the pre-briefed timeline, we were daringly on time.

Matt saw what I saw and quickly went to work. "I'm heads down looking for targets."

We enjoyed an amazing and unsuspected success, defined by the massive explosions and the flood of light that overwhelmed the cockpit. The brilliance of the explosions briefly reduced the efficacy of the NVGs. Ironically, if the NVGs get too much light, they become less effective, but the reduction lasted less than a breath.

I looked up long enough to get a glimpse of the entirety of Safwan Hill silhouetted. I also had an instantly perfect view of two Cobras, Howdy and Flash. They looked oddly frozen in space and time off to my front left. The low acoustic rumble of the bomb blasts came only seconds later. It sounded and felt like a thunderclap followed by the slight overpressure that rippled all around the cockpit.

I verbalized my observations. "Damn, Matt, maybe we were too close."

At least we were not alone.

The radios immediately erupted with chatter. The bombs were our wakeup call. The F/A-18Ds of VMFA(AW)-121 had woken us up, and the second salvo on bombs told us to get up and get moving. I'd have thought the "shake and bake" would have been a bigger event. The explosions gave all of us an immediate sense of discomfort. They were welcomed in the same way a tsunami was to the desert. We embraced the change, and the second bombs exploding was a needed salute, but too much of a good thing was...well, too much of a good thing. The chaos they created was as random and as unsuspected as their departure. The tsunami was our nighttime blessing and curse.

The bigger victory was having them, VMFA(AW)-121, here at all. These were just the second signs that HMLA 269 and MAG 29 were not going to start this war alone. That sense of relief, like the light from the bombs, was short lived.

The brightness of the bombs impacting targets brought us a welcome but temporary respite. That brilliance was immediately followed by darkness—a darkness that signaled we were all, once again, alone. The moonlessness of the night and the never-ending blackness of the desert crept back as soon as the bombs stopped falling. All that remained of their once impressive explosions were a few unceremonious brush fires.

A now familiar dread had quickly replaced the vision and clarity brought by the F/A-18s. Either ironic or foreboding, the several thousand pounds of US firepower, which had just lit up the skyline like a traveling circus, had disappeared and left us in darkness with a few clowns, the bearded lady, the lobster boy, and maybe the elephant man.

Once again, I could only see the dim strip lights of Flash in the second Cobra and felt blind. I couldn't reacquire him in the HUD and got that familiar sick feeling in my gut.

I immediately keyed the radio or, more accurately, yelled, "Flash, turn on your damn smack lights."

That light provided a regular Federal Aviation Administration (FAA) overt, or visible, anti-collision light. It meant that I would immediately see him, and I did. In a second, I saw his bright rotating beacon, the light that announced Flash off my nose about 150 feet. I almost simultaneously saw Howdy's light come on. He must've known I wouldn't have asked for it unless we really needed it.

Howdy and Flash, and their big red rotating light of situational awareness, was also clearly visible to the enemy on and around Safwan. I had made a big ask, but they didn't hesitate or say a word in protest. Their lights just came on and gave a big F-you to the Ghost. Now, it was almost a taunt.

Some would consider their actions both remarkably dangerous and remarkably courageous. It was nuts for me to ask anyone to turn on their overt lights. It defeated many of the reasons we operated at night. I could guarantee that US military weapons school certainly didn't teach that procedure, but we were desperate. With only a few seconds until the flight unleashed a manifold of 2.75-inch rockets and upwards of one thousand rounds of 20mm HE cannon fire, I needed to know their precise location. No sooner had Flash's lights come on when, about three hundred feet to my left, two hundred feet above the desert, and flying at 120 knots, Howdy called, "Leads in hot."

The "in hot" call meant Howdy had found his target and readied to fire on enemy positions. Matt remained head-down using the FLIR in our front seat and had the target entered via our GPS. With the laser range finder locked onto the target, it automatically put the reticle, or crosshair, in my HUD. Inside that reticle was the target. I remained too busy to even consider nervousness.

I only needed to maneuver the Cobra to center the reticle, select rockets, arm the weapons systems, and then mash the rocket trigger with my right thumb. I saw the reticle but not the target. The target, one of several, slowly closed in. Every second, the HUD told me more details. Every second, I could see more, but I couldn't see it all. They had briefed our first target as an Iraqi infantry trench line, but I couldn't identify it. Intelligence analysts had painted a picture that we couldn't see.

Trench line or not, the HUD displayed the time, distance, and about everything else I needed to put the rockets on target. Next, I only had to select the correct 2.75-inch rocket pod, move my master arm switch to the arm position, put the rocket reticle on the target, and punch the trigger. Too easy, right?

Incidentally, the trigger wasn't a traditional trigger but a thumb-actuated button on top of the pilot's controls. The master arm switch was located about a foot directly in front of me and moving to the arm position was accomplished by the rear seat pilot moving a half-inch metal and self-locking switch forward.

Those may seem like minute details, but they represented a big action. That action would "arm" all of the weapons systems and allow Matt to fire the 20mm cannon or engage targets with the TOW or Hellfire missiles. It would also allow me to shoot the cannon using my helmet-mounted sight or fire the cannon in the locked forward position, like an old World War II fighter. I could also fire, on rare occasions, the Hellfire missiles from the rear seat, and finally, the HUD allowed me to fire the AIM-9 Sidewinder missile.

The Sidewinder was an air-to-air weapon designed specifically for dog fighting. Coincidentally, there were Cobra pilots who dreamed of fighting an air-to-air fight against Iraqi MiGs or helicopters. Some of those pilots were my friends, but they were what I called daydreamers and night screamers. Both the use of AIM-9s and our chance of dog fighting an Iraqi fighter or helicopter remained slim. Even after the most liberal debate of enemy scenarios, we would never carry Sidewinders in Iraq. Even with that point made, every pilot secretly wished there were an Iraqi air force out there to hunt.

The Cobra could carry a wide variety of weapons, and finding the perfect loadout was unachievable. Even with the Cobra tactics manual providing guidance for ordnance loads based on the mission, the terrain, and the enemy, it was up to us to find the right mix. The aircraft couldn't be armed for every potential scenario, and we also had to find a mix that wasn't limited based on weight.

Our squadron WTIs debated loadouts, and these debates got detailed down to the specific warhead types, but we eventually came to an agreement. The loadout had to pass the "ilities" test. Reliability, sustainability, repeatability, maintainability, it goes on, but building a Gucci loadout needed to be tempered. We needed a Leatherman approach.

I saw the rocket reticle line up with where Matt had aligned the laser on the target and announced, "Matt, master arm is going to arm."

I hesitated and called out to the flight, "43's in hot." Then, I fired.

Whoosh!

The rocket came out with the near immediate flash of light from the rocket motor followed by the distant smell of the propellant. I felt a slight kick in the pedals and a subtle sway of the Cobra. I immediately judged the first rocket's impact point, made a slight adjustment, and fired another, then another.

Whoosh. Whoosh.

Damn it, this is taking way too long, I thought.

We pressed dangerously close into the target area, no further than two hundred meters. I looked down at my weapons panel, selected the ALL button next to the rocket pod, and pressed the trigger again. This time, the remaining sixteen rockets spat out into what felt like a single volley.

Whoooooosh.

Matt pushed his foot switch. "I'm going hot on the gun."

He immediately began to engage the trench line with the 20mm cannon. With a backdrop reminiscent of the darkest side of the moon, Matt sent a rope of 20mm HE and tracer rounds to the target. The electrically driven three-barrel M-197 cannon rotated, and the trigger responded to Matt's inputs.

Tuck. Tuck. Tuck. Tuck.

I heard and then felt the vibrations in my feet and in my seat. The cannon made more of a deep churning sound as it hurled hundreds of three-inch HE projectiles to their target at one thousand meters per second. The cannon's three-foot flame was perhaps better described as a dragon's breath of 20mm fire. No matter the hundreds of ways to describe the M-197, it was as fearless as it was inspiring.

I had fired my first pod of rockets, and Matt had just released the trigger. So far, so good with a total of seventy-six rockets and a few hundred 20mm rounds down range from the four Cobras. We had—or, better stated, MAG 29 and HMLA 269 had—announced their entry into the war.

I had little time to think about the rockets and 20mm fire. I could see Buss's rockets and 20mm rounds had impacted his target just to my right, the same direction I had intended to turn. It made no tactical sense to overfly a target since we'd immediately become vulnerable to pretty much anything the enemy could shoot at us, particularly at three hundred feet. So, we overflew the target. It wouldn't be our last time.

With the continued adrenaline rush from having just engaged those positions, I unceremoniously announced, "Matt, master arm going safe. Marjo 43 and 44 off safe."

I had been a Marine for nearly fifteen years, traveled across the globe, flown the Cobra on armed and on "real-world" missions through the Persian Gulf, Somalia, and Bosnia, but tonight was different. For the first time, I'd moved the master arm switch to the arm position and fired on real targets. These were bona fide targets with unfeigned consequences. I knew something big had just happened, but I wasn't exactly sure how I felt about it. The Wallflowers' song captured something that would register much later: "I feel just like somebody else…I ain't changed, but I know I ain't the same."

We started an easy turn to the northeast of Safwan Hill, so I announced, "43 and 44 headed northeast."

What hit me immediately, and what should have been obvious, was there had been no return fire.

I was still looking into a black abyss. "Matt, what are you seeing?"

"I got nothing in those positions moving. No hot spots either," he replied.

In fact, we couldn't see any enemy fire at all. Either the storm had masked the tracers, or the Iraqis had hunkered down in their positions, avoiding the weather. We passed Safwan to the left. I could only see a slight silhouette of the hill. I expected heavy machine guns or anti-aircraft artillery (AAA) fire to erupt at any second.

I needed an answer. "Matt, where are they? It's way too quiet."

"Sir, I don't see anything yet. Let's keep east of Safwan. I'm looking for Howdy and Flash. Check your airspeed. We are at three hundred feet and in a slight descent." Matt sounded slightly annoyed.

We kept our eyes peeled for any infantry fighting positions or armored vehicles. I simply couldn't see much, even from three hundred feet. I corrected the descent with a slight pull of the collective and gentle pressure on the stick to level us. I heard the engines whine just a bit louder. I was not about to make the same mistake twice. I increased my scan through the HUD and down onto my lower instruments.

Over my left shoulder, I could still see the embers from our first rockets and gun pass but saw nothing else other than an eerie calm. Where were the Iraqi defenders? Not that we needed another variable introduced into that already unsolved equation, but we found this little mystery a bit unnerving.

"Buss, I'm slowing down to one hundred knots. I'm not seeing anything," I passed.

A short, "44 copies," came back from Buss.

No sooner had we rolled out of the northeastern turn when we saw movement and then headlights.

Matt called it out first. "Target on the move, right to left, six hundred meters."

Only Matt could see that far, and I couldn't really tell exactly what it was. We had been briefed that the Iraqis used Russian-made UAZ scout trucks and other SUVs. Perhaps it was one of those. I was counting on Matt to identify it in the FLIR. I couldn't get sight of it through the HUD, but Matt worked to keep it tracked on the FLIR. With the Phrogs reporting two minutes out from the LZ on Safwan, I wouldn't or couldn't let this potential threat drive directly toward Safwan Hill.

"Matt, master arm's going to arm. Can you hit 'em with a TOW?" I asked him, but I knew we were too fast and too close.

The storm continued to blow sand and debris into the night sky east of Safwan Hill. All three provided critical seconds of cover for the fleeing scout.

Matt responded, "I can't track him. I can't get a good picture on the FLIR."

We didn't consider the TOW missile ideal on a moving target at night in that weather, but it would certainly do the job. The TOW was effective out to almost four thousand meters and had a shaped charge designed to destroy most armored vehicles. We also found it effective on buildings, and it certainly had enough destructive power to obliterate a lightly armored scout vehicle, or whatever was in front of us.

"Marjo 44 in hot," came across the mission's common frequency, and immediately, 20mm rounds began impacting what looked like an Iraqi military truck.

Buss and Rosie entered the game, and within a second, the vehicle had burst into flames and careened off the road. They flew to our right and about one hundred feet behind us judging from the flash coming from their 20mm cannon.

I didn't then, but I would later reflect on that driver's decision. What was he doing? Did we simply spook him? And why didn't the driver know enough to stay quiet and stay cool, off the FLIR? I would have time later to review the gun tape and maybe glean a few lessons. Each Cobra carried a high-definition VHS video recorder secured in the tail boom of the helicopter. Every time I moved the master arm to the arm position, it recorded. Plenty of time for that later.

"I have another target, two o'clock, seven hundred meters." Matt immersed himself in the FLIR, which gave him a distinct advantage.

The night still limited my capabilities. Through my NVGs' lenses, I could only see the grainy and greenish outline of the target Matt described to me. I thought to myself, *Are you serious? You see another vehicle?* I could feel my sweat-saturated gloves instinctively push the stick to the right and pull in more power.

A wise Marine general once proclaimed that "calm, like panic, is contagious." If he could only see what we saw. If only he could have our god's-eye view of an infantry unit being overwhelmed, overexposed, and under-led. The Iraqi units on Safwan Hill made critical decisions—decisions I couldn't understand or anticipate, but their own "flight or fight" choices were obvious. The pictures seen through my HUD and NVGs—and, for Matt, through his FLIR and NVGs—told a story. A story of men at their worst—at their most desperate. Trapped. Panicked. You could almost smell it. The disorder was obvious, with vehicles moving in all directions, some lights on, some lights off. The sounds of US Marine gunships overhead, searching for their next target, must have terrified them.

The sounds and shockwave of the F-18s' bombs, followed by our rockets, then guns, then the guttural and unnerving sound of rotor blades approaching, crushed their resolve. Panic ruled the night, and any thought of fight had evaporated into flight. The remaining defenders must have assumed we were hunting them, a fair assumption considering what we had just done to their comrades.

We both scanned for the vehicle. "Matt, you see it?"

"I'm looking," he quipped. "Sir, target 040 at five hundred meters, but we need to come hard right."

Snap or abrupt turns were not on tonight's menu, and I sure didn't want to make a hard turn into my wingman. I was ready to shoot, but Marjo 44 had the better position unless he couldn't see what we saw.

I kept my heading and called to Buss, "44, can you get a shot?"

We could still engage it, but it would mean a 30- to 40-degree change of heading across his flight path.

In what would become his typical calm demeanor or, more accurately, deadpan response, Buss said, "Stand by one." Then, he confirmed my request with a simple, "44 is in hot."

That call was followed by a rush of light. The 2.75-inch rocket motors temporarily flooded my cockpit as Buss engaged what was now identified as a truck. One rocket, two rockets, impact. *Boom.*

Buss quietly announced, "44 is off safe."

We were in a slight right-hand turn with Buss maybe fifty yards off my right wing.

"You see anything else?" I asked Matt.

Nothing from him at first. Then, he countered with, "Let's come left, roll out 330."

I asked Matt again if he saw anything, but the smoke from the impact obscured both the NVGs and the FLIR. I took a second to get my bearings. We needed to move closer to the airfield.

I keyed the radio. "Marjo 41, Marjo 43 and 44 are pushing to hold west of the airfield."

I took my first deep breath in what felt like a few minutes and took note to lighten the death grip I had on the stick. The cockpit was likely a cool 75 degrees Fahrenheit with air-conditioned seats and temperature dial on full cold, but my sweat-soaked flight suit and gloves told another story. No response from Howdy in Marjo 41 meant he was busy, but I knew he'd heard me. I also knew that if he had something important to say, he'd say it.

I also didn't need to tell Buss anything. He'd heard the call I had made to Howdy. We had agreed, during the mission briefs, that we would enter a left-hand turn pattern and await the arrival of the Phrogs. Flying in a left-hand pattern reduced my workload, as well as Buss's, by establishing and maintaining a predictable flight path.

That flight path put us in between Safwan Hill to our west and the reportedly abandoned Safwan Airfield just to our northeast. I hoped it would provide a manageable landmark to orbit as the Phrogs edged closer to their LZ.

Before we could appreciate the sound of silence, we heard the Phrog flight lead, "Scooter," calling, "One minute out," on the mission's common frequency.

We used two frequencies to communicate, one for Cobras and another for everyone else flying the mission. The mission common frequency provided situational awareness for every crew, along with a means to announce any obvious dangers or changes to the mission. The Phrogs also had their own private frequency as well as the mission common frequency to monitor. Finally, the command-and-control Huey had multiple frequencies. It monitored all of our frequencies and also communicated directly with higher headquarters.

No sooner had we made our turn to the northeast than the headlights of another scout vehicle came on. It immediately accelerated from the airfield's western edge directly toward Safwan. Matt saw it as well, and I promptly rolled out of my turn.

"Too close for a TOW. I'm going to gun," Matt stated.

I mustered a, "Copy."

From Matt's announcement, I simultaneously selected the second rocket pod and rolled left to be Matt's backup. I could see the target right in front of us, three hundred meters away, and we closed the gap fast.

"Master arm to arm," I said as I keyed the ICS and then announced, "43's in hot to the northeast," on the tactical frequency.

The mission command Huey would determine whether to pass along that Cobras continued to engage targets to the northeast, but Scooter and his crews could see the obvious. The brilliance of rocket motors as they fired, the flames coming from the 20mm cannons and then the tracers, had to mesmerize, or alarm, anyone watching. The drifting smoke, the dying flames, the distant images of targeted vehicles combined with a growing level of radio chatter would be as clear a picture as they would get.

Lieutenant Colonel Scott "Scooter" O'Mera served as the Phrog flight lead and the operations officer for the Golden Knights of HMM 162. He was also a WTI and led as one of the Golden Knights' most experienced flight leaders. He was no fan of the plan or the weather. He'd lived through a similar experience some twelve years previously during *Operation Desert Storm*. He had already danced with one Ghost, and this new Ghost was turning out to be more than we wanted. He had been pushing his flight through the same storm and over the same ground and had made it to the same place, but his mission had just begun. He was now a flight of two, as the CASEVAC orbited several miles in a trailing position. This meant the CASEVAC would find its own place to orbit and wait. Wait for a call they hoped would never come.

Scooter and his copilot, Captain Brian "Sugar Ray" Robinson, had seen both Howdy's flight of two Cobras and our section engage targets on the southern face of Safwan and had also seen additional cannon or missile fire coming from the east. In any event, the mission was a "go," and they headed for the LZ. On their right side flew their wingman, piloted by Captain Brian Koch and Captain Rick Azanon, two talented aviators leading their crew and their "customers" into an LZ.

The inside of a Phrog was nothing like that of the Cobra. The Cobra had a closed cockpit, which dramatically reduced noise from both the engines and the transmission. The Phrog was open air, open wires in the cabin, open hydraulic pumps, open doors, open ramp, simply open to all the elements. It was also incredibly noisy with both turbine engines sitting above the crew and passengers. Those turbine engines, while providing the necessary power for flight, also generated a high-pitched whine. That whine or moan became audible every time the pilot added or removed power. It was simply an unnerving and haunting sound.

The Cobra had armored and air-conditioned seats, while the Phrogs had been built before the discovery of air conditioning. Did the Phrogs come in 2003 models? Nope. Those were not even recently off the Boeing production line. Instead, they had come off the production line circa 1966. Riding in the back of the Phrog, the passenger could almost see, smell, and hear every drop of fuel, engine oil, and hydraulic fluid. Each passenger saw a seemingly endless number of metal lines, braided plastics, tubes, and pipes running down the side and ceiling of the cargo bay, creating a unique smell and unconfined sense of chaos. The smell reminded me of the dankness of your ole Aunt Judy's brown couch. The couch that had been in the basement for years, saturated with sweat, spills, stains, and other unthinkable substances. Now, imagine that heated to 100 degrees, and then lay down on it.

Inside that controlled chaos sat two sticks or squads of eleven Marines each. Their coolness showed more the acceptance of fate than a lack of fear. Once you go in, and the ramp comes up, there's only you and your thoughts. Tonight, they had a special ride with the added bonus of the blowing sand coming through the cabin and the sight of the crew chiefs manning the .50 caliber heavy machine guns. They had communications with their headquarters and received regular updates to the timelines, almost like the scene from *Band of Brothers* on D-Day as they acknowledged they were two minutes out and then one minute out. This could have been 1944 with the crew chief yelling, "thirty seconds," but this was 2003.

I saw the lights on the vehicle heading toward the LZ. I put the rocket reticle just ahead of the vehicle. "Matt, master arm is going to arm." The foot switch from the front seat responded with only a *click, click.*

Again, I called out on the mission common frequency. "Marjo 43's in hot, just east of Safwan Hill."

With the Phrogs now on short final to the zone and Howdy's section only about a half mile to the west, I wanted our calls to be both descriptive and directive. They would immediately understand we were engaging more targets. Neither Howdy's section nor Scooter's section would come in our direction unless absolutely necessary.

The heaviness of the night continued muting our efforts, and it remained nearly impossible to track the vehicle without Matt's help on the FLIR. Finally, I caught its side profile. I fired.

Whoosh. Whoosh. Whoosh.

The rockets impacted long, short, and right. What was the problem? What was my problem? We were no more than three hundred meters away and closing in fast. I would never claim to be the best rocket shooter, but was I really this bad?

I looked down to my instrument panel to see the rudder or the "ball," which kept the helicopter in balanced flight. The ball was out to the right—*way* out to the right. I was essentially flying sideways. I pushed the right rudder and quickly glanced into the HUD. The HUD showed eighty knots and slowing. I immediately thought about Buss, and no sooner had the thought crossed my mind than Buss went flying past me on the right.

Buss calmly radioed me. "Four-four is passing you on the right side, and check your airspeed."

How was this happening? I had become disoriented again. Even more notably, I'd made my wingman's job nearly impossible. As Buss overran me, I switched from rockets to the 20mm cannon and locked the cannon into the fixed forward position.

The infamous M-197 20mm cannon had been and remains the mainstay of the Marine Cobra. It's chin mounted, meaning it's attached under the nose of the front seat pilot. The cannon sits, literally, under their feet. It can fire at a rate of 650 rounds per minute and is aimed with a helmet-mounted sight from either cockpit, fired from the front seat using the gyro-stabilized camera, or the FLIR, and lastly from the rear seat with the cannon locked in the forward position. The gun turret can articulate about 100 degrees either side of the centerline of the Cobra and can shoot almost directly down and elevate up to a mechanical stop. That mechanical stop prevents crews from shooting off the main blades. Fine thinking.

Firing from the rear seat in the locked forward or "fixed forward" mode was a pilot's favorite. No one debated that the 20mm was the most enjoyable weapon to fire from a Cobra. Add in the chance to shoot it old school from the back seat in fixed forward mode, and it felt like we were shooting from a WWII Corsair or Mustang. But right now, I needed new school and a new option to hit this vehicle.

I switched from rockets to guns—yes, a bit cliché, but it happened in nearly every engagement. As I made the switch to gun, the gun reticle replaced the rocket reticle in my HUD, and I was once again aiming at a moving target. It turned northwest, so I looked at the taillights, headed 355 degrees, 5 degrees nose down. *Here we go.* The master arm was still in arm. I could only concentrate on the vehicle's taillights as we pressed closer. I scanned the altitude, three hundred feet above the desert floor and in a slight descent, so I added power.

We dove inside of two hundred meters, and I called, "43's still in hot to the northeast."

I saw the silhouette of the vehicle more clearly. We could both finally recognize it as a military SUV. "Matt, going hot with the gun. He's turning back left. We are 150 meters."

I began to fire.

The flames of the cannon were mostly covered by the nose of the aircraft, but the three-foot flame would emerge as I pulled the trigger and held it. The 20mm HE incendiary rounds soon began exploding around the truck, and tracers quickly followed in rhythm to gently remind me where to adjust my aim. I still flew slightly sideways, which meant the Cobra yawed to one side. I centered the ball one last time, moved the stick to the right, and walked the stream of 20mm fire to about five feet ahead of the target.

The truck exploded as the driver and his crew had the misfortune of steering directly into my cannon fire. The vehicle slowed, quietly veered off the road, and began to burn. I moved the master arm switch back to the safe position and looked for Buss.

"Good hits, good hits." Buss's voice jarred me back into reality.

Buss had extended out to the northeast, reacquired me, and moved back into position.

"Four-four, let's hold closer to the airfield. I can see it better. Left-hand turn and ninety knots." I released the radio switch.

Click. Click.

Two clicks from his radio said it all. We started a lazy left-hand pattern until the Phrogs could get the Marines onto Safwan.

I had barely rolled into the first turn when our radios cracked. "On guard, cease fire, cease fire…cease fire. Cobras, you are engaging friendly forces. I repeat, you are engaging friendly forces!"

That call sounded both desperate and pleading. It was immediately followed with a ten-digit map grid coordinate, and that grid would let us all plot the position. We would know in a few seconds and within a few feet where this was happening. Broadcasting on guard meant anyone with a radio would hear the call. I stopped breathing and felt sickness building, bile creeping onto my tongue. Who was that, and what had just happened?

I responded immediately. "Matt, what the fuck was that? Plot that position. Marjo 44, you hear that? Check our position."

Click. Click.

Buss and Rosie were way ahead of me.

Rosie was the first to respond to us. "Hey, 43, that's eight clicks from here. That's either another west coast section or one of ours."

Panic, dread, despair. I still couldn't breathe. I was trapped with a thought and a vision. There's no way US Marine Cobras fired on friendlies. Eight clicks meant eight thousand meters or roughly five miles from our position.

Matt confirmed. "Sir, I concur with Buss. We are almost nine clicks from that position."

It did little to ease my mind. What was happening?

It would have to wait. The Phrogs were inbound, and there were certainly more Iraqis in and around the LZ.

CHAPTER 12

Location: Safwan Hill, Iraq
Date: 20MAR03
Time: 1850L

The CH-46s, aka Phrogs, and Scooter headed inbound to the LZ. Both crews had seen flashes from our engagement of Iraqi vehicles to the northeast. Simultaneously, Howdy's section looked directly into the LZ. They scoured the area for enemy infantry, armor, and any obstacles. After several minutes scanning the LZ, they became convinced that no manned enemy positions remained and moved back to their holding position to the northwest. The Phrogs slowed and turned inbound to the LZ. They would begin their first of several attempts to land.

As the Phrogs began their third or maybe fourth and last pass into the LZ, the blowing sand and near zero visibility caused them to wave off a final time. Though they were only a thousand meters or so from us, we couldn't see either of them. We could barely make out Safwan Hill.

Scooter called, "Waving off to the north. Resetting for another try."

I strained my eyes through the NVGs, but I could only hear them. I could hear the stress. I could almost feel the apprehensiveness. His voice, masked only slightly by the high-pitched whine of the Phrog's powerful Dash-16 engines, was determined. We could only listen as they made their repeated approaches. I wished there was some way we could help.

Scooter's voice was calm, but strained, tension pulling on his vocal cords. These were talented pilots and aircrew, and they were not in the business of being vanquished by weather or winds, but we needed a new plan. The Phrogs had battled the terrain, the elements, and now likely a drifting confidence. Not a lack of confidence in their abilities but a slow sapping of their abilities. Fatigue became a factor.

I noticed a pause in the radio calls from Scooter and his flight. We sensed they were looking at their options, making decisions and formulating their next steps. No way they should try again, and I was sure they'd come to the same conclusion. Not quitting but living to fight another day. More of an acceptance of the realities. It takes a mature and seasoned flight lead to call or cancel a mission, especially a mission with that level of visibility from everyone up and down the chain of command.

Finally, it came over the mission common frequency. "This isn't working. We can't see anything. We are RTB."

RTB meant return to base. I took a mental note. I needed to tell Scooter what a great call he'd made. The Ghost teased him and all the Phrogs, dared them to push their luck and to try to accomplish the impossible. It's hard to explain how difficult it is to land a helicopter at night in a sandstorm on a specific piece of terrain on top of a hill while under the direct threat of enemy fire.

As the flight of two Phrogs turned south, I felt a sense of relief. I also got the feeling that we were not alone. The Ghost was out there somewhere, and she had watched everything, her head still cocked slightly to one side, almost in a pensive pose. If I closed my eyes, I could visualize her hovering over Safwan. I could see her mouthing something in a toneless whisper. "Don't be disappointed...don't be too disappointed. Maybe I'll get you next time."

It had been more than an hour of burning fuel at a high rate, and fuel was now a concern for the entire flight. We needed to regroup and bow out gracefully, or at least bow out while we had the fuel to get home. As the mission commander passed the codeword, which canceled our mission, I suspected we all silently breathed a similar sigh of relief. I knew then that the tactical portion of the mission had ended, and a new mission had begun. The new mission was to get safely back to and land at Joe Foss. Both Scooter's section of Phrogs and Howdy's section of Cobras were out of sight.

We needed to squeeze one more piece of luck from our four-leaf clover or rub even a sliver of serendipity from our rabbit's foot if we were going to get back. We still held to the northeast of Safwan and immediately made the turn south. Howdy announced that he was pushing from his northwest position and headed south. He and Flash were not close enough to see on the NVGs, and we had no luck finding them on the FLIR.

He called out, "41 and 42, three hundred feet, heading 170 at one hundred knots," and added a ten-digit GPS plot.

Matt quickly tracked their position and realized that Howdy and Flash were more than a mile ahead of us. There was no way we could expect them to slow down for an attempted four ship rendezvous. I agreed that we should not try to rejoin them.

I made the decision for all of us. "Four-one, this is 43. Four-three and 44 are linked up and will follow a mile in trail."

In typical Howdy fashion, he simply replied, "Copy. See you on deck."

I was looking for Buss when he appeared off my left side and just ahead of us. Matt continued scanning in front of us with the FLIR and putting in the coordinates for Joe Foss.

Buss's copilot, Captain Mike "Rosie" Roseberry, keyed his mic first. "Joe Foss, 170 at eight miles."

The weather and this endless desert remained our most dangerous threat, and trying another lead change was unwise. With Buss already ahead of me and to our left, I tucked into the right side of his Cobra.

That was all I needed to hear. "Buss, you good getting us back?"

Click. Click.

I had just asked him to fly us directly to Joe Foss, and he had accepted. I remained on his right as Matt worked our route home on our GPS. A simple system, it gave us time, distance, and heading to the next point. It was also linked directly with the laser. When we locked on a target and squeezed the laser, it recorded an eight-digit grid coordinate for the target. We could use that to confirm location, adjust artillery or mortars, have fixed-wing aircraft drop onto that position, or engage it with our own laser-guided missiles.

Matt's GPS was populating data to Joe Foss in my HUD, and it told me how far it was and how long it would take us to get there. We still had enough fuel; it was still another twenty minutes before the pucker factor would kick in.

Based on the lack of a runway and a heavy ordnance load on takeoff, we had not taken a full fuel load. Because Joe Foss Field didn't have a conventional runway, we couldn't use the runway to execute a "running takeoff." It both reduced the power required to take off and would let us take off at maximum weights. We didn't have that option and had no choice but to take off vertically from Joe Foss, which increased the danger by requiring 100 percent of the power. If we had overloaded the Cobras too much, we would have knowingly invited disaster.

With fuel now a potential concern, and Howdy's flight out of sight, we rolled out aimed directly at Joe Foss. Howdy was now ahead of us by about four miles, which was a fortunate turn of events and would make our landing a bit easier. We saw no improvement in the weather, and the landing helicopters would blow more sand into the air, but if we had some time and distance between landings, it might help.

The Marines had tried to put lights and other markings on the ground, but it had provided little value. Buss, before our takeoff, had instructed the ground crews to scatter "chem lights" in the LZ, along with lighting a small bucket of flammables to provide a beacon. That would become a trend for Buss, thinking one step ahead and considering things that could potentially kill us. As Buss and Rosie led the way back to Joe Foss, we stayed tucked in tight on their wing. We had long crossed back into Kuwait, with ourselves being the only remaining threat.

The Phrogs flew well ahead of us, and Howdy and Flash had already touched down. We made a slow approach to the field because we couldn't see much until we hovered right on top of Joe Foss. I could recognize the faint outlines of the other helicopters, and Buss made a shallow turn to land. I took this as my cue to drop behind him into the trail position and stay just out of his dust cloud.

With no parking spots or lines to use to gauge distance or drift, I just lowered the power, kept the nose level, and waited to hit the ground. The sand quickly overwhelmed us, and we continued our slow drift forward. I tried unsuccessfully to find a reference point. I knew we were drifting. I decided to take out all the power by pushing the collective to the floor.

Thump. Thump.

That muted sound signaled our landing. It was followed by the sensation of sliding through sand. And then, we stopped. Another uneventful touchdown.

"Well, Matt, that was interesting. Not sure how many more of those we have to look forward to," I attempted in my most relaxed tone.

I knew Matt had heard me, and he tapped his foot switch.

Click. Click.

It spoke volumes, those two quick presses of the foot switch. It said, "I hear you but don't have anything to say."

Perfect.

Matt and I went into checklist mode. The ordies ran under the still-turning blades to de-arm the Cobra. Matt exhaled, a long and deep breath that I could hear through our voice-activated intercom (VOX). It spoke volumes.

We both used hand and arm signals to communicate with the invisible plane captain. We could see him with NVGs, but I could only imagine what we looked like under the naked eye. We saw him give the horizontal cutting motion with his flashlights. I reached to secure the throttles to both engines. I felt for the throttle release switch, then rolled each throttle counterclockwise, which shut off fuel to the engines. The engines nearly simultaneously went silent, and as we were the last to shut down, the soft sound of our rotor blades replaced the chaos. The blades slowed and gradually crept to a stop.

It was surreal. Had we been gone for one hour or two hours? It felt like we had been gone for days. Had we ever been here before?

The fact was it had been only about an hour and a half. Gone from my aircraft were twenty-six 2.75-inch rockets and about two hundred rounds of 20mm ammunition, but also gone was my belief that I would ever survive another night like this.

The plane captains popped open the canopy and greeted us with the usual smile before going to work. They excelled at their job. Those guys were excited but resolute. On their first deployment, they once again began the hard work of refueling and rearming the aircraft for the next mission.

Right behind them was Gunnery Sergeant Jim Cafarella. The Boston native was our senior NCO ashore for the operation and one of my most trusted leaders within the maintenance department. A rabid Red Sox ("Socks"), Celtics ("the C's"), Bruins ("the B's"), and Patriots ("Pats") fan, he was given a long leash to ensure the maintenance of all our aircraft and ensure the Marines were taken care of. He was one of the few who could recite the lineup of the 1976 Red Sox, 1984 Celtics, or 1972 Bruins. He could never understand why people could possibly be anti-Boston. Titletown was only America's twenty-fifth most populated city, but somehow, it had captured untold numbers of championships. Even the tormented Red Sox were on the cusp of a championship, breaking an eighty-five-year drought and the "Curse of the Bambino," but that too would have to wait.

I sat in the cockpit for a few extra minutes. Nothing dramatic. Nothing reflective. Looking back, I wasn't particularly aware of my surroundings. I simply sat there. My body and mind sort of took a knee. Not sure I could have gotten out of the cockpit at that particular moment anyway. I was thirsty to soak in the calm and the quiet.

Adrenaline is an amazing thing. I didn't recall ever feeling a sense of "fight or flight," but I did remember being intensely focused, and all that focus had exhausted me. So, I sat in the cockpit, spent, tired of focusing, tired of the dread, and certainly tired of that bullshit weather. I don't know how long the rush of adrenaline lasted, but I could feel it leaving my body. Fatigue replaced it, but along with that came something I might classify, in hindsight, as clarity.

Perhaps I knew right then how difficult that war would be. This mission had been anything but simple or sexy. It had been unpleasant and tediously dirty work. It had required absolutely every ounce of concentration and focus, and that almost hadn't been enough. If this was any signal of the days and nights ahead, we needed to make some changes. No way we could do that for more than a few more nights. With that revelation as my accepted new normal, I once again began to feel a heavy weight slowly pressing down—the same feeling I thought I had left behind at Safwan Hill, but maybe not.

I didn't remember the moment when that feeling of corruption had briefly lifted—probably as we'd opened fire and the adrenaline rush had kicked in—but now it had returned. I still hadn't unstrapped from my seat. The feeling was like a weighted blanket, or maybe it was, more appropriately, a force-fed cocktail of despair and dread. Once I stepped out of this cockpit, nothing would ever be the same. I had no immediate recognition, and it wasn't an epiphany, but I had changed. I didn't know how, but I knew my life had taken an extraordinary turn.

I released my shoulder harness and then my lap belts, took off my helmet, removed my drenched gloves and kneeboard, and pulled myself out of the cockpit. I collected my M4 carbine, checked to ensure my M9 pistol remained in the holster, and grabbed my water, maps, helmet, kneeboard, and NVGs. After thanking our plane captains and ground crews, I gave a distant wave to Gunny Cafarella and walked to my tent to drop my gear before the planned mission debrief.

I made one last quick trip back to the Cobra to retrieve our gun camera film from the tail boom. That film and the story it told could become very important. It would have recorded video and all voice communications from the FLIR for any time I had moved the master arm switch to the arm position. The tape I held in my hand would eventually tell quite a tale.

CHAPTER 13

Location: Joe Foss Field
Date: 20MAR03
Time: 2155L

We made our way into the operations tent, and I found a seat in the back row. The entire flight and every pilot spent the few next hours debriefing—a debriefing in what seemed like only a blur. The situation didn't require me to say anything, and I had nothing to say, so I remained silent. I stood and listened to our CO and other flight leaders recount their missions. I also listened to the air group staff and crew of the command-and-control Huey, along with the mission commander. They discussed options to try the mission again in about an hour. *Hmmm.*

One thing remained clear and would have been obvious to the most casual observer. Each flight lead, including the mission commander, talked in a softer tone and cadence. Just ten to fifteen decibels lower, calmer, and more metered, as though poised to not "spook the herd." Almost saying, but without saying, there's got to be a better way.

We had nothing to be chest thumping about. We had all done our jobs, and we all had the same level of disbelief and anxiety. The discussion quickly turned to whether we should get back into the helicopters and try again, wait for sunrise, or simply cancel.

The pod of lieutenant colonels and other staff officers considered the options. One thing none of them knew was the reality of attempting to fly men and machines back into a literal black hole. These were talented officers who had planned and then listened to the mission play out on the radios, but none had flown it. Even as the mission commander, Lieutenant Colonel Darrell Thacker, who was flying in the command and control, knew he was close but not that close to the reality that was Safwan Hill. Thacker was Boomer's XO, or the number two most senior leader within MAG 29. He was also a former MAWTS-1 instructor and talented pilot, but even he likely felt the pressure to put us all back out there.

They—we—weighed the pros and cons of another attempt. One option was to prepare the crews and make another flight back into Safwan immediately. Another option was to wait until dawn. The last option was to use ground vehicles and no helicopters. No one asked me, and I didn't need to add to the confusion. Truth was, I didn't have a better answer. In my mind, it was either go now before these wounds scabbed up or go in full daylight.

I took a position on the sidewall of the planning tent and listened. Next to me stood Matt, Buss, and Rosie. Beside Rosie stood Howdy's front seat Pez, along with Flash and Country and the Huey crew of Andy Dyer and Len Walker. Howdy edged his way forward, a few paces back from the planning table, to get a better sense of the conversation. If a new strategy hinted at or smelled like an unrehearsed plan (*i.e.*, a desperate one), Howdy or I had the job to raise the "bullshit flag," a flag that was easy to raise in training missions, but this was unfamiliar territory for everyone.

This discussion stayed between our CO, the Safwan mission commander Darrell Thacker, the Phrog flight lead Scooter, the ground commander, and the assorted staff planners with input from a few others. Those others included senior commanders and staff located either on *Saipan* or massed on the Iraqi border or still others with permanent headquarters in Kuwait. Satellite phones and emails were a far cry from effectively communicating the picture on the ground. Painting a picture of our actions on Safwan seemed nearly impossible, and communicating the impact of the weather and sandstorm we'd encountered on the mission remained a challenge. I listened and got the feeling a plan was being developed.

We also didn't know the impact the friendly fire incident had had on ground commanders. Additionally, we had just received reports of a Marine helicopter going down somewhere closer to Basra. It would take some time, but that report would later be confirmed. Tragically, we had lost a Phrog assigned to HMM 268, their crew, and eight of the United Kingdom's finest on a mission into the Al-Faw peninsula.

The mission to secure Iraqi gas and oil platforms had been deemed essential—essential to prevent the Iraqis from committing another environmental disaster similar to the ones in 1991. In 1991, Saddam Hussein had ordered the destruction of his oil fields, lighting them on fire. With those lessons learned from 1991, coalition planners had sent both United Kingdom and US Marine forces into the area. The Royal Marines 3 Commando Brigade with the direct support of the 15th MEU had been assigned to secure those oil fields and other key locations.

Tonight, those aircrews of the 15th MEU and HMM 268 were fighting the same conditions and enduring the same environment we had. I didn't want to admit it, but the Ghost had secured her first victory.

The makeshift command center at Joe Foss Field buzzed with calls, secure emails, and sidebar discussions. We watched, listened, and waited. After several hours, with much hand wringing and gnashing of teeth, cooler heads prevailed. No mission tonight. The new plan and the insertion of 1st Force Recon would wait until morning.

Those who had flown the mission said little during the debrief and added only some commentary during the subsequent discussions to launch again. None of us said the obvious, but it only took a quick glance at any one of us to see that we were glad it was over. In a glance, you could see relief. It wasn't fear because we all would have gone back out, but it was a relief to know we weren't going to unnecessarily put lives at risk for a mission that would not succeed.

I walked back to our tent and sat on my cot, amazed at what we had survived and amazed that more aircraft flying that night hadn't been lost. It may sound callous, but I was surprised that we, the collective we, had lost only one aircraft.

I didn't know any of the aircrew flying the HMM 268 Phrog, but there was an immediate sense of loss. It could have been any of us. There was always an immediate gut punch any time we lost Marines, but this one had been close. We knew someone's life—in this case, many lives—would be changed forever. It was also a call to every flight lead to straighten up, tighten up, and don't screw it up. We had our crews to take care of. I also knew that every one of the thirty plus Marine helicopters flying that night were trained, professional, and doing their absolute best to fight the Ghost, but sometimes, the Ghost simply gets you.

Looking from the outside in, others wouldn't have found the mission particularly significant or memorable, but it had astounded me. The level of effort by every planner, every pilot, every aircrew, every maintainer, and every sailor or Marine associated with the mission had blown me away. I had already packed away some key lessons for Matt, Buss, and Rosie. We would debrief the night later in the morning and then turn to planning for the next night's launch.

Though daylight was hours away, I began to think about tomorrow. Tomorrow morning, the 21st, was not only a new day but also the opening of the ground war. Thousands of Marines and machines would push through the opened gates into Iraq. Back on board *Saipan,* the remainder of the squadron would wake and listen to news of our mission while planning for their own. The ship planned 0600L launches. The remaining HMLA 269 crews would fill every cockpit. Launching in waves, the deck of *Saipan* would burst with activity, ready to support Marine forces heading north and west into Iraq.

My focus returned to the present as Buss and I shuffled back to the tent and found our cots. I had settled myself into mine, taken off my boots, and closed my eyes. It was almost 0200L.

No sooner had my eyes closed when we got our wakeup call via the tent flap opening and a voice booming, "Let's go."

I couldn't tell who it was. It was likely one of the staff officers, one of MAG 29's two or three spare lieutenant colonels ashore as Boomer's liaisons and planners. It didn't matter who had roused us because this was a new day.

"Matt, grab Buss and Rosie. I'm heading out to preflight," I said.

Matt instantly sprang up.

I rose and gathered my gear. We were not flying north right now. Rather, we needed to get these aircraft back onto *Saipan* where other crews waited to fly them right back into Iraq. We also needed to get some more sleep and then prepare for our next launch. We would be taking off again in less than ten hours. The sun was already up, and we couldn't avoid the already familiar morning air, moist with a heavy, dank smell of desert.

Howdy and I hadn't had much time to debrief the mission the night before, but we really didn't need to talk. What we had to say to each other was obvious and could wait. We were roommates on *Saipan*. We had also deployed together aboard the USS *Wasp* in 1995. We had both been assigned to the "Black Knights" of HMM 264 with the 26th MEU supporting operations in the former Yugoslav Republic.

As the overall Cobra flight lead for the opening night on Safwan, he had the responsibility to debrief the intelligence officers and eventually Boomer. Right now, we focused on getting our sections back aboard the ship and planning for tonight's mission. Howdy would take his section back to *Saipan*, and I would take mine. All the arrivals had been coordinated via a tight and detailed arrival and landing plan.

Matt, Buss, Rosie, and I walked to the flight line. As mentioned, the flight line wasn't traditional with pavement and painted lines and numbers. Instead, it was an open desert with helicopters parked everywhere at different angles, as we had landed anywhere we could find open space last night. The helicopters' positioning reflected the previous night's chaos. We had all landed in our own slice of open desert.

We began the ritual of flying Cobras. It started with finding our plane captains, completing a preflight, and then climbing back into the cockpits. We executed an SOP administrative brief. That included startup, radio check-in, and flight formations back to the ship. We had picked up our current frequency cards and identification codes. We were back into the cockpit.

The flight back took us through Kuwait. As the oil fields left our view, we could see the towering skyline of Kuwait City on our right side, a beautiful sight to behold. We had a quiet flight with Matt and I running through checklists and doing a bit of sightseeing. We noted fishermen, oil tankers, and commercial boats. Once we got our "feet wet," we dialed in *Saipan*'s navigational beacon or TACAN, followed the head of the needle that pointed in her direction, and started looking.

Finding a capital ship was not that easy because the almost nine hundred feet of steel runway seemed to blend into the hazy brown sky. We flew at three hundred feet above the Persian Gulf and a mile offshore. "Four-three and flight, switch button seven," I said to an expecting wingman.

Click. Click.

We'd previously checked in with the airborne command-and-control (ABCCC) aircraft, who then had us check in with the ship-assigned radar duties to protect the naval task force. They had assigned us a "squawk," an identity code so US Navy radar operators—and, more importantly, US Navy weapons operators—did not mistake us for enemy aircraft.

We were finally picked up by the ship's radar. "Marjo 43 and 44, flight of two, cherubs three, eight miles to the northwest."

The radar operators were located in *Saipan's* helicopter direction center (HDC). HDC came back. "Mother is 120 at eight. You are cleared to switch tower."

That meant the ship cruised at 120 degrees from our position at eight nautical miles. I pushed my transmit button. "Four-three flight, go tower."

Buss responded with a "44."

I saw the ship and made the turn toward *Saipan*. "Tower 43 and 44, five miles for a catch and kill."

A catch and kill implied that we planned to shut down versus executing a "hot seat." The hot seat involved keeping the aircraft running, having the new aircrew get into each seat one at a time, and then taking off again.

The Air Boss responded, "BRC 250, you are cleared to cross the stern. Report in position for the break."

The BRC, or base recovery course, identified the direction the ship sailed, similar to the tower of an airport announcing the active runway in use.

I quickly acknowledged the Air Boss. “Four-three and flight wilco.” Wilco meant I understood and would comply with their instructions.

Finally, at three miles, we could see her through the haze. I was excited to lay eyes on *Saipan.* The sun bounced off the pale green water that seemed to flow endlessly to the west. An ocean defined by trade routes, fishing lanes, history, and untold drama. I saw the fishing boats, the sea snakes, and the other random boats called dhows. The once innocent or innocuous watercraft now seemed more ominous.

Threats were now abundant, and after only a few days and nights, I saw them everywhere. My perspective had changed. I saw the deck of any boat transformed from displaying the proud catch of local fishermen to acting as an Iraqi or Iranian gun platform. Iran was as close to us as Iraq. US warships from multiple amphibious ready groups and carrier air wings dotted the Persian Gulf, Indian Ocean, Arabian Sea, Gulf of Aden, and Mediterranean Sea.

The United States Navy had sent five aircraft carrier battle groups to support *Operation Iraqi Freedom*. They included the USS *Kitty Hawk* with Carrier Air Wing 5, the USS *Constellation* with Carrier Air Wing 2, the USS *Theodore Roosevelt* with Carrier Air Wing 8, the USS *Abraham Lincoln* with Carrier Air Wing 14, and the USS *Harry S. Truman* with Carrier Air Wing 3. Those sixty-five warships carried more than three hundred F-14A/B Tomcats, F/A-18A/C Hornets, EA-6B Prowlers, E-2C Hawkeyes, and SH-60S Seahawks. They were accompanied by another two dozen guided missile cruisers, frigates, and destroyers and a complement of submarines. The US Navy had also sailed fifty mine-hunting, supply, and support ships in the area of operations. This armada covered thousands of miles of the open ocean, a very tempting target for any foe.

Those carrier air wings brought an undeniable level of commitment from the United States and her allies. There were also the four amphibious ready groups composed of twenty amphibious assault ships. Those ships carried tens of thousands of Marines and sailors. They also were capable of launching AAVs and the nearly 150 helicopters and AV-8B Harriers carried on their flight decks.

This was brinkmanship, the ultimate chess match between the Iraqi leadership and the United States-led coalition, daring Saddam or any of his potential allies to exercise their fight-or-flight response. There was no doubt we were now in the middle of it.

There was *Saipan.* It seemed as if it had only been a few days, but it could have been months since we had flown off. It felt more like years.

We accelerated, and I pushed the nose of the Cobra down to our break altitude of three hundred feet. Close enough to the light chop of the ocean but not low enough to become distracted.

I called the Air Boss and reported, "Tower, Marjo 43 and 44 in position for the break."

Once cleared, we turned hard to the left and flew across the bow. The break meant a 45-degree angle of bank turn to enter the landing pattern. That break gave the aircrew time to prepare for the landing, provided separation of the flight, and also alerted the deck crew to where they should expect us to land.

Buss waited three seconds and did the same.

Matt and I did our final check lists, and I again called the Air Boss. "Marjo 43's abeam."

The Air Boss, normally a senior Navy commander charged with running the floating airport, cleared me to land on spot two reflected by his call of, "43, Charlie, spot two." I turned to final, reduced power, and slowed my airspeed, keeping it between fifty and sixty knots until I crossed the flight deck. We found it important to focus on the flight deck and landing crews, understanding the ship continued to move at about fifteen knots and pitch and roll slightly.

Once over the deck, I pushed on the left rudder pedal to ensure the nose turned, and all fourteen thousand pounds turned into the wind. Aligned, the aircraft pointed directly down the flight deck. Once over the landing spot, I watched the commands of the yellow shirt and reduced power. The sound of the Cobra landing was the skids grinding on the steel deck. Since we didn't have wheels, the quick jolt from the impact let us know we were down.

The landing was uneventful, and again, they de-armed us, called for chains, and shut down. Everything on a flight deck, especially aircraft, is chained to the flight deck or attached to a towing vehicle.

No sooner had they chained us down than our maintenance crews, other pilots, and Boomer greeted us. Boomer was excited to count as many aircraft returning as he had sent off just a few days earlier. I didn't have anything to say, and the noise of the flight deck would have made it useless to try.

I began my solo walk through the maze of passageways and stairwells, stepping over and through knee knockers and stepping around the chaos that is the design of most capital ships. Large doors with watertight fittings are the norm, there to prevent water or fire from compromising the ship should a missile, mortar, mine, or anything else strike us.

As I walked through *Saipan*'s corridors, I sensed a noticeable change in the atmosphere. Or maybe there wasn't a change. Maybe the only thing slightly different was me. The flight deck crews had taken a long look at us, like we were strangers, but maybe I was imagining that too.

Yes, our faces may have had some dirt on them. Our tan desert flight suits might have had some encrusted dust and grease smears. I would admit the helicopters were covered in desert sand and needed a fresh wash. Perhaps it was the empty rocket pods and the gunpower stains on the fuselage from the 20mm cannon fire, but that was it, right?

As I closed the steel door behind me, I was jarred back into the normalcy of the ship. I tried to comprehend how or why normal could still exist. The ship ran as though we were still cruising off the coast of North Carolina. A complete absence of intensity or urgency existed, along with a perceived blindness to what was happening just miles away. Maybe that was how it was supposed to be. A steady sameness based on US Navy discipline, daily routines, and operating procedures that made every day on *Saipan* nearly the same. I found it unnerving, and in some strange way, I needed to get off the ship and back to Joe Foss—or wherever the next Joe Foss would be.

CHAPTER 14

Location: USS *Saipan*, Persian Gulf
Date: 21MAR03
Time: 0800L

We needed time to eat, grab a shower, and brief the upcoming night's mission. But first, we had a short face-to-face with Boomer and our CO after landing on the flight deck. There wasn't much time to talk with either of them—just enough for a thumbs up and a few back slaps. The noise and chaos of the flight deck otherwise overwhelmed us. I also knew we had little time to prepare and brief before we were scheduled to launch for tonight's operations. However, that would have to wait a few more minutes because, right now, I needed to execute our post-flight routine before we could do anything else.

I had shuffled forward with body armor, flight vest, M4 carbine, M9 pistol, gas mask, extra ammunition, and my helmet bag. Again, I continued through a series of passageways, knee knockers, airtight doors, ladder wells, and ramps until I cleared my weapons and returned them and the ammunition to the armory. Next came the flight equipment department to drop off my vest, helmet, NVGs, batteries, and chem lights. I made a final stop at the maintenance department to write up any maintenance issues with my aircraft and have a quick talk with the maintenance team.

I still had the tremendous responsibility of leading the maintenance department, and we couldn't anticipate how much time I could dedicate to provide daily support to them. That also meant a gap of officer leadership in nearly every department. See, each department was led by a pilot and a senior NCO. Each of those pilots was expected to support the mission of the department as well as fly. In peacetime, pilots normally flew three or four times a week and only one mission per day. Now we were expecting our pilots to fly seven days a week and six to eight hours per day. This was unique to naval aviation—maintenance departments led by pilots filling key billets.

As I mentioned, I had attended the formal school for training as a maintenance officer. This was the course that arms officers with the specific micro and macro skills needed to perform essential functions as well as understand the supply and aviation-specific parts ordering and delivery processes. In addition, the pilots in the maintenance department served as the primary post-maintenance functional check pilots, specially trained to test and evaluate aircraft after both minor and major maintenance work. Fortunately, the actual work and expertise in aviation maintenance came from senior NCOs and the few select ground officers assigned to the squadron. In this case, 269 had a talented core of senior NCOs, warrant officers, and, of course, Captain Monty Campbell.

Whether he knew it yet or not, Monty had now become the de facto leader of the maintenance department of three hundred plus Marines. Monty stood behind the counter in our maintenance spaces. It looked like a counter where you could go and order a burger and fries. Instead, it was where they issued pilots their aircraft and was what we considered the epicenter of the department.

"Hey sir, come back in an hour or so, and I'll brief you on the fleet and some issues we need to get ahead of." Monty delivered his words in a rhythm just calming and slow enough to reveal he had been born somewhere south of the Mason-Dixon Line. I just wasn't sure where, and I didn't ask. The relationship with Monty was critical, and I knew I could not earn his trust with a back slap and a simple, "So, where are y'all from, son?" mentality. This would be a long road trip. I had to be comfortable with choosing the destination and then letting Monty pick the roads to get us there.

That sounded good to me. "Thanks, Monty. I'll be back after I drop some gear."

I walked away amazed, but I shouldn't have been. It astonished me that Monty acted as though nothing special had happened somewhere over the horizon in some faraway desert. However, I should have anticipated his level of insight and instincts. I don't recall looking at myself in a mirror or even visualizing what I looked like, but Monty saw something. He saw something that said I needed normal—or what we had created as normal on the ship. Normal was good. Routine was good. Safe and familiar.

Monty Campbell was no average Marine captain. He had twenty-six years of service and experience. He served as an LDO, which meant he had enlisted, earned promotion through the enlisted ranks quickly to gunnery sergeant, and then been selected as a warrant officer. From there, he'd been selected again as an LDO. In the Marine Corps, the LDOs served a variety of technical or expert roles. Primarily used in aviation, the LDO rank ended at lieutenant colonel but allowed those officers to advise and serve beyond the thirty-year limitation of a senior NCO or warrant officer.

As a warrant officer, he'd attended The Basic School in Quantico and been given nearly the same training I had received as a 2nd lieutenant. Though I was a major who had recently been selected for promotion to lieutenant colonel, I still brought nearly every large or seemingly small decision before Monty. I'd take his insights and experience over my seniority any day, and I did.

It wasn't just Monty and me. We had a team of seasoned warrant officers led by Chief Warrant Officer Luke Crouson. We also had master sergeants and gunnery sergeants, all with decades of aviation maintenance experience. We had developed a playbook to phase aircraft, supplies, ammunition, and Marines ashore while planning to maintain a small team on the ship. With operations only beginning, it fell on Monty and that team to create a new normal both on *Saipan* and wherever we landed inside of Iraq.

I finally made it back to my stateroom. I shared a two-hundred-and-something-square-foot space with three other majors, one being

Howdy and another being Scott Jensen. Scott was the most senior and experienced Huey pilot in the squadron. The Idaho native was the previous 269 maintenance officer and had left me with a well-tuned and disciplined department. Scott and I had been classmates at the Amphibious Warfare School and the Command and Staff College in Quantico, Virginia. Both schools were ten-month courses designed to educate and prepare captains and then majors for positions of more responsibility. The schools were also great opportunities to make professional and personal connections.

Having landed a few minutes ahead of me, Howdy was sitting at his desk. We had been friends for more than ten years, and I felt fortunate to have him on this deployment. As a former weapons school instructor, he not only had every qualification and designation in the Cobra, but he also had thousands of hours of experience leading and problem solving in the Cobra.

Howdy turned toward me slightly. “Sup?”

With a slight head nod, I quipped, “Nothing. Sup with you?”

Head turned back to his notes. “Nothing. Just sitting for a minute.”

Our standard greeting—exactly what I needed.

Four single beds or “racks,” a sink, four desks, and storage made up our stateroom. I found it a humble but welcome sight. I had enough time to shower and put on a fresh flight suit and was looking forward to relaxing for a bit when I heard a knock. I opened the door to find the headquarters squadron commander, Lieutenant Colonel Roy “Ozzie” Osborn. He worked directly for Boomer.

“Gents, Boomer wants you both in his stateroom in five minutes.” He quickly turned as the door slammed behind him.

I looked at the ceiling. “What the fuck was that all about?”

Howdy knew I wasn’t really asking him, so he didn’t answer.

I sensed we were walking into an ambush. I did a quick mental review of the past three days. We had done everything right, or at least nothing terribly wrong, and certainly everything they had asked us to do.

I began to write down a few thoughts and readied to make the walk. Maybe it was nothing—just a normal debrief. But the door slam… What was that?

We both started the walk to Boomer's room. I pushed my door shut. As it closed, it made the same metallic slamming noise. Every interior shutting door—aka hatch—on the ship sounded like it slammed. Maybe I was being a bit tough on Ozzie. He had spent several sleepless nights on *Saipan* trying to track everything we were doing ashore. Plus, it wasn't in his personality to be petty or ill-tempered. I didn't have enough time to ask why, and it didn't matter.

Location: MCAS New River, North Carolina
Date: 31JUL95
Time: 1345L

I pulled off the final target as the other two Cobras maneuvered onto my wing. We were a flight of three, flying back from a live fire range just off the North Carolina coast. It was the end of summer or perhaps just the end of the summer for me. Command had called me off leave to head out for another deployment. Not just any deployment but another six-month shipboard deployment. This one was with the 26th MEU to support the beginning of an increased presence and upscaling of the US mission in the former Yugoslavia. I'd enjoyed my last flight with 269. This was my last before joining the new squadron—a new squadron that was deploying in a month.

The squadron had been given a plus up of four additional AH-1Ws and four additional CH-53Es. I was now a "Black Knight" of HMM 264, assigned as the aviation combat element to the 26th MEU. I'd joined the squadron as one of the plus up crews and was not particularly enthused about adding another six-month deployment to my résumé. This would be the fourth deployment in nearly as many years.

That particular flight was a check flight for the CO, then Lieutenant Colonel "Shooter" Spencer. We had completed all the prerequisites and executed a three Cobra attack with 2.75-inch rockets and the 20mm cannon. We'd finished the last few minutes of what had been a successful requalification flight for Shooter. We had spent the previous thirty minutes of the flight making the required radio calls to various agencies, maneuvering the flight through standardized routing back to our base at New River, North Carolina, and reached the last ten minutes.

Shooter spoke with a calm, flat North Carolina accent. "Ferris, I appreciate what you have done, not just for me but for the squadron over the past four plus years."

I didn't like that. It felt like an unfinished sentence, so I said nothing. I sensed that statement was just one slice, the first slice of what was the glad sandwich, which is best served as a three-part club. The first layer is an opening compliment. The second is the meat or the real message, and the last is another compliment or slice of bread to take with you. Hmmm.

Shooter continued. "Ferris, I observe, listen, evaluate, and make professional and career decisions every day, and some decisions are never easy."

Shit, this was going south fast. My brain maneuvered to full reflection and recall mode. I ran the film in my mental projector backwards. Someone must have told him about my cliff diving in Greece when I was assigned to 365, or maybe the incident with the moped in Barcelona, but most likely the golf cart SNAFU in Rota. They'd said we were all paid up, and I certainly wasn't the only golf cart driver to have found his way into a sand trap at Naval Station Rota, Spain.

He continued. "Watch out for certain people. They don't always share your enthusiasm and don't always appreciate your methods. I'm telling you this because I think you have a bright future."

There it was. The meat and the last slice of bread.

"Copy that, sir. I appreciate that." I needed to close this open door and close it fast.

What I wanted to know, and what I wanted to say, was, "Hey, Skipper. Who are those chickenshits who won't talk to me about my 'enthusiasm'?"

But I said nothing, and the flight ended uneventfully. I knew someone had talked to him, and those "someones" were not lieutenants or captains. I had my suspicions. Nonetheless, I got his point to say less and observe and listen more.

CHAPTER 15

Location: USS *Saipan*, Persian Gulf
Date: 21MAR03
Time: 0920L

Ozzie's summons sounded ominous, but what the hell did Boomer want with us? It was true that the opening night had not all gone to plan, but it wasn't on us, was it? Not much to think about—the boss wanted to see me, and I had to go. It wasn't a request. No god-fearing major wants one-on-one time with the Colonel, the Old Man, the Boss, the Big Cheese, El Hefe…you get it.

I had learned to steer well clear of senior officers, though I was not always successful. I did that instinctively, an automatic defense to being caught and tried for the laundry list of high crimes against the Crown I had likely committed. Truthfully, I was not a natural rule follower, and I had certainly colored outside the lines on more than one occasion. Hence my callsign "Ferris," similar to the character Ferris Bueller in the film *Ferris Bueller's Day Off.* I had historically managed to weave my way out of tight spots and avoid taking any direct hits from senior officers, but my time may have just run out.

To be candid, most trouble found me when I dealt with serious people—or, more accurately, people who took themselves too seriously. I generally didn't trust those types of personalities. They hid things. They used arrogance, abrasiveness, and sometimes an abusive personality to hide their own inadequacies. They used that as armor to prevent juniors and peers alike from questioning them—from finding out they don't know and perhaps never knew. They harnessed their own inadequate version of reality to become a forced truth.

I certainly took my work seriously, but I joked and smiled. My gut told me that seriousness often got in the way of ideas. I was naturally optimistic, and I also saw that seriousness often manifested itself as pessimism. Plus, I was simply too stubborn or too stupid to fake it. I had seen too many who walked a complete bullshit walk, talked a complete bullshit talk, and never had the skills, balls, or talent to execute what they not only expected but often demanded their subordinates to accomplish.

I had to remind myself that smiling and keeping people confident had nothing to do with lowering standards or accepting poor performance; in fact, it was exactly the opposite. It was about building a team that was never afraid to fail.

Boomer, from my increasing observation of him, was not afraid to fail, not afraid to change, and not afraid to smile. I would only remember that later, but not now as I found myself knocking on his stateroom door. I stood there anxiously waiting, having already suffered a significant confidence drain. I frankly didn't need an ass-chewing or lecture.

"Enter," a voice called from inside.

I pushed inward on his hatch, stepped through, and looked down. No plastic on the floor...that was a good sign. So, the chances of me getting the *Godfather* or *Goodfellas* mob hit treatment was reduced. The idea of being somehow professionally assassinated, shot right there, rolled up in the plastic, and tossed overboard, was less likely. Anyway, I think you get the picture.

Howdy and I arrived to find that Boomer had an audience. In his stateroom, most of the flight leads and planners from the opening night had assembled. As the senior officer, Boomer had a large stateroom by ship standards with enough space for a briefing table and chairs. This room was normally reserved for the MEU commander, but in this case, and with no expeditionary unit embarked, it went to the air group commander.

We had been called to tell our version of the night. Did we have any lessons learned that would benefit the group? Did we have any epiphanies or revelations to share now that we were back aboard *Saipan*? Of course, we did, but somehow, we didn't. We stood there, exhausted. I couldn't concentrate on anything anyone said. I was trying to visualize how we could ever survive the next mission, which was beginning in just a few hours.

Standing in the back of the room, I listened to a few of the aircrew outline what they had been requested to recount, but I couldn't clearly hear the conversation. There was too much static, too much sidebar noise. Truth was, I didn't care either. The stories may have seemed enlightening and likely inspiring, but I investigated every flight leader's eyes. They wearily told their tales, but it was obvious that, for most, their hearts were not in it, and their minds were miles away.

Boomer could sense it. He listened to everyone but wasn't swayed by the random opinion or the purported glorious achievements of the blowhard. He was most concerned with finding the ground truth. That truth was elusive. We didn't have it and we didn't know what it was. Thankfully, Boomer wasn't the type of leader who demanded details—at least not now. He mostly wanted to thank us and ask us what we needed.

Hubris aside, I knew one simple truth. What we needed, he didn't have, and he couldn't get—either we already had the "it," or it was too late. The Ghost would see to that.

His staff had briefed him on as many of the opening night's details as they could, but it would take weeks to dissect and understand all the drama of the first night. The atmosphere in the stateroom loomed heavy, just the dankness and discomfort of all being in the same place.

The Cobra flight lead who had engaged friendlies last night also stood in the room, but we would have never guessed what he'd been responsible for from his demeanor. Apparently, he was already playing the deflection game, beginning to blame others. Scheming to find his own personal and professional escape route, an easy out on the backs of his crews. Sickening.

The normal smartass rhetoric had been replaced by a more intense silence. When my turn came, I answered questions as briefly as possible.

"Yes, sir. We engaged several vehicles with 20mm and rockets." "No, sir. We didn't see anything else." "Yes, sir. It was dark out there, and yes, we initially engaged our assigned targets with rockets and guns."

It was clear to everyone in the room that I was tired and distracted. What I didn't say had more impact than my verbal message.

Boomer was doing exactly what good leaders do. He was listening, learning, watching, and likely trying to consume as much of the mission he could. He had the immense responsibility of sending us all back out tonight and the next night and the next. In hindsight, he was trying to help us improve without telling us we needed to get better. He had the advantage of looking from the outside in. I was simply too tired and too distracted to believe that anyone could say anything that would change our futures. That was up to us.

In some strange way, I didn't want to share my thoughts, so I kept my answers short. In those brief moments, I began to understand the enormity of the previous night. Maybe I was enamored with what was only a peek into the future. In any event, I kept my musings to myself. Those reflections were private, a shared experience for me, Matt, Buss, and Rosie. These were neither state secrets nor critical lessons learned but rather my initial thoughts, and thoughts I had not completely processed yet.

I wanted out of that stateroom. I sensed the pressure building until I felt vulnerable and somehow alone. I wanted to be back in the Cobra with Matt in the front and Buss and Rosie back on my wing. It would all make sense then. I looked over at Howdy and the other trusted flight leads, and I could tell they were already visualizing tonight's mission, preparing for another long night.

As the sun began to set on the 21st, our launch time approached. There had been no great revelations, no universal truths exposed, no proclamations made since we had landed several hours earlier. No resolution on the reported friendly fire incident, no changes to our

SOP, nothing. It seemed as if yesterday was already forgotten, and that was fine with me.

Location: Persian Gulf on USS *Saipan*
Date: 21MAR03
Time: 2130L

The mission for tonight was wide open. We had been briefed on the multiple Iraqi divisions in the south. The basic plan was to launch fully armed and check in with the ship's direction center. From there, we would check in with a shipborne command center and finally an airborne command-and-control Marine KC-130 named "Sky Chief" once we went "feet dry" or reentered Iraqi airspace. The flying command center would push aviation assets to specific areas while other attack aviation assets were given specific missions or cleared to conduct deep air support (DAS). Deep implied going beyond the front lines to conduct reconnaissance and engage enemy units. That also meant going beyond artillery support and certainly beyond any friendly units to recover us should we get ourselves shot down.

The wing gave us the simple mission to attack to the north with a focus on artillery to clear a path for the fast-moving 1st MARDIV. The division was led by a crafty infantry officer. He brought a contagious enthusiasm and sense of purpose that Marines felt not only in the division but throughout the MEF. Major General James Mattis commanded the division and had made his intent well known to the air wing. He had confidence that his tanks, fighting vehicles, and infantry could handle Iraqi armor and infantry, but we needed to kill Iraqi artillery.

We all had copies of "No Better Friend, No Worse Enemy." It was his personal letter to the division, and I took to heart many of his observations. For me, that meant being the hunter and not the hunted. General Mattis had written the letter to the Marines of the 1st MARDIV, but I think we all had a copy and pulled from his powerful message.

Our mission tonight was to conduct armed reconnaissance around the port city of Basra and around the southwestern city of Nasiriyah. Both had significant Iraqi mechanized units located in and around the cities. We planned to engage a total of eight Iraqi divisions with a combination of infantry, tanks, artillery, and fighting vehicles. We'd accomplish this with one Marine division and the British 7th Armored Brigade to our right, but also with the 3rd MAW at 335 aircraft strong—all combined and attacking north. Beyond those forces, we expected to find the Republican Guard mechanized divisions and Saddam's Special Republican Guard divisions as we moved closer to Baghdad.

The intelligence planners and targeting planners had created a matrix of the country and divided it into alphanumeric locations, which we had plotted on our maps and loaded into our navigation system. We also used the first of many forward arming and refueling points (FARPs). Those were genius and the brainchild of the Marine wing support group. They gave Marine helicopter aviation the ability to generate an unprecedented number of flights or sorties. The FARP teams would have a fuel truck, an ordnance truck, light security vehicles, and several mechanics who worked on any of the four types of Marine helicopters in theater. Led by a major or lieutenant colonel, the FARPs frequently became vulnerable to enemy fire and often co-located with the most forward Marine combat units.

BOOK TWO

Shame on the Moon

When the will defies fear, when duty throws the gauntlet down to fate, when honor scorns to compromise with death—that is heroism.

— Robert Green Ingersoll (Author, Abolitionist, Attorney, Civil War Veteran) 1872

In the absence of specific guidance, attack north!

—Lieutenant General Jim Conway (Commanding General I MEF) 19 March 2003

CHAPTER 16

Location: An-Nasiriyah, Iraq
Date: 23MAR03
Time: 0700L

"Reveille, reveille, reveille. All hands heave out and trice up," poured from every speaker via the ship's loudspeaker system or 1 Main Circuit (1MC), which was received in every part of the ship. The routine had begun, but recovering from last night's nearly eleven hours in the cockpit would take a few more hours. Yesterday, Saturday the 22nd, our first permanent base had been established at Jalibah, a former Iraqi MiG-25 base located just miles south of another Iraqi air base, Talil. Both bases had been the home of Iraqi MiG-25 interceptors, along with Russian-built SU-23 and SU-25 attack jets.

Though reveille had only just sounded, the ship and crew had been at work for hours. In fact, we had already begun launching helicopters ashore. Plus, we had sent several of our Hueys to join the 1st MARDIV for what we called direct support. We provided Hueys to the division and to the four regiments. In turn, they kept the aircrew and aircraft fueled, armed, watered, and fed.

The Phrogs and Marines of HMM 162 also flew ashore, lugging parts and people into our new home of Jalibah, or "Riverfront." We—more accurately, the wing planers—had agreed to give names of American baseball parks to all temporary air bases or arming and refueling points. We named Riverfront first, an honor for the Cincinnati Reds, but we soon followed that with the likes of Fenway, Comisky, Coors, Wrigley, Tiger, Astrodome, and others.

Our mission remained simple: to fly in support of the advancing 1st MARDIV and Task Force Tarawa units. That included both CAS and armed reconnaissance missions. Part of the latter involved going ahead of friendly lines while also screening their eastern and western flanks. Keeping pressure on the defending Iraqi units would prove simpler than resupplying and maintaining aircraft.

Iraqi Army's 3rd Corps commanded Nasiriyah and the adjacent areas of southern Iraq. A mix of 1960s and 1970s vintage main battle tanks called T-54s, T-55s, and T-62s comprised their most mobile and lethal force. With tanks were hundreds of 1970s Russian-designed infantry fighting vehicles, which were labeled based on their designs and capabilities and called BTRs, MTLBs, and BMPs. For example, BMP was an acronym for "boyevaya mashina pekhoty," which translates to English as "infantry fighting vehicle." Alongside those were associated artillery and infantry units. Though upgraded over the preceding decades, not a single armored vehicle would be a match for modern missiles, Marine tanks, and Marine anti-armor crews.

Those forces also did not reflect Saddam's best troops. The Republican Guard and Special Republican Guard divisions served Baghdad and other dedicated cities. Those left to defend the south were young conscripts led by too few warrant and commissioned officers. Saddam Hussein had placed a priority on the capital and left the undermanned and outgunned 3rd Corps the unrealistic and near suicidal mission of stopping the coalition.

Three divisions made up the Iraqi Corps: the 11th Infantry Division, the 51st Mechanized Infantry Division, and the 6th Armored Division. We had engaged portions of the 51st on the opening night and following days and nights. The 6th maintained a position further to the northeast, and that left the 11th to defend Nasiriyah. US forces would encounter three brigades assigned to the 11th, along with numerous paramilitary units in the streets of Nasiriyah.

The 23rd of March began with a sense of familiarity. The early morning launches from *Saipan* were followed by afternoon sections headed feet dry. Of course, our planned launch was scheduled for just before sunset.

What we didn't know and would not know for several hours was that the US Army and US Marines in and around An-Nasiriyah had kicked a hornet's nest. While bypassing the city to the west, one unit of the US Army's 3rd Infantry Division (3rd ID) had driven straight into downtown Nasiriyah. The US Army's 507th Maintenance Company, in light-skinned or unarmored vehicles, had simply missed a turn along Highway 8. Instead of traveling to the west of Nasiriyah, the convoy had driven north, straight into the heart of the city. Over the next hour or so, they had become disoriented and separated while under continuous fire from Iraqi irregular forces.

By 0800L, several vehicles of the 507th had made it back out of the city to the south. Their desperate calls for support put the Marines of Task Force Tarawa on high alert. With Task Force Tarawa being the 507th's only option, Brigadier General Rich Natonski and his task force turned their focus on both the 507th and the enemy forces inside and around Nasiriyah. One thing remained clear: The 507th had been watched, analyzed, and then engaged.

They suffered heavy casualties with an unknown number of soldiers captured or missing. As the task force made plans, the aircrews of HMLAs 169, 267, and 269 were being pushed toward the city. Additionally, Boomer had prepared HMMs 162 and 365 to ready their Phrogs for casualty evacuations and resupply missions likely very near or inside the city. The message traffic sent via satellite phone and secure internet told the MEF commander and the wing commander that Nasiriyah was now a serious problem. This put more squadrons on notice that something significant had unfolded in the otherwise innocuous southern Iraqi city. Before arriving overhead, they initially watched, waited, and wondered. They would not have to wait long.

Brigadier General Natonski and the 2nd Marine Regiment's CO, Colonel Ron Bailey, pushed forces up toward the stricken convoy. Marine units—specifically, the 8th Tank Battalion and other lead elements of Task Force Tarawa—made contact with the 507th south of the city. News from the 507th's commander, a US Army captain, was not good. There remained an unknown number of 507th soldiers fighting for their lives somewhere in the city. A melee would ensue, and by the end of the day, more than thirty US Army soldiers and US Marines would make the ultimate sacrifice. There would also be another sixty wounded and still more unaccounted for.

The command-and-control KC-130 was up on all radio networks, scrambling air support into Nasiriyah. HMLA 269 Cobras and Hueys were already on station, along with HMM 162 Phrogs. Burning Humvees, US supply trucks, and other destroyed or disabled vehicles around the city's southeastern bridges greeted the crews. That represented the first of several wakeup calls. These were not flag-waving Iraqis awaiting liberation but well-armed and apparently well-led forces.

The pounding fist on the door woke me up, and the sound of the door hitting its steel backstop provided the punctuation.

"Sir, let's go. You need to get to the ready room. I'm not sure what's going on, but we've got a bunch of shot-up Cobras."

"Thanks." *Whoever you are*, I thought in my dreamlike stupor. "Let 'em know I'm on my way."

It was one of our operation's lieutenants. He vanished, and the door slammed shut as fast as it had opened. I sprang out of my rack, swiftly dressed, and, taking a quick pace over knee knockers, ducked under airtight doors and through passageways to the ready room, the heartbeat of any squadron. I pushed through the door, my heart beating faster and faster. I could feel the tension and knew something big or bad or both was happening.

I wanted to ask the first person I saw what was going on, but that would only add to the confusion. Instead, I turned to see both of our flat-screen TVs showing coverage from CNN's and NBC's embedded reporters filming from a few miles outside of an unknown town. It would not be unknown for long. Nasiriyah would capture our focus—and the nation's focus—for the next week.

We had four sections briefing for the afternoon launch, which had now accelerated. Some paced, others watched, and a few simply stood and listened. Everyone looked for someone to provide updates. Unfortunately, in a situation like that, little intelligence existed, so we could only count on spot reports from those with eyes on the ground.

Before walking to the flight deck, I stopped at our maintenance control to review the logbook of the Cobra I had been assigned and to talk with Monty and our senior NCOs. I expected to be gone until the next morning, so I also needed to brief the CO on anything critical.

Walking through the doors into the maintenance control room, I found quite a scene. The energy was electric. Buzzing. The day crews had done some incredible work, but we also had proof of the accuracy of that famous Marine general who'd once said, "The enemy gets a vote." After landing on *Saipan*, the pilots and maintenance crews had discovered Iraqi bullet holes in tail booms, FLIRs, engine cowlings, fiberglass panels by the cockpit, and other holes near the main transmission. The Iraqis had voted and would likely vote often.

Pilots were talking a hundred miles an hour to mechanics and supervisors about where Iraqi gunners had hit them or what ordnance systems needed fixing or recalibrating. Pure mayhem! I wish I could have stayed longer, but I needed to get back to the flight deck of the ship. So, I grabbed Matt, Buss, and Rosie from the ready room, and we made our way topside.

We all grabbed our gear, climbed a series of ladders, and entered the flight deck from a balcony access point. Finally, we made it to our destination. We were back where we belonged. In what felt like no time, we were once again in a Cobra, getting ready to launch for night three operations. Wash, rinse, repeat.

Strapped into the cockpit—check. Canopy closed and checklist started—check. Purple shirts fueling—check. Ordies or red shirts arming all weapons systems—check. White shirt safety overwatching for safety violations—check. Blue shirts removing chains—check. Big light by the Air Boss's perch has gone green—check.

Where were the knots in my stomach? Where was the sense of dread that I'd felt just hours ago? They'd left me in peace for now, but I had the distinct feeling that dread waited for me "feet dry."

Over the noise of the flight deck, we heard the Air Boss announce, "We are launching skids off spots three, four, five, and six." He quickly followed that with a call on the tower frequency. "Deadly 31 and 32, winds are 5 degrees to starboard at eight knots, cleared to launch spots three and four."

Matt and I had lost track of each other over the past hours and had only rendezvoused in the ready room to receive the intelligence brief with Buss and Rosie. The plan called for us to check in with Sky Chief once we became "feet dry" and just shy of the Iraqi border. Sky Chief would send us to support specific units, vector us into the predesignated "kill boxes," or essentially kick us loose to conduct armed reconnaissance.

The day shift had trickled in over the last few hours before our mission. We still had several sections out as we, the night shift, began to launch. I saw Captain Bob "Rider" Finneran, one of our more seasoned captains and a respected flight lead, at the maintenance control window. The maintenance control window was a six-by-eight hole, complete with commercial-grade rolling security shutters. It resembled a Burger King drive-up window, not a place to conduct aviation maintenance, but there Rider was. His voice was calm but intense. Several senior NCOs were listening intently to him. The conversation was animated, and I knew that his sense of urgency and intensity might just get lost in translation.

I walked to the counter and stood close enough to be recognized but only listened. I could hear his message, but I could also see myself speaking the same words. Rider was still processing the details of the day's missions while simultaneously trying to paint the clearest picture to the maintenance teams of what needed fixing. These were insightful and important points. Some could wait, and others needed immediate action.

Rider was a proud Auburn University Tiger and had returned from another full day of combat flight operations. He and his crew had delivered rocket, missile, and 20mm cannon fire to Iraqi forces; been shot at; been hit by Iraqi ground fire; and made it back to *Saipan*. It had been a full eight hours of flying for him and his crews, and as quickly as I'd stepped up to listen, he'd disappeared. He had made his points and then faded away. In all likelihood, he was headed for a shower and some sleep. After all, he was, like all of us, back on the flight schedule tomorrow.

Our squadron flight schedule was linked with the bigger air tasking order (ATO). The ATO and, therefore, our schedules were designed to have a continuous presence of HMLA 269 aircraft supporting I MEF. This meant having five to six Hueys and twelve to fourteen Cobras flying at any given time over a twenty-four-hour period for the duration of the conflict. A tall order for sure. It made us all vulnerable.

In fact, we were vulnerable based on our location, on a limited supply chain for high-end parts, and on Murphy's Law. Our maintenance team had game-planned for high-demand parts and built teams of mechanics that could fix aircraft not only on the ship but wherever was needed in Iraq. That included having communication with damaged aircraft and effectively explaining what they needed on site. Finding, securing, and moving high-end parts such as FLIRs, rotor blades, transmissions, and engines became a grave concern.

Time accelerated, and we sat strapped into the Cobra. Truth was, we wore the Cobra more than we buckled, belted, and hooked ourselves into it. The more we flew it, the more the controls became an almost natural extension of our hands and feet.

I gave a quick call. "Matt, you set?"

Lost in thought, Matt shot back, "Sir, I'm set."

We didn't need to say anything else. The deck crew was moving in and out of our rotor arch as the bow of *Saipan* gently pitched up and down at a comfortable 5 to 6 degrees. It was time to launch. We had already removed the chains and armed the weapons. Matt gave a thumbs-up to the yellow shirt. I pulled slowly into a hover while Matt checked the engine performance and did a scan of the cockpit. As he looked inside, he said, "100 percent torque, gauges green, and the panels clean. Clear to slide left."

I pushed the stick to the left with a coordinated addition of the right rudder pedal to counter the torque while simultaneously challenging the twin GE turbines by pulling up on the collective. We pulled until I hit 100 percent torque, demanding that more than two thousand horsepower be transferred from the engines to the transmission. Matt saluted the yellow shirt, and I eased the nose forward. Away she climbed.

I keyed the mic. "Tower, Deadly 31 ops normal for the turn." Then, I looked to my left as Buss climbed up to our altitude and closed fast.

I heard Rosie from Buss's Cobra. "Tower, Deadly 32 ops normal. I have lead insight."

The Air Boss responded matter-of-factly. "Three-one and 32 left turn out approved, frequency change approved." He paused for another second in case we needed reassurance. "We'll see you soon."

Ha! What did he know? How the hell did he know that? That unsettling feeling began to seep back into my bones.

"Deadly 31 flight, go button six," I said.

Rosie responded with a simple "Two," which is called a front side check. We would also get in the habit of doing a backside check-in to ensure we had the proper frequencies.

"Three-one check."

Rosie again responded with a "Two."

I made the next call. "Center, Deadly 31 a flight of two, cherubs three, heading 320."

Center responded, "31 and flight, radar contact, report approaching feet dry."

I had turned over the radio to Matt, and he got the call. "Center, 31 wilco."

Matt would take the responsibility for talking to most of the external agencies, while I would talk directly to Buss to control the flight and our fires. I would also talk to any tertiary units such as fixed-wing attack platforms, mortars, artillery, or tanks. Either I would control them or pass one of those responsibilities to Buss and Rosie. We didn't know then, but our ability to orchestrate and coordinate fires would become our greatest skill.

I began arming our defensive systems per our checklists. These prepared crews and their systems for combat. They also included a weapons check. For us, that meant shooting a quick burst of 20mm rounds to ensure the gun worked as advertised.

I called it. "Three-one flight, go spread for weapons checks."

Rosie once again responded, "Two."

I followed that with, "31 is hot. Matt, master arm is going to arm."

The cannon immediately began spitting out approximately twenty 20mm rounds.

Once complete, I called back to Buss, "31's fenced in," meaning all checks complete. That included our defense systems designed to defeat heat-seeking and radar missiles.

I trusted the blankness of the horizon as well as the familiarity of the flight to feet dry. That should certainly have given me a newfound sense of confidence. I wasn't so sure, but when I looked up through my NVGs, I recognized stars and the lights of Kuwait. I also looked off my nose past Matt's shadow in the front seat. We both could see the oblivion that was Iraq. Maybe March 23rd would be a better day, a better night, with no nightmares ahead.

Those fading Kuwaiti lights combined with the glow of the coastline were an illusion. The Ghost had returned and certainly recruited some new believers—some disciples. Nonetheless, the retreat of the March 20th sandstorms gave me a splinter of hope. We flew at nearly 130 knots and five hundred feet over the ocean on a moonless night, headed for the Iraqi coast. *Hmm.* My pulse instinctively quickened. *Who had she recruited to do her bidding?*

I felt a twinge in my gut—a pinch. Were we now on the B side of a "one-hit wonder"? We had spent last night singing our A side to the backs of a disinterested audience, and now we had a B side to sell. Neither song would ever be a hit, but it was time to start singing.

Screw them all, I thought. Our flight of two carried eight Hellfire missiles, eight TOW missiles, fifty-four 2.75-inch rockets, and twelve hundred rounds of 20mm HE incendiary rounds. We were a radio call away from raining down death and untold destruction. We had our laser and GPS to designate a weapon for any threat. We could drop bombs, artillery, mortars, rockets, or cannon fire at will, all accurately on nearly any target. It sounded clear and simple, but the Ghost lurked out there in concert with an army of nearly one million Iraqis.

As we turned back to a familiar northwestern heading, I made another unenthusiastic call. "Center, 31 flight approaching feet dry for the switch."

The muted response came promptly. "Roger, 31. Cleared for the switch. Safe flight."

I needed to get this moving along and get us feet dry. "Three-one switch."

Click. Click.

Time to get the backside check. "Three-one flight check."

"Two," Buss answered.

Perfect. We are over the Kuwaiti border, armed, about to check in.

Based on the CNN footage and descriptions from the aircrew during our turnovers, we knew the carnage of An-Nasiriyah. What made that different and more compelling was the overnight bags in our tail booms along with our other worldly possession in the back of the Phrogs flying into Riverfront. I had checked out of the Hotel *Saipan* and checked into a place that was unfamiliar to me. We were in the land of not quite right. Things were changing fast.

By 2030L, we were feet dry and fenced in with our combat checks complete.

"Sky Chief, Deadly 31 up as fragged for your work."

A frag or fragmentary order is an abbreviated version of the much larger and more complicated operations order. Typically, you can think of it as a short update. So, "up as fragged" was slang indicating we knew the basic plan and carried the ordnance requested.

Never had a longer sentence come out of my mouth, and never had Matt, Buss, Rosie, and I found ourselves so unimaginably unprepared for the next order from Sky Chief.

CHAPTER 17

Location: West of Basra, Iraq
Date: 23MAR03
Time: 2350L

Sky Chief had work for us. "Deadly 31, proceed to B2 and contact Mouth on Plum."

I acknowledged the call. "Three-one wilco."

That call was a welcome change. We had navigated across southeastern Iraq for the past six hours, covering an area measuring nearly five thousand square miles, the size of Connecticut. We had exhausted the limits of visual reconnaissance around Basra and southeastern Iraq. As a result, we were weary of overflying the same locations and fatigued at looking at the same small islands that dotted the Euphrates River.

"Three-one flight coming left to west and climbing to five hundred feet," I announced.

Click. Click.

We headed west, about ninety miles from Basra to the outskirts of Nasiriyah, with only the sight of a dark, open, and lifeless desert. Where was everyone? Where was the 1st MARDIV, the US Army's 3rd ID, or any sign of life? Prior to arriving, we turned slightly south to Riverfront for fuel.

We called for the radio switch. "Three-one flight, switch Riverfront."

"Two."

I continued our calls for clearance to land. "Riverfront, Deadly 31 is a flight of two from the west in for gas."

We remained about ten miles out, but we could hear the hurried calls of helicopters landing, refueling, rearming, taking off, and repositioning. That place was hopping with Marine helicopters along with Army Blackhawk and Apache helicopters. Interesting.

Riverfront had Marines from the 3rd MAW's communications squadron, so the sound of seasoned air controllers reassured us.

The controller must have seen us, as he called out to us as we came closer for landing. "Deadly 31, push midfield and to the north of the runway. There is open ramp space with some Cobras shut down. That's your gas."

"Three-one flight copies," I replied.

Buss could already anticipate our call, but I made it anyway. "Three-two, go trail, and let's land east of those AHs parked on the ramp."

Click. Click.

I knew the two clicks on the radio were from Buss or Rosie. With two radios in the Cobra, I kept the volume turned up just a bit on our discrete frequency. It was a minute detail, but it allowed me to immediately recognize the two clicks came from 32. It was one of the hundreds of small things. Call it an unwritten SOP, call it familiarity, call it anything you like, but it reduced unnecessary communications, increased efficiency, and built trust. Trust was the real fuel of this section, and every day, we built a little more.

We approached the ramp from a high hover, which meant about fifty feet and a thirty-knot air taxi above the fine dust we'd agitated below us. I had flown us slightly south of Jalibah to keep the entire view of the airfield in front of us. I wanted to ensure the directions the controller gave us matched what we saw through the NVGS and FLIR.

"Matt, you see anything on the ramp?" I asked.

I could see his helmet and NVGs pivoting. "Yup, I see a few Cobras shut down and a bunch of Blackhawks further to the east on the ramp."

We flew across the long east- and west-oriented runways, heading north.

"Come right, and there's plenty of space away from those Cobras," Matt said.

No linemen, no signals from anyone, and no fuel trucks. An interesting start. We had ambient light from all the Army and Marine ground vehicles contributing to our standard landing. Matt and Rosie hopped out of their front seats to de-arm us. Then, we shut down, meandered out of the cockpit, and met at the nose of my Cobra.

All of the 269 helicopters had nose art—that is, hand-painted pictures and designs. The Marines had asked, and the CO had approved, so something resembling WWII B-17 art adorned each Huey and Cobra. My Cobra had a simple graphic: a yellow smiley face with a bullet hole in the forehead. An odd image, but when you ask Marines to get creative, they get creative.

The four of us had a brief chat about the uneventful arrival. What we found notable was the number of helicopters arriving from the east and departing to the northwest. Dozens of Army UH-60 Blackhawk transports and even more AH-64 Apache attack helicopters. They were units of the Army's 3rd ID, all moving along Highway 8, bypassing Nasiriyah, and heading straight for adventures in exotic places to the north.

What we considered odd were the other four Marine Cobras that were shut down. The aircrew all listened intently to a briefing. The tail marking clearly identified them as belonging to MAG 39. It surprised me that no one had approached us. Not that we needed a welcome party or any care and feeding, but idle curiosity would have been expected. Didn't they want to ask where we had come from, what we had seen, what lessons and intelligence on the enemy we potentially had? Anything? Nothing.

We walked closer to see what they found so interesting. After a few seconds, I realized it was just one guy giving an admin brief. He was not the Great and Powerful Oz. Instead, he was someone completely unrecognizable. He said nothing about an enemy or tactics, but that was fine. I was sure he'd covered all that before we'd arrived. I said nothing, finding the scene both fascinating and strange. Strangest of all was the lack of acknowledgment we received.

I approached one of the pilots standing in the back. "Hey, how do we get fuel trucks here?"

He turned as though I had bothered him like an uninvited guest. "Can you keep it down? We are briefing."

It was a young pilot, a random lieutenant or captain. I could feel my blood boil. Who was this pissant? No one wore rank on their desert flight suits in combat, but this guy should have known better.

I prided myself on not ever using my rank as a weapon, but he really tempted me. I wanted to say, "Hey, asshole, I don't give two shits about you or your fucking brief. I'm tired, and now I'm pissed off. I want to get gas and then get as far away from you dipshits as possible."

I was about to bite his face off, ready to pass on my opinions, but instead, I turned around as an unnatural wave of calm and maturity washed over me. It was a rare occurrence indeed. I had no time for these people. My concerns focused on the three silhouettes leaning on the FLIR of Deadly 31, chatting like we were on the flight line in California or North Carolina.

I looked east and began walking toward a small convoy of idling Army Humvees about a hundred yards down the ramp. Then, I called out, "You guys got any JP we can steal?" I must have looked pretty strange with my helmet on and NVGs down, walking alone out of the darkness on the ramp.

Out of the Humvee popped an Army captain. He took a quick look at me before responding. "Yes, sir. We got fuel trucks about a quarter mile down the ramp. I'll get one down here, but we are not gonna be here much longer."

Well, that was a refreshing change. I turned and began the walk back to 31 and 32. Out of my periphery, I saw a flash. It began as a quick burst of light. There was a millisecond pause, then a longer stream of bright yellows and oranges followed by the burping sound of Iraqi AAA fire trailing the initial lights. I found it as shocking as it was unexpected. The early morning sky wasn't alone anymore, and neither were we. Finally proof the Iraqi 3rd Corps was out there. I stepped up my pace as an Army fuel truck passed me and stopped next to Buss.

Buss looked to the north. When he saw me, he turned. "I think that was either a 14.5mm ZPU-4 or a Zeus."

Buss was already way ahead of me. I could tell what he was thinking: Get gas, get back in the air, and go kill that AAA. Before the thought was complete in my head, another three- or four-second burst of AAA sprayed upward and to the east. That confirmed it. It fired with four barrels and had to be the towed 14.5mm ZPU-4 or the self-propelled ZSU 23-4. I wasn't sure which one though. We had both studied the threat systems as students at the weapons school, but I had never seen or heard one actually firing. I stepped toward my aircraft to check on Matt but didn't mention the conversation I'd had with the other aircrews.

In either case, a ZPU or ZSU made for a helicopter's worst nightmare. The ZPU-4 was deadly at ranges out to about two thousand meters. But they could fire effectively out to nearly eight thousand meters and to five thousand feet. However, their need to visually acquire and engage their targets limited their effectiveness, particularly at night. The gunners had to first see their targets and then track them visually. The Iraqis didn't have any briefed night vision capabilities, meaning they couldn't put a night site on the ZPU to engage low-flying helicopters. Unfortunately, that didn't seem like such a limitation now. The ZPU crews only needed to point in the right direction and pull the trigger. The nearly seven-inch HE or armor-piercing incendiary rounds traveling at one thousand meters per second would make quick work of a Cobra. The ZPU was a weapon for any war and the same weapon that had downed Marine helicopters from Vietnam in the 1960s and 1970s to Grenada in 1983.

The ZSU-23-4 "Shilka" was another imported Russian weapons system commonly referred to as the Zeus. The engineers had mounted four 23mm radar-directed cannons to a tracked and armored chassis similar to a tank. With a skilled crew, attack helicopters had little chance to defeat them from close range. A Hellfire from long range gave us the best chance to beat the Zeus. Otherwise, we could mask the Cobra from its radar using buildings or terrain and simply hope the ground clutter allowed a gun or TOW shot. Actually, the best way to kill a Zeus was with other people's ordnance (OPO), fixed-wing bombs, or artillery.

The fuel truck pulled up. "Matt, I'm grabbing the hose. Can you hook the lead to the skid shoe?"

Matt grabbed a long and coiled metal line designed to ground the aircraft and prevent static electricity from sparking the nearby fuel. The gravity nozzle looked similar to what you'd see at a gas station. The Cobra had two refueling points—one was pressure refueling and the other was gravity refueling. I removed the fuel cap and pumped in two hundred additional gallons of JP-5. Then, I hauled the big rubber hose to Buss, and he did the same.

On board *Saipan*, the "grapes" or refuelers used a pressure refueling system. The long hose was similar but had a locking attachment that fit into the Cobra's left-side fuel receptacle. The pressure refueling prevented fuel spillage and allowed for faster refueling. Tonight, we simply needed gas and were thankful for the US Army.

Once Buss had finished, the four of us met at the front of my Cobra. I started with, "We are going to start, check in and take off SOP, and head to Nasiriyah. Any questions?"

Nothing. After a slight pause, Buss and I turned to enter our cockpits. Matt and Rosie would act as both plane captains and ordnance crews until we were ready to take off.

All four of us had renewed focus. If the Ghost and Iraqis were not enough, I think the reception from our fellow pilots had pissed us all off. Any great team needs a common enemy. Now we were up to three and counting.

Our startup and arming followed the SOP with Matt and Rosie arming both Cobras. Once back in the cockpit, Matt and I closed both canopies. The miscellaneous noises of the outside quieted. We now enjoyed the familiar sounds, sights, and sensations of a turning Cobra. It provided a blanket of calm, but a building sense of anticipation filled both cockpits.

I kept an eye on Rosie and Buss. Once their position lights went from flashing to steady, I knew they were ready.

Time to confirm that with Buss. "Three-one check."

Rosie keyed their radio. "Two."

We then turned off all visible lights in each Cobra except for the NVG visible strip lights and the NVG visible anti-collision light. The latter, positioned just aft of the main rotor hub and attached to the highest point of the helicopter, gave Buss and Rosie a continuous flash to announce our position. Again, a rotating beacon that was only visible when wearing NVGs. To the naked eye, it was invisible.

"Sky Chief, Deadly 31 on deck at Riverfront for tasking."

After a pause and the familiar static, I heard, "Deadly 31, push to the vicinity of 210 310 and contact Inchon on magenta."

"Deadly 31 copies. Inchon on magenta," I replied.

The 210 310 represented a six-digit grid that gave us a general area of where to fly to. Normally, we would be given a larger "box" to operate in or a very specific position, but this would work. Once airborne, we would contact the FAC, get his assessment, and then come to terms with a plan.

Buss worked fast. "Three-one, that's about thirty-five miles to the northeast. I'm not sure who Inchon is, but that position is south of the city."

"Copy. You set?" I released the radio switch and got ready to taxi out.

Click. Click.

It was time to call the air traffic controller. "Riverfront, Deadly 31 and 32 are on the northern ramp. Request a present position departure to the north."

Their clearance had the professional sound of an FAA controller. It was another small comfort. "Deadly flight, winds reported 320 at eight knots from your present position. You are cleared to the north. Report clear of the pattern."

"Deadly 31 wilco." That meant we would be taking off from the ramp and not taxiing onto the runway.

I pulled into a ten-foot hover, then checked the power. We were good. I added in some left pedal to put my nose directly into the wind. The torque reading in the HUD immediately dropped, meaning the wind had worked to reduce the amount of power we needed to take off. As I added more power, I eased the nose forward.

The Cobra edged ahead, gradually picking up speed. Finally, a slight bump or burble let me know we'd passed through translational lift. The main rotors now chopped into clean and undisturbed air, and we swiftly climbed and accelerated.

The flight north passed quickly, and the check-in with Sky Chief and the FAC, callsign "Mouth," was uneventful. Mouth gave us a short update of the situation and asked that we push out east and north of the city. At nearly 0230L, we were only a few hours from sunrise. We had a simple mission: an armed reconnaissance of the city. Start to the east, then work north. Go from the northwest to the south. Report anything of interest.

Buss could guess the plan, but I didn't want to leave any doubts. "Three-two, let's push east until we find Highway 8, then work further east to the canals."

Click. Click.

The city had some lights. With the main power cut, these were likely from generators or a few other random sources. Any light helped us see the city and quickly identify friendly positions. They certainly helped to outline the city center, but to the east and north, we saw only darkness. Where was that ZPU-4?

The city had canals that bordered it to the east and to the north, all supplied by the Euphrates. We descended to three hundred feet and kept up the speed. We couldn't hide our sound, and going faster only made the blades bite harder into the early morning air, generating even more noise. We could see some of the Marine vehicles stacked up on Highway 8 to the south. As we overflew them, we noted that most were clearly marked with orange panels and specialized glint tape, a reflective tape we could see through our NVGs that designated them as friendly. I pushed to the east, passing directly over the Euphrates. Nothing out there except dry desert.

Matt saw the northern city border. "The canal's just in front of us, and it turns north."

Matt was using both the map and the FLIR to pick out landmarks. He also slewed the cannon to the canal and pushed the infrared laser. Separate from the targeting laser, we used this as a pointer. Like the strip lights, the infrared laser was also only visible with NVGs. We could also use it to visually mark targets for 32 or other attack platforms or to assist either cockpit when using the helmet-mounted sight. Tonight, it kept both 31 and 32 oriented, and a continuous dialogue followed.

We continued the counterclockwise reconnaissance east of the city with NSTR—nothing significant to report. It wasn't until we came north of the Saddam Canal along the north side of the city that we began to see clues of the day's events.

Buss broke the silence. "Three-one, you seeing what I'm seeing?"

I said nothing. Matt mustered, "Yup."

Devastation. We couldn't see everything, but everything wasn't what we needed to see. The devil was in the details, but the carnage was obvious with the remnants of Marine Humvees, AAVs, and random trucks of unknown origin. Those were 1st Battalion 2nd Marine Regiment vehicles. Those were Task Force Tarawa vehicles. Those were Camp Lejeune, North Carolina, Marines—our Marines—and we should have been here earlier.

I flew too far outside the city to identify specific details through my NVGs, but both Matt and Rosie could see. Too many Marine vehicles were destroyed and lay cold on the FLIR. Twisted metal told an otherwise unimaginable story painted on an immature canvas, splashed with the colors of horror and tragedy.

I felt sick. The Ghost had found a soulmate.

Time passed slowly, but we were running low on fuel, and we needed to leave. "Mouth, three-one's checking off station. If you need us, we will be on strip alert at Riverfront."

A different voice responded. "Three-one, any chance you can fly north of the Saddam Canal and take a look out there?"

Take a look out there? That wasn't a mission familiar to us, but we got the message.

I immediately replied, "Roger. We will do one more lap up the east side of the city and then look north. I'll let you know what we see."

"Thanks."

Thanks? Not a normal response, but normal was long gone.

We checked with Buss and Rosie. "Three-two, how's your fuel?"

The fuel gauge is only in the back seat, so I waited for Buss. "Three-two's got about twenty minutes, but I'm not sure if Riverfront has any more gas."

Damn, he was right. The Army fuel trucks were headed back west on Highway 8.

"Three-two, call Sky Chief and see where we can get gas."

Click. Click.

The voice on the radio hadn't come from the Mouth or one of the other FACs or air officers assigned to the battalion. I'm sure the planning for the next day's combat operations consumed them. No, it had sounded like a younger voice, maybe the radio operator. I wasn't sure, and I certainly wasn't going to ask. The call had been less a request and more a hope. A hope that we would keep turning "gas into noise" and continue searching for the Iraqis. That would buy everyone more time before the sun began to rise in about an hour.

I thought about that voice and figured one more response to him would be reassuring. "Three-one and flight is going to recon to the north of the city. We will pass on anything we see. Matt, we are coming left and going to go north of the last friendly pos."

Click. Click.

Buss came back. "Hey, 31, Astrodome is open for fuel. Think we can do another fifteen minutes here and top off before heading back to mother."

Okay, that was good. "Thanks and copy all. We are turning north."

We didn't expect anything to the north, but I also remained unsure about towers or wires or other hazards not marked on the vintage paper maps we used. I liked to believe that I made the right decision as opposed to my definition of a choice.

Choices are easy, made using a pretty simple process. As a Marine, I had learned the importance of choices. Start with common sense, sprinkle in some basic awareness of your surroundings, then top it with your version of a moral compass. Use that formula, and you'll generally make the right choices. *BAM*, life is simplified. Make the wrong ones, and life's going to get more complicated, but wrong choices are generally recoverable.

Not so much with decisions. Decisions seem to bear more weight, more gravity, more consequence. They seem to happen in ambiguous circumstances with more unknowns than knowns under time compression and stress. Making a decision implies you have taken a 360-degree view of the problem, weighed risks against rewards, mulled it, discussed it, and then come to a conclusion. The problem was that chance and uncertainty also played a bigger role when decisions needed to be made quickly, and time was something we rarely had. In any event, I needed to keep thinking, keep preparing for the next unknown.

We flew over the Saddam Canal and then over Highway 16. We planned to follow Highway 16 west until it merged into Highway 7, which ran north and south. There had been reports of buses and taxi cabs bringing Saddam Hussein loyalists called Fedayeen Saddam and other irregular forces into the city throughout the day. This was more than hearsay since Cobras from 269 had engaged multiple taxis, trucks, and vans loaded with armed military-aged males (MAMs) driving into Nasiriyah. FLIR videotape that showed them engaging coalition aircraft with automatic weapons and rocket-propelled grenade (RPG) fire answered any question of their intent. All that cemented our decision to recon north.

We could see the burnt-out husks of a dozen buses, pickup trucks, and cars as we made the turn north. With Iraq's mature highway system, those men could have easily come from Baghdad, Najaf, Diwaniyah, or places much further away. It didn't matter now. Those same roads sat empty, and those forces lingered somewhere in Nasiriyah.

I caught a glint off to my left—a Humvee, the last of the 1st Battalion 2nd Marines, and the last time we would see them tonight. My pulse began quickening, a slight pressure building as I looked into endless black and wondered what lived out there and, more importantly, *who* lived out there.

Gunrunner pilots and air and ground crews pose before launching (20 March 2003).

Final team huddle before we launched (20 March 2003).

Conducting flight operations from the USS *Saipan.*

The view of Task Force Tarawa entering Nasiriyah (23 March 2003).

Gun camera of Buss firing in Nasiriyah. We are pictured at the eleven o'clock position (29 March 2003).

HMM 162 aircrews evacuating wounded Marines (23 March 2003).

HMLA 269 Cobra at a forward arming and refueling point (24 March 2003).

The remains of Mongoose 22 minutes after their crash (25 March 2003).

Our brothers from HMLA 267 sweating out the sandstorms of 25 and 26 March.

Captains Shenberger and Budjreko "opening" Jalibah.

The crew of Mongoose 21, four of our nation's best. Words can never describe their heroism.

The HMLA 269 flight line in Jalibah, Iraq, on 30 March 2003.

Sergeant Mike McGuire, the twenty-one-year-old Marine from Camdenton, Missouri.

Author posing next to Lance Corporal Radcliff's Cobra. I was honored to take his helicopter into combat.

Plane captains doing inspections on a Cobra getting ready for a combat mission.

Commanding officers picture: Fuzzy, Ozzie, Mad Dog, Boomer (MAG 29 CO), Huey, Yoda, Zipper, and Cubi.

Officer quarters at Jalibah, Iraq (2 April 2003).

MAG 16 crews who supported the Jessica Lynch rescue with United States Special Operations Command assets (1 April 2003).

Marine gunships engage Iraqi positions east of Baghdad (6 April 2003).

HMM 162 commanding officer, "Fuzzy" Hedelund (R), with his executive officer, Jose "Outlaw" Vazquez (L). Fuzzy flew 200 miles unescorted to save Marines outside of Baghdad (1 April 2003).

HMLA Marines enjoying a short break east of Baghdad (11 April 2003).

Our brothers and sisters from HMLA 267 just east of Baghdad.

HMM 263 "Thunder Chickens" evacuate Marines near Baghdad (6 April 2003).

Iraqi tank about to be engaged by HMLA 269 Hellfire missile (7 April 2003).

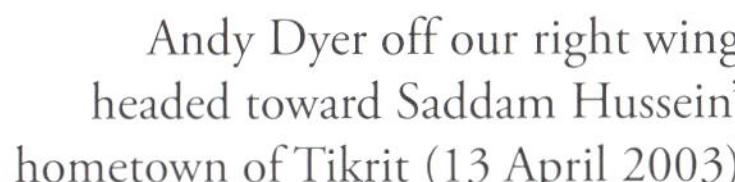

Andy Dyer off our right wing, headed toward Saddam Hussein's hometown of Tikrit (13 April 2003).

Saddam Hussein's custom castles and palaces on the Tigris (14 April 2003).

Rosie, Ferris, and Matt back aboard *Saipan* (30 May 2003).

Our alter-egos – Country, Flash, Howdy, and Pez often did the possible when it was impossible.

Captain John "Buss" Barranco. The Boston native's contributions were invaluable.

Ferris, Boomer, and Howdy on the deck of *Saipan* at Naval Station Rota, Spain (6 June 2003).

USS *Saipan's* flight deck as we headed home (22 May 2003).

A final view of *Saipan* leaving for Norfolk (25 June 2003).

CHAPTER 18

Location: On Approach to USS *Saipan*
Date: 24MAR03
Time: 0540L

"Tower, 31 for the break," I announced.

The boss was up early again. "Deadly 31, continue upwind. Your interval is company traffic departing at your ten o'clock position."

We passed the ship, keeping it on our left, or port side, and looked to see two other Cobras departing to the northwest. Another five seconds passed.

The boss came back up on the tower frequency. "Three-one and flight cleared for the break. Expect spots four and five."

Buss and Rosie flew off our right wing in a tight parade position. I took a quick look over my shoulder. They were less than one rotor blade distance from us with about ten feet of step-up, which kept their rotor blades from meshing with ours. That's a sporty distance considering we had been up sixteen or seventeen hours and had been flying the past eleven.

Matt put his right hand up against the canopy. With three counting motions, he signaled to Buss when our Cobra would break across *Saipan's* bow and away from 32. One, two, three, and I heard Matt's gloved hand slap the canopy for a fourth time. That was my cue to break left. I rolled at a 45-degree angle and at 140 knots as we cut across the front of the ship at three hundred feet. We rolled out on the downwind and slowed to one hundred knots before calling abeam, the landing spot.

"Three-one's abeam," I said.

The boss responded rapidly. "Winds are six knots to port. Three-one, Charlie spot four."

The same calls came from Buss in 32. Landing, de-arm, chocks, chains, shutdown.

In the eleven plus hours since we'd last seen *Saipan*, we had traversed all of southern Iraq. We had contacted nearly every major ground combat unit and covered more than one thousand nautical miles. We had not seen a single moving enemy soldier, tank, armored vehicle, or artillery tube. We had seen the destruction in Nasiriyah, but done by whom? Where were they? How had thousands of Iraqi regular and irregular troops vanished into the neighborhoods and side streets of Nasiriyah? There was something clearly bigger than us at work here. No way we hadn't gotten a chance to exact some form of payment from the Iraqis. They had overdue bills.

I'd almost forgotten that we collected debts. Things had changed so much over the past few days. The memory of Safwan Hill remained tattooed into my memory, but it was nothing fresh. The picture was clear, but the ink was already fading like it had been there for years. Four nights ago—that was it. One hundred and something hours had passed since the opening night. We had just landed after sunrise for the fourth straight day—thirty-five hours in the cockpit in four days, a new record for all of us. Of course, all records are meant to be broken.

Life on *Saipan* changed swiftly as we pushed supplies and Marines into Riverfront by the Phrog-load. We had already sent a small aviation maintenance detachment of thirty Marines, along with parts and supplies, ashore to Riverfront. They had gone "in country" a couple of days ago—dropped off onto the otherwise abandoned Jalibah Air Base with nothing but water, MREs, GP tents, and sledgehammers. Maybe a shovel. GP tents were large olive drab tents, and that was it. Marines from 269 and other MAG 29 units set them up using sledgehammers, sandbags, and three-foot tent pegs. We now had several small repair and maintenance tents on the airfield, and they were open for business.

I strode into our *Saipan* maintenance spaces, having walked across the flight deck, down a set of stairs, and directly into where my office was technically located. The noise of the flight deck subsided as I pulled, closed, and latched the watertight steel door. The natural noise of the ship interrupted the brief calm. Octaves of low-frequency energy produced a constant and audible hum. More human sounds quickly drowned that out, coming from the office space just a few feet ahead.

I turned the corner and surmised that the trading floor on Wall Street had nothing on HMLA 269's maintenance control. I was immediately consumed with the overwhelming sound of activity: Marines yelling across desks or on intra-ship phone lines, papers being tossed into inboxes, files being yanked out of outboxes, and the tick, tick, ticking of fingers tapping on computer keys. Boxes cleverly labeled "Intake" and "Exhaust" were being filled as quickly as they were being emptied.

The number of simultaneous conversations was bewildering. I found no one upset or panicked. The sheer noise level showed how difficult it was for fifty people in a forty-by-thirty-five space to communicate. These were fifty people all working toward the same goals. They thought nothing of outshouting the Marine next to them in claustrophobia-inducing back office spaces already cramped with desktops, laptops, printers, temporary desks, and vintage 1980s technology that hadn't been maintained for years. The bulky, metal-encased technology was seemingly welded into the floor and into the sides of the bulkheads. Those offices never ceased to be rockin' and rollin' with the waves of the Persian Gulf.

I did a quick search for a seat to complete my naval flight recording system form, or NAVFLIR—the paperwork that logged data on the Cobra. That information was used to track hours for dynamic components. These were critical aircraft parts that needed constant inspection and replacement. This form was also used to track the number of missiles fired and other specific events that put added stress on the aircraft. A copy would subsequently be sent to the operations department to track pilot and aircrew training codes, combat codes, and flight time—all important elements for million-dollar weapons of war.

Unfortunately, there were no seats, so I grabbed a blank NAVFLIR and found space on the wall. This took longer, as the ink would go dry after a few lines, but writing on a wall was nothing new for anyone who spent time on ships.

I had nearly finished that part of the process when I heard the voice—not just any voice but a very particular one. I had been found. I had wondered how long it would take him to find me.

"Good morning, Major. How was it out there?"

I didn't need to turn because I knew this voice well. It dripped with sarcasm. It said, without saying, "I'm amazed any of you made it back again—surprised your dumb ass didn't get shot down or somehow punt it."

I didn't turn my head. "Good morning, Top. How are we doing?"

Top is an accepted term or way to address a master sergeant, similar to a gunnery sergeant being referred to as "Gunny." Warrant officers are also often referred to as "Gunner," a throwback to the gunnery days when assigned to naval warships. Plus, pilots have their own acceptable slang with their use of callsigns.

The booming voice that had bounced off the bulkhead and penetrated deep into my eardrum was still ringing through my brain. It had come from my maintenance chief, Master Sergeant Jim Quirk. Quirk and I had a unique relationship. I didn't take his irreverence to my rank personally. Nearly every word out of his mouth offended someone. At five foot five with the build of a wrestler, a shock of red hair, and a questionably regulation mustache, he was a terrorist of the highest order. A born windmill chaser, Quirk always tilted at windmills. He always pursued his version of reality or justice. He exhausted me at times, but on other occasions, I found his attitude refreshing and actually uplifting.

Despite my best efforts to understand him, cajole him, appease him, fire him, or otherwise minimize his self-destructive tendencies, he was a good leader and took even better care of our Marines. I had no issue with him venting in my direction. It took all kinds to build and run our village, and if he was with me, it meant he wasn't carving up some unsuspecting captain or lieutenant. I was happy he was on our side. He was a natural smartass and gifted ass-chewer, and there would soon be times we needed both skills.

I got through my paperwork and walked deeper into the ship. The 2nd Battalion 8th Marines had long since disembarked, leaving empty staterooms in "officer country" and hundreds of empty beds in the berthing area where the Marines had made their homes at sea. Except for personal effects kept in large storage units in the bowels of the ship, those Marines carried everything they owned with them into Iraq. HMLA 269 Marines, just as I had, planned to do the same.

I needed some time alone to gain perspective on what was happening outside my section of two Cobras. So, I grabbed a stack of maintenance reports and looked for a quiet nook. Since we had flown continuous operations since the night of the 20th, it was the first time I'd had some white space in my calendar to both help with the planning to move maintenance ashore and to better understand what the squadron had been doing. The ability of Monty, Luke Crouson, Jim Quirk, and the entire team to generate sorties was unprecedented.

I carried my maintenance brief, which included parts status, readiness, and overall aircraft availability for the next day and likely the next several weeks, to the ready room. I selected a seat on the back left wall, finding solace in the fact there were no seats behind me, and got tucked in for a good read.

What I perused, page after page, showed an evolution. Not only had our goals changed, but the expectations for the squadron had changed. It should have been obvious to a casual observer watching from the ship or from the shore. For those on the inside, we were blind to the changes. We were so close that they were harder to see. Momentum and pace had swept us away. What had started as a jog had become a sprint.

Marines love large formation runs. Not really. COs and senior enlisted advisors like formation runs. These are usually formations of a few hundred Marines going for a run in columns of three. In those instances, you rarely notice the speed increase, and in fact, you want to increase the speed to make the run predictable. That allows Marines to settle into a pace, a cadence, and breathing. On such runs, the CO and the sergeant major set the pace, but even the slightest slowing of the pace causes an accordion effect with Marines in the back slamming into the Marine in front of them. By the time everyone recovers, those same Marines are sprinting to catch the formation.

I saw that same thing happening on the pages of my maintenance files and from the operations briefs. I followed the Marine in front of me, Jeff Hewlett, who ran behind Boomer. Two formations ran behind me. Closest was Monty and the three hundred maintenance Marines, and the other formation was Matt with Buss and Rosie. I needed to keep a steady pace but slow on the gas and brakes to save us a ton of wasted effort, but how? Whoever said that expectations are the foundations of failure and disappointment never went to combat with Marines.

The statistics said it all. It sounded dramatic, even in my head, but for four nights and at the start of the fourth day, we had blackened the skies with our Cobras and Hueys. The squadron had operated everywhere tasked, ordered, or needed. We had been armed with the firepower and expertise in each cockpit to execute nearly any request. I continued to read.

March 22nd in Basra: HMLA 269 generated 103 combat sorties.

The following day quickly eclipsed those. We had fuel and ordnance available on *Saipan* and ashore.

March 23rd in Nasiriyah: HMLA 269 generated 214 sorties, another fifty-four theater wide.

March 24th: As of 0810L, HMLA 269 expended 126 Hellfire and TOW missiles, 1,080 2.75-inch rockets, and nearly sixty-five thousand rounds of 20mm, .50 caliber, and 7.62mm rounds.

Those statistics were inarguably dated but an impressive snapshot in time. We had no fewer than fourteen Hueys and Cobras currently airborne and ashore. That equaled nearly four hundred combat sorties or flights with no aircraft losses. Impressive numbers, but impressive only like reaching one mile into a marathon. We'd find time later to wax eloquently about the tenacity, fearlessness, and outright heroism of our aircrews, but nobody looked past today. For me, Matt, Buss, and Rosie, we could only think about tonight.

Those early successes hadn't come easily. Once we got feet dry, nothing was free. The Iraqis had their own version of debt collectors. The maintenance teams had already repaired four bullet-ridden Cobras, and there were two more recovering from more serious wounds. Proof that the enemy gets a vote.

We had also tapped into lady luck. Several of the rounds had hit perilously close to dynamic components, and a few others had just missed the cockpits. Captain Matt "Burger" Shenberger and his copilot 1st Lieutenant Travis "Lionel" Richie had been hit with 23mm cannon rounds over Nasiriyah, and one round had blown off a chunk of their main rotor blade. Alarmed but undeterred, they'd continued to fly for another eight hours. Along with their wingman, Captain Tom "Bull" Budrejko and 1st Lieutenant Mark Vincent, they'd delivered a devastating mix of missile, rocket, and cannon fire in support of Task Force Tarawa.

Burger and Bull, and their copilots, were already tank "aces" from the first two days of combat. They had destroyed a platoon of tanks outside Basra and then turned their sights on Iraqi fighting vehicles, supply vehicles, and several enthusiastic but misguided squads of infantry in Nasiriyah. They exemplified the gritty, in-your-face, roll-your-sleeves-up kind of work that we not only needed but demanded in the close urban fight. I found Burger and Bull impressive, but even more amazing was how quickly they had melded their strengths and weaknesses to form that perfect team. It would take weeks and a short break in the war to fully understand how close Burger and Bull had come to the Ghost.

We typically launched a section of Cobras and Hueys on a schedule or via a call for support. With twenty-four-hour operations, we had half the squadron flying nights and the other half flying days. So, we rarely had the time or the opportunity for formal debriefs. Instead, we counted on crews debriefing the intelligence department or getting a turnover over the radio as one 269 section checked off station and another checked in. It was the rare occasion when two sections landed for fuel or ordnance at the same FARP and could talk face to face and pass along intelligence or lessons learned.

The inability to see enemy fire during the daytime gave us all concern. Exceptions to that were heavy-caliber machine gun and cannon fire or random RPG fire. Heavy-caliber machine guns and cannons used tracer rounds, and tracers were universally visible, both day and night. So, that left Iraqi crews in their tanks, in mortar positions, or in otherwise hidden positions with the ability to fire AKs and light machine guns with little chance of being spotted from our cockpits.

The ability to see tracer fire was only one of the night crew's multiple advantages. The FLIR showed anything hot or even warm, which included the silhouettes of armored vehicles, hot gun barrels, and people. Night crews, also camouflaged by the darkness, could more easily pick out muzzle flashes and tracer fire. However, the night crews were also exposed when engaging enemy positions. The Iraqis could see the position in the sky of where a 2.75-inch rocket was fired from, and they could also trace the stream of 20mm cannon fire or 7.62mm mini gun fire back to the source.

Today, we were getting a little bit of day and night. We were scheduled to launch in the late afternoon, which would give us some appreciated daylight prior to night operations. Little victories.

"Sky Chief, Deadly 43 is feet dry for tasking." Today, Buss served as the voice of the section.

The four of us had found time to talk about issues beyond the standard briefing topics. I wanted to open the aperture on flight leadership a bit. After the first night, I knew I didn't have all the answers, and I told them as much. We would need all of us to be exceptionally active members of each cockpit and the section. Though I was the section lead, we would practice a direct democracy where we all got a vote and the majority ruled. If I did something stupid or became unpredictable, they needed to speak up. It also became clear, to me anyway, that fatigue was starting to nest deep inside each of us.

Matt and I slipped back into the wingman position. I had full confidence in Buss's leadership, decision-making, and judgment. That didn't relieve me of the responsibilities as the assigned section lead, but I had passed the authority to Buss and Rosie.

Buss made the call. "Four-four, we are going into Safwan for gas, and then we'll push west."

"Four-four copies." Matt took the primary on radio.

I'd asked Matt to swap seats, so today, I rode in the front, and Matt flew from the back. I thought it would give me a better chance to scan the terrain with the FLIR. It also gave me a fresh perspective outside the sometimes myopic view of a section lead flying from the back seat.

Safwan had a FARP labeled Busch Field. Busch was owned and operated by our friends from the United Kingdom. Though it had plenty of jet fuel, it lacked any of the ordnance we would need. I took a mental note. We didn't have a concern about it that day, but in the very near future, it would be an issue.

Landing there in daytime and far enough away from any known enemy positions made Busch Field a welcome diversion. I peered off the nose to see Safwan Hill. It looked much smaller than I remembered. I was tempted to search for the vehicles we had engaged, but I quickly forgot about those as we set up to land.

With Safwan Hill off to our left, Buss called, "Four-four, go trail."

Matt dropped behind Buss and gave him a quick "44" as we set up for landing.

We touched down on the fully paved and nearly sand-free runway, just a few feet from the fuel lines.

Matt ran through his checklists. "Sir, I'm shutting down number two."

Click. Click.

We shut down the number two engine as a standard practice when using a pressure refueling hose. I unstrapped, opened the canopy, and dropped the three plus feet to the runway, instantly feeling all 105 degrees of the late afternoon sun. Damn, it was oppressive. About the time I stepped a few paces out of the air-conditioned comfort of the Cobra, I found and installed the pins to "safe" the rocket pods, TOWs, and Hellfire. Then, I crawled under the chin and disconnected the electrical wires to the gun.

This was a good day to switch things around. Although I had sensed a need for change and to get everyone another vantage point, it wasn't intended for Buss to experience the challenges of leading. He was a MAWTS-1 instructor pilot, meaning he was as or more qualified than me. He was a seasoned flight leader and a combat veteran of Afghanistan, as was Rosie. Matt and Rosie were certainly capable of flying and fighting the Cobra from the back seat, but this was different.

This was a chance for everyone to build more confidence and showcase another side of their skills. I already knew we were good—not just good in our current roles but good in any role. That might have appeared as a test, a challenge, but it wasn't either. We'd simply found a window where the view might only change slightly but enough to offer a new perspective and appreciation of how each of us contributed in ways difficult to see and even harder to quantify or qualify. I hoped that with just a minor shift of roles, we would see major improvements to what I already considered a highly functioning team.

What was the problem with having Matt in the backseat and passing the tactical lead to Buss for the day? If things went south, no doubt many would question my decision and hold me accountable. I was fine with that. It was a risk worth taking.

I had previously served in the roles of maintenance check pilot, flight leader, mission commander, and FAC and had held every qualification and designation in between over the past ten years. That didn't make me the best pilot, leader, decisionmaker, or planner. I clearly wasn't. However, it did imply my COs trusted me to ensure every Cobra pilot became qualified and ready to execute, and I took that responsibility seriously.

Without highlighting the obvious dangers after four days, it had become apparent that we'd flown less than one bullet away from catastrophe. No one said it, and no one needed to. Stating it aloud would have come across as dramatic and weak. My end state focused on a combat capable section with or without me or anyone else. Again, nothing melodramatic but a reality and a responsibility I took to heart.

CHAPTER 19

Location: USS *Wasp*, 2 Miles Off the Coast of Somalia
Time: 03APR93
Time: 0500L

I had met another Ghost ten years prior—or maybe it was the same Ghost. It didn't matter which Ghost she was, and she certainly didn't care. The vastness and the emptiness of this desert, with its complete lack of contrast and texture, was both beautiful and intimidating. I got the sense that we could unwittingly be trapped and devoured by what lay just outside of my view in the shadows.

A Somali proverb may best describe my thoughts as I pumped jet fuel into the Cobra. "Nin fadhigaaga arkaya looma sare joogsado" translates to, "Don't ask for help from a man who sees you need it." I certainly wasn't asking for help but I sure as hell felt someone was watching. In fact, even within the endlessness of the southern Somali desert, I always got the feeling that someone was observing us. I felt exposed and somehow, ironically, unguarded.

It had been three months in the desert, three months in the river valley, three months of escort missions and reconnaissance, three months of searching for elusive warlords. Those three months had not been in vain because we had captured thousands of pounds of khat, a stimulant that Somali footmen chewed. The drug would produce extreme highs and even lower lows. Khat was traded in every bazaar and market as an informal form of currency. The Somali shilling was nearly worthless in an economy that had otherwise collapsed.

The past three months had served as an extended prelude. It was then that an exiled Osama Bin Laden, operating from Sudan, made his first of several overt moves against "American occupiers."

Bin Laden stayed hidden, far away from the Americans, but he clearly had observers and sympathizers planted and reporting to him from every city.

We'd also recovered thousands of rifles, pistols, bayonets, light machine guns, and even rusted Russian heavy machine guns. Some weapons were new AK-47s with shiny 7.62 x 39 Russian-made bullets. Others were family relics and should have long been in museums. They ranged from British bolt-action Enfields to US-made Thompson submachine guns, Chinese-made SKSs, Belgian G3s, and some unknown Italian manufactured rifles.

It had been three months of coming up short. Three months of only finding weapons and drugs. We knew this was a United Nations (UN) mission, but the details of exactly how we executed those mandates was a bit fuzzy. The United Nations had been in Somalia for more than thirty years, looking for new ways to end the cycles of violence, corruption, famine, and human right atrocities. For most of us, this was a welcome adventure. We flew equipped with sidearms and body armor. Today, we conducted another deep reconnaissance. Who would guess that ten years later and 3,500 miles north, I would fly similar missions.

I was assigned to HMM 263, the famous "Thunder Chickens," who'd gained their fame flying the same Phrogs in support of Marines from Marble Mountain in Vietnam some twenty-five years earlier. HMM 263 served as the aviation combat element assigned to the 24th MEU. Collectively, we flew in support of the United Nations mission in Somalia or UNISOM II.

The current mission in Somalia had been established in 1992 to stop the historic famine, which had gripped the country. We had arrived off the Somali coast in February to support *Operation Restore Hope.* The 24th MEU had joined the multi-national force operating under the United Nations Task Force (UNITAF) mandate. With a failed central government and virtually no public services, food distribution and supply networks needed more security to be effective. Of course, more security required more United Nations forces, so changes needed to be made.

The United Nations mission continued to evolve in size, scope, and complexity as the result of the transition to UNISOM II in March. UNISOM II began to execute a more US military focused mission. Throughout the spring and into the summer of 1993, the US and UN continued to add more dedicated combat forces, causing their combat missions to expand accordingly. This addition of more United Nations forces threatened the already delicate balance of competing warlords.

Today, our mission included a deep reconnaissance from the southern port city of Kismayo 150 miles west, deep in the Jubba Valley. We had been chasing factions led by Colonel Ahmed Omar Jess, one of the longest serving military officers at the time.

I was a freshly minted captain and flew as the combat copilot and front seater with Captain Bob "Scheister" Darling, an NCAA college hockey player and native New Yorker. His sarcastic sense of humor made us a perfect fit. We flew off the wing of our detachment officer in charge, Major Tom "Preppy" Ellis, and his front seater and copilot, 1st Lieutenant Ken "Kid" Maney. Kid, a Florida Gator, and I would spend the next several years deploying with various squadrons and on various US Navy ships.

This was an NVG launch from *Wasp* as I continued recovering from my first encounter with the Ghost.

We had conducted similar operations only two weeks earlier but, that time, west of Mogadishu, the nation's infamous capital. West of the city was an open desert, endless nothing minus the occasional Bedouin and his flocks anchored to the unmapped and easily identified oasis. The squadron had tasked us with looking for small convoys infiltrating the city at night.

We found the once booming city easy to navigate but hard to observe. Besides *Wasp*, we used the Mogadishu International Airport as our prime refueling and support base. The city of Mogadishu sat boxed in by the international airport to the south, the Indian Ocean to the east, 21 October Road to the west, and the "old embassy row," along with a series of internal roads, markets, and districts, to the northeast.

The 1993 Cobra had no FLIR or NTS. In addition, our NVGs were a previous generation and not nearly as capable as they should have been. Regardless, we had a mission to search for weapons caches and warlords attempting to secure weapons already locked up by the United Nations.

We never saw it coming. No warning. No signs. Less than an hour into what was to be a two-hour mission, we were swallowed by what the Somalis called a haboob. This was a fast-forming and nearly undetected wall of winds and sands that gave us no way out. We were completely enveloped and encased in the haboob within seconds. The flight immediately broke into two single Cobras fighting to stay aloft while trying to find a way over, under, or around the storm.

Then, almost as quickly as it had swallowed us, we were spat back out. Shaken wouldn't even begin to describe how we were feeling, but I knew there was more to it. My fears of being tracked and shadowed by the Ghost were not just the fears of a child. It was clear that we were being watched. I immediately recalled those early mornings and late afternoons in the desert when I could feel eyes burning into me. If I could have replayed this scene, rewatched and relistened, I would have seen and heard her. I should have recognized her scent, somehow tasted her presence. She was there, just out of the periphery and perversely out of focus. I would have heard her voice scarcely an octave above the winds. "Be not afraid. I am only here for you!"

How we were caught so unprepared, so unaware, and so defenseless would go unanswered.

That had been two weeks ago, and the Somali desert was no less forgiving. Today, we had an early morning launch, flying convoy escort for 1st Battalion 2nd Marines, a few AAVs, and LAV-25s from the LAR detachment. Sound familiar? It was a 150-mile escort mission flying over the Jilib Highway, which connected southern Somalia to

Kenya. We planned to run the entire highway from Kismayo to the town of Dhobley.

The Air Boss and the flight deck were ready to get us moving. "Thunder 31, 32, winds ten to port at twelve, cleared to launch."

We knew we had a long day before us, but first, we needed to get feet dry, link up with the convoy, and get communications with the FAC. The ground units had pushed out from the port a few hours earlier, and our first stop was a fuel bladder to top off the Cobra. Fuel bladders had been muscled into the back of 263's detachment of one of the four CH-53E Super Stallions. The Super Stallion, or Big Iron, was a seven-blade, three-engine monster. Designated a heavy-lift helicopter, it could carry more than its weight. The CH-53s had launched about an hour earlier with a small security detachment and now waited for us. Nothing quite like flying to a point in space only to arrive and find Sikorsky's finest ready to pump fuel. The vast Somali desert shrank dramatically with our unconstrained ground, logistics, and aviation capabilities.

This extended reconnaissance and show of force demonstrated that Marine forces were capable of reaching any place in the country. Though our mission had originally focused on providing security for humanitarian aid, it had clearly morphed, branching into missions deemed important to the United Nations.

We were now writing sequels to otherwise unwritten chapters, and that was dangerous. At the Command and Staff College, "Blackjack" Matthews would have called it a slippery slope. We had initially been tasked with executing convoy escorts for humanitarian aid in Mogadishu. That mission now fell into the hands of UNISOM II ground convoys. That left the 24th MEU to find other missions that may or may not be aligned with UNISOM II, which was no model of efficiency or clarity but rather a cabal of loosely aligned and often uncooperative nations. They faced severe challenges now, and those challenges would only multiply over the weeks and months ahead.

We had moved well south of Mogadishu along with a contingent of Belgians. Together, we extended the UN mission to Kismayo. We had been here for more than a month, and even though we were three hundred miles south of Mogadishu, we were expanding further west. Despite feeling eager for the adventure, I wasn't sure what armed attack and utility helicopters were expected to find. That mixing of missions and potentially ambiguous intent opened the door to confusion and misinterpretation. This humanitarian mission was taking on a distinctly different flavor, but it was a decision made far from me, and I was glad to be flying it.

I barely noticed anything out of the ordinary as we landed for fuel, but I should have. I didn't know it then, but the Ghost took it all in. Even in the vast Somali desert, she hid there, just over the horizon, hovering behind the last mirage, observing, analyzing, and devising her next move. Oblivious to the danger, I unstrapped. As I jumped from the cockpit down into the desert's soft sand, a small dust cloud broke over my head like a wave. I immediately felt like I was drowning in the heat and the sand. I ran toward the fuel bladders and away from the Cobra. As quickly as it came, it disappeared. The same queasy and defenseless feeling I had experienced flying outside Mogadishu had returned. That feeling was no longer foreign to me; it was a warning, and I knew the Ghost had sent it.

CHAPTER 20

Location: Safwan Hill FARP, Iraq
Date: 25MAR03
Time: 1230L

The Iraqi sun beat down mercilessly; it was more than 100 degrees out. The heat of the metal fuel nozzle went right through my gloves. Seeking relief, I reached to grab something non-metallic, even the hot hose. Then, I dragged the fuel hose fifty feet to the turning Cobra. That became quite a workout, and I felt my internal temperature rise even further. Matt had done that dozens of times already. Mental note to throw out a "Thanks, Matt" to him every now and again.

I signaled the fueler with a thumbs up, and then Matt gave us both a thumbs up to confirm fuel flowed. Another ten minutes in the sun plus standing next to the Cobra's two jets and the noise. Phew!

When Matt gave the fuel cutoff signal, I relayed the message to the fueler, and the fuel shut off. From there, I disconnected and returned the hose, removed the grounding wire, and armed the flares. Finally, I reattached the gun's electric wires, removed the pins from the rocket pods, and armed the Hellfire and TOW missiles.

"Four-four's up." Matt had the radios.

"Four-three and 44 departing. Thanks for the gas, fellas," said Buss. "Heading straight out with a left turn to 280, three hundred feet, call on board."

Click. Click.

Buss made the radio calls as we took off from the FARP and checked in. "Sky Chief, Deadly 44 up as fragged and ready for tasking."

I sat in the front seat with pen in hand, ready to take notes—ready to plot our next destination on the map and back up Buss's route to the target with our GPS.

Sky Chief gave us an all-too-familiar request. "Deadly 43, proceed direct, and contact Mouth on orange."

I didn't need to hear any more or write anything down. We were headed back to Nasiriyah. It was going to be a quick flight. Our intelligence briefs showed where Task Force Tarawa units had repositioned. It included the same units located north near the Saddam Canal, along with others positioning themselves to the south of the city. They also had both light armored and armored Marine units attached to Task Force Tarawa holding the two southern bridges that crossed the Euphrates. This encirclement of the city was ongoing, and after the 23rd, it was going to be fight or flight for the Iraqi 11th Mechanized Division of the Iraqi 6th Corps and any Fedayeen Saddam fighters. Flight was no longer an option.

Buss checked the flight in. "Mouth, Deadly 43, fifteen to the east for your work."

Mouth was ready and had multiple targets prepared for us. "Four-three, stand by to copy a 9-line."

The intelligence team on board *Saipan* had briefed that Nasiriyah, now referred to as Al Naz or simply Naz, had been relatively quiet for most of the day. Berger and Bull had done some work earlier in the afternoon. Collaborating with Inchon, they'd struck a building with TOW missiles in the north of Naz and subsequently pursued fleeing infantry. They'd also discovered unmanned artillery pieces east of the city and destroyed several before returning to Riverfront. Demolishing those artillery pieces had been one of several critical missions that Major General Mattis had asked 3rd MAW to execute. Those were Russian-made D-30s, a single-barrel 122mm cannon that could fire HE rounds ten miles. At seven thousand pounds, they could be pulled by a military truck but also by a sturdy SUV or pickup truck.

Howdy and Flash had also been working north of the city. We got a debrief from them for what we called a battlefield handover. Over our squadron common frequency, they spelled out exactly what they'd done and seen. The FAC, callsign Inchon, had called them in "danger close" earlier in the day. They had engaged a heavy machine gun position and observation post on the northeastern side of Nasiriyah. Danger close meant they'd engaged Iraqi forces within six hundred meters of Inchon or any friendly position.

No one—no one flying and no FAC—had actual experience calling in danger close missions in combat, but that would change. That specific mission created a dilemma up and down the fire support decision-making chain. A danger close mission could be called using mortars, artillery, and fixed- and rotary-wing CAS platforms. Cobra and Huey crews could also do the same by acting as the FAC(A)s and employing their own ordnance or whatever else was available. It was not as simple as it might look in the movies where the hero calls in artillery fire on his overrun position. Effectively orchestrating direct and indirect fires requires a detailed understanding and coordination of timing, geometry, and ordnance effects. The speed at which US forces were moving and maneuvering made detailed coordination more difficult and made executing danger close missions both more likely and more dangerous.

From my perspective, I wanted to avoid any situation where we needed to deliver fires close to friendly positions. I also wanted to avoid calling in mortars, artillery, and fixed-wing fires close to friendly positions. Lastly, I didn't want to be close enough for an errant friendly mortar or artillery shell, not to mention the explosion or fragments of a fixed-wing aircraft's bomb, to hit us. We would avoid danger close missions for now, but that wouldn't last forever.

Engaging an enemy within six hundred meters of friendlies would become more common than we expected. However, right now, I had more concerns about what Mouth would say. What did he have for us? The impending 9-line meant he had enemy targets under observation and would use us to address them.

"Matt, I'm only concerned with lines five, six, and eight." I wanted Matt to know.

Click. Click.

Mouth was ready to give us a complete 9-line brief, and so were we. "Deadly 43, Train Station, 220, three point six, twenty, 436

822, observation post, one round Willie Pete, north one thousand, egress west then north." After Rosie repeated the entire brief back to Mouth, he wasn't long in confirming. "Four-three read back is correct. Remarks to follow. Request 20mm and rockets. How copy?"

"Four-three copy all," Rosie responded. "Standing by for TOT."

Our specific TOT gave us a tight window to be in position to engage the Iraqi observation post. The timing ensured the 60mm mortar's white phosphorus or Willie Pete round would hit the target thirty seconds before we arrived. The Willie Pete round would mark the enemy position. Once it hit, the FAC or observer would give us immediate corrections while simultaneously trying to provide us a "talk-on" to the target from where the mark had landed.

Then, we had the responsibility to use that five- or ten-second window to identify the target and provide the FAC with a "wings level" call. That call was a covenant, the bond between the Marine aviator in the cockpit and the Marine aviator on the ground. It fundamentally told the FAC we had the target in sight, our weapons were pointed at the enemy, and we were past any friendly positions.

Lines five, six, and eight gave the target's description, the location, and the location of friendlies. Buss led while Rosie ran the mission from the front seat. We could hear Rosie read back every detail to Mouth. Buss had the responsibility to analyze our position and figure how we would hit the target. My role wasn't to look outside yet but rather to input data for Matt to see in the HUD and for me to get a sense of distance to the target.

I jotted down notes, read the map, input data into the GPS, then began scanning with the FLIR.

Matt gave me a heads up. "Coming left. I'm gonna wrap it up a bit."

I heard the big General Electric motors whine followed by the distinctive sound of the blades biting into the thin late afternoon air. Matt had rolled the Cobra into a sharp 50-degree angle of bank turn. Not like an F-18 pulling seven Gs but with enough airspeed and angle of bank that I knew I would feel it.

The sharp turn pushed me down into my seat with more than enough G-force to distract me from my current day job. I'd forgotten how much work it was in the front seat. The turn made it particularly annoying while trying to write, but I had to trust Matt. I needed to stay focused inside and let Matt stay focused outside. The beef and bean MRE I'd consumed at the FARP didn't sit well as I fought to maintain my concentration.

Soon enough, I started to become overwhelmed by doing my front seater job, taking a mental note of Matt's flying, rechecking Rosie's math, and bracing for Buss's plan for the attack. I followed our intended flight path on the map. Damn, that was a 3,300-meter run to the target. Quick bar napkin math. At 140 knots, that was about forty-five seconds until we were over the target, likely thirty seconds of overflying scenic northeastern Nasiriyah before we needed to "pop."

The FAC was back on the radio. "Deadly 43, TOT 26."

"Copy, TOT 26."

All in six minutes. The FAC had also coordinated the artillery mark. There was no mention of any front or back door suppression—common when there were known AAA or other air-to-surface threats. In that case, it would have meant several mortar rounds fired onto the target to protect our final attack. Doctrinally, it would stop one minute prior to our TOT and then start again once we were off the target. It was amazing when it worked. Not on the menu this afternoon.

Our flight path put us on a nearly two-mile straight line run over the FAC's position to the enemy position over the city. We flew in a left-hand orbit north of the Saddam Canal, still offset to the north and west of the northernmost Marine units.

Matt didn't need a map, a compass, or any advice from me. "Okay, I think we are going to need to get above five hundred feet to see anything. Otherwise, we are going to be on top of it before we can shoot."

I was tracking our progress with my finger on the map. "I agree. I think a slight offset to the left with a climb to about one thousand feet for a good dive angle and time to see the position."

Click. Click.

I continued my plans. "Matt, I will be heads down and plan to go hot with the gun once I either see Buss's hits or get corrections from the FAC."

Click. Click.

The 9-line brief is formal doctrine designed to provide the aircrew with everything they need to engage enemy positions and to avoid any friendly positions. It sounds simple enough. However, CAS in the open desert is one thing; CAS in an urban environment is anything but simple. At our altitudes, we had wires, towers, buildings, civilians, questionable geometry, and a low-level ingress and egress. We also had the unknowns, the assumptions made in the absence of facts or anything resembling a truth. Where were those ZPU-4s? Where were the missing soldiers from the 507th?

Buss had the plan in his head. Rosie and I both had portions in our targeting system and on our maps, but now it was Buss's time to sell it. "Four-four, we are gonna push at time twenty-five, max speed, two hundred feet, right offset with a left turn back to 220, slight pop and left pull to the east. If we need to extend for an immediate reattack, I'm thinking in from the east and another left pull to the south, then egress east. How copy?"

Matt validated the plan. "Four-four copies all. Twenty-five push time."

A strange calm and silence developed between the current time and the push time. Nothing needed checking. There was nothing more to discuss. Contingencies and what ifs were wasted thoughts, and it simply became about execution. All I needed was a second or two in the wide field of view on the targeting camera. Time to identify the target, switch to a closer field of view, and pull the trigger.

"Four-three's pushing." Before we could respond, Buss and Rosie were out of their holding turn, headed south in a slight dive down to two hundred feet and clearly pulling maximum power.

"Four-four copies," Matt said, pulling 100 percent torque as we quickly passed through two hundred feet and 140 knots. Buss remained too far ahead. We were no longer in the suburbs. I attempted to use the targeting systems camera, but we flew too low and too fast. I transitioned to an outside scan but kept my right hand on the turret's steering joystick and my left hand on the trigger.

On my right, the streets appeared empty—nothing, nobody. I could feel the city from that altitude. I could see every building, see the Arabic writing on storefronts, see into windows, see down streets, but the natural sightseer in me snapped back to reality.

"You see that?" I pulled my head around in time to catch the white plume of the Willy Pete mark.

Buss pitched his nose up slightly and called, "Four-three's wings level."

Holy shit. Buss and Rosie had already pitched their nose high 40 degrees and stayed in a 60-degree angle of bank turn to the left. Within a second, they'd risen to a thousand feet and were now in a 40-degree nosedive towards the target.

Matt echoed my thought. "Master arm is going to arm."

Click. Click.

"Four-three, you're cleared hot." The FAC saw us, and that's all we needed to hear.

I watched, waited, wondered. There was 43, completely silhouetted over the Nasiriyah skyline and in their most vulnerable state.

I felt Matt pull the nose of the Cobra into a near identical vertical climb, then make a hard left turn. The sun blinded me, and even through my dark shaded helmet visor, I strained to see anything off the reflections of the sun-bleached buildings. After a climb like this, there was a second when the Cobra almost floated. It forced Matt to add more left rudder. That rudder input "kicked" the tail of the Cobra to the right and allowed the nose to fall back below the horizon. With the nose pitched down, we were close to a 220 heading, picking up speed. We could feel the ground rush toward us. I couldn't see Buss's rounds impacting, and I couldn't hear Mouth, the FAC, making any corrections.

Matt called us in next. "Four-four's wings level."

Nothing. No response. Twenty-degree nose low and building speed. We had another three or four seconds.

Again, Matt reported, "Four-four's wings level."

Buss broke the silence. "Four-three's off cold, no shoot."

What was happening?

Buss quickly clarified. "Mouth, we couldn't see anything. Resetting to the east."

Mouth suddenly came back. "Four-four, you're cleared hot, south of the mark."

The call had come too late because we were less than a hundred meters away. The tracking angle and speed made it too fast to acquire anything in the camera.

I couldn't see anything. "Matt, I got nothing. Go safe."

Matt reported us off. "Four-four's off safe, no shoot. We couldn't see anything."

This was followed by another 60-degree angle of bank roll combined with the leveling of the Cobra at less than two hundred feet while turning to the 100 plus degrees of heading back to the east. It was a handy piece of flying by Matt.

"Mouth copies. Reset to the north."

Buss had already headed west, still at maximum power, and we were now about two hundred meters in a trailing position, actually good spacing. That put us in a position to support Buss should he be fired upon, and if we turned back for an immediate reattack, he would be in position to cover our run.

Cobras are most vulnerable in the last few seconds of an attack run since they are generally flying straight and level. It's the time when the front seat pilots need a stable platform to engage targets with TOW and Hellfire missiles or sometimes the gun. Even though the gunsight, via the camera, is gyro stabilized, it's very difficult to deliver accurate fire when moving on multiple axes. The wings level profile also provides the same increased accuracy when delivering unguided 2.75-inch rockets and cannon fire from the rear seat.

Every CAS profile onto a target is a tradeoff. I preferred to go in once and get it done versus doing a lot of excess maneuvering only to go back two or more times. Every situation is different based on the mission, enemy, terrain, and other considerations. It demands your best judgment. It's a decision.

Mouth came back quickly. "Hey, 43 and 44, our observers saw tracer fire all over you on the egress. I think you guys took some rounds. I suggest you push south and check that out."

Rosie was back on the radio. "Four-three copies. We are safed up and headed south."

Before we had time to think about any battle damage, I saw a flash of light off to the left followed by a contrail of smoke.

Buss was back on the radio. "Four-four, you see that? Let's push direct south now."

Click. Click.

We turned south and made the now familiar trip back to Riverfront to refuel and shut down. We needed to give the aircraft a good look-over. It was frustrating to have spent all the time and effort to come up short. Though we didn't shoot, there was satisfaction in knowing we were very visible to both the Marines and the Iraqis. Maybe it was less a failure than I had initially believed.

"Sky Chief, Deadly 43 off station inbound Riverfront. No battle damage assessment (BDA) to report. Took possible SAM or RPG fire about two clicks north of the southeast bridge."

Sky Chief acknowledged our intelligence report and pushed us for the radio switch.

We checked in with Riverfront. By now, we had a small detachment of air traffic controllers, along with a MAG 29 operations tent, both welcome additions. Prior to shutting down to refuel, the tower passed that we should expect to be put on strip alert, meaning we should be ready to launch when requested. There are levels of readiness expected based on times, but in our case, this involved being fully armed and fueled with the crews a reasonable distance from the aircraft. We didn't actually time ourselves to see how fast we could get airborne, but if called, we could have rotor blades turning, engines running, and ordnance armed in under ten minutes. What normally took the longest was getting a situation report (SITREP) as well as the unit's location, callsign, and frequency.

Strip alert implied urgency, giving us the feeling that, when called, we needed to be there five minutes ago. That was a bit of an exaggeration. As much as we wanted to be on station whenever

Marines needed us, we also didn't want to arrive ill prepared. We wanted to avoid flying into a situation blindly or with a false sense of urgency. That could lead to hasty decisions, and with ordnance being delivered and Marines always in close proximity, we needed to have a little patience.

We considered it more important to arrive on station with as much information as possible. Even an extra few minutes allowed the section leader to think through plans to support the ground commander. It also let the section lead build contingencies enroute and potentially arrive with a more complete support plan. It was not our job to drive the fight, but it was our job to arrive with awareness, expertise, and ideas.

Buss and Rosie had shut down and walked toward the nose of our aircraft. I could tell they wanted to talk, so we completed the shutdown and hopped out of the cockpit.

"Hey, sir, come check this out." Buss turned and strode back toward his Cobra.

Matt and I glanced at each other. Then, we put our helmets on the ammunition bay door and followed about fifteen feet behind them.

The first was easy to see—a nice, clean bullet hole. The others took more time to notice. It was similar to searching for the differences between two pictures that initially appear to be identical. Obscure anomalies hid in plain sight. With careful study, they eventually unveiled themselves.

We found another impact in the left skid tube just above the skid shoe, a piece of metal attached to the bottom of the skids of all Hueys and Cobras. They were designed to take the damage caused by sliding landings and other abuse best not given to the actual skids. The skids themselves were bolted onto the airframe. Replacing those was a major maintenance evolution, one we wanted to avoid. The round off the skid shoe and skid looked to be from someone shooting nearly straight up. Fortunately, we found no damage on the main or tail rotor blades.

One, two. Ahh yes, there it was—three. Another blemishing mark on the right side. That round had impacted the TOW missile rack and hit at an angle. It was a small divot, but scarring showed how the Iraqi bullets had deflected off the rack. That shooter had looked nose on to Buss and Rosie, offset slightly to the right. Buss had got it from both sides, so maybe it was time to take a look at 44.

"Sir, you got a second?" Buss was stepping toward me.

It was rhetorical, but I stopped. "Sure. What's up?"

"Did you see that SAM shot or RPG?" He didn't look concerned, just curious.

I didn't have a good answer. "I didn't see anything until it was way above me and long gone out to the east. I couldn't say what it was. If I had to guess, it was an RPG. There was no corkscrewing, and the smoke trail wasn't too long."

Buss thought it through. The RPG-7 was a Russian-made and shoulder-fired portable grenade launcher. It hurled a grenade at about three hundred meters per second but didn't have an accurate range past three hundred meters. It was a subsonic round, and based on our altitude, I thought the RPG had the best chance of hitting one of us.

I didn't believe the Iraqis would waste a SAM shot. A SAM would likely be the shoulder-fired SA-7 "Grail." Also Russian made, it was a heat-seeking missile that tracked hot engine exhausts. It was unlikely that we had seen an SA-7 for several practical and technological reasons. First off, we had flown too low, and the missile seeker would have had a hard time picking us up flying at two hundred feet. The missile preferred to track the exhaust of an aircraft against a blue-sky background. Plus, I doubted the Iraqi gunners had had the warning time and ability to attach the required battery onto the SA-7. That battery cooled the missile's seeker head, and the process took time. We assumed they used the SA-7s in a less reactive mode, but I was spitballing.

Buss, still considering what I had said, responded thoughtfully. "I think you might be right. I wasn't expecting that, and I certainly was not expecting to run that far downtown on the 9-line."

I didn't want to interrupt him because he had been spot on all day with sound tactical choices and judgment. This was the first time Iraqis gunners had actually hit either of our aircraft.

I saw the look on Buss's face. Maybe he'd expected more of a reaction from me, but I wouldn't have changed anything. We would follow up every flight, including that one, with a debrief, and in those moments, we dealt honestly and directly with one another.

Marine aviation debriefs are things of legend. They are take-the-gloves-off, no-holds-barred assessments of everything that went as anticipated compared to what actually happened. The tone of a debrief varies from unit to unit and often reflects the commander's priorities. Some commanders are calm, metered, and reasonable. Others are a bit spastic and irrational. However, a few elements are common to all debriefs. They generally start formal and disciplined and eventually get ugly. Everyone is offended, everyone learns, and everyone, minus those who cannot accept the handshake, gets on with it.

Since the morning of the 21st, the debriefs had been short, to the point, and delivered in ways to make us better. Out here, we simply tried to maintain the standard, and we didn't have all the resources. We certainly did not have the time to wax on about how screwed up a flight had been.

The mistakes I'd made over the past few days and nights had become amplified by the environment, fatigue, and repetition. Most mistakes I made, whether navigation, communication calls, or tactical decisions, got corrected on the spot. I needed to get better regardless of how well the actual flight went. That orderly and dispassionate review of our performance as a section and as individuals was critical, but today was different.

We couldn't dissect today's flight now since we were anticipating another two or three sorties. Not that I relished taking random gunfire from places unknown, but there was no simple answer. It was a combination of my decisions, my assumptions, and a desire to support the FAC that had pushed me to take unnecessary risks. Matt, Buss, and Rosie all knew what we had done and what I had asked them to do. They also knew the enemy got a vote. Meanwhile, I tucked away a few additional thoughts on future daylight engagements over the city or over any urban areas—not as a judgment or comparison to what we had just done but more as observations to simply be better the next time.

We made our way to the operations tent to check on our strip alert status. Over my shoulder, I noticed the changing weather. The sky began to display a slight shift in color. As an unwelcome but familiar reddish and brown hue slowly formed on the horizon, I started to get that feeling again.

Unbeknownst to us, a cyclone was approaching. A low-pressure system dragged sand, dust, and debris north across the Egyptian and Saudi Arabian deserts, and it was headed straight for us.

MAG 29 had several GP tents already set up. That included one for operations, one for logistics, and one for the staff to brief and congregate. The operations tent had several of Boomer's staff ashore. They were preparing for the eventual influx of more than a thousand Marines and tons of additional parts, supplies, tools, vehicles, ground security units, desks, computers, generators, water, and sixty odd helicopters.

Having Riverfront fully operational would also include getting an air traffic control capability established. We needed procedures for entering and departing the airspace around Riverfront. That included specific headings, checkpoints, and altitudes to prevent midair collisions. An increased capability also included more formal procedures for arming, de-arming, refueling, and parking. Riverfront already felt like a regional airport, handling hundreds of inbound and outbound flights per day, but it would soon handle thousands of airplanes, helicopters, and unmanned aerial systems, along with the constant flow of vehicles and personnel on the runways, taxiways, and tarmacs.

As the weather turned, few noticed, but Deadly 43 and 44 could see it and smell it and had just received a request from the direct air support center (DASC). DASCs were responsible for formally processing air support requests for ground units. Though located in Kuwait, they could relay those requests via a secure computer system to any flying unit. They also extended their reach and communication capabilities with Sky Chief, who used the ample space inside the Marine KC-130 to fit extra communications equipment. That created an airborne DASC.

In our case, the DASC's request was acknowledged by the MAG 29 staff, and the mission was given to 269. From there, they assigned it to an available section of Cobras or Hueys. We pulled the strip, or piece of paper that had everything the requesting unit wanted, and walked back to the flight line.

I found myself pacing back and forth as I read the strip. It gave us the location, the frequency, and other unit-specific data. That mission had come from the 1st LAR Battalion. They operated north of Nasiriyah, and I suspected that they wanted to go further north. It was time to get back to work after the hour break.

Midafternoon had come by the time we arrived. 1st LAR was essentially doing what we were doing. The missions of the LAR battalion and an HMLA squadron bisected at many points, and I always looked forward to working with them. Armed with the LAV-25 reconnaissance vehicle, these were not armored or mechanized units but scouts or reconnaissance in force. Built by General Motors and powered by a three hundred horsepower diesel engine, the LAV-25s required three crew members and carried several infantry Marines. The vehicle was reliable, durable, and packed with legitimate firepower. Although they were normally equipped with a 25mm Bushmaster cannon and several machine guns, there were other specialized variants as well.

Today, we linked up with a "Highlander" platoon and planned to push out north along Highway 1 to extend their vision. The battalion had been attached to Regimental Combat Team 5 (RCT-5). I knew the 1st LAR battalion commander, Lieutenant Colonel Duffy White. We'd met through mutual friends while both students in Quantico. As a captain, I attended the Amphibious Warfare School and Duffy, a major, studied at the Command Staff College. It had been years since we had talked. I almost wished I had time to land and say hello face to face. I found him an impressive officer in all respects, and he had returned more recently to the operating forces after having served as an aide to the president. Strange place indeed to be running into old friends.

Buss checked us in. "Deadly 43 checking in. We have about an hour."

The FAC came back to us. "We copy. Need you to take it up the highway as far as you can."

Well, that seemed simple enough. We headed north at full speed, fewer than twenty miles south of Nasiriyah and less than ten minutes from their positions.

I suspected Buss had a strategy, and it wasn't long before he shared it. "Four-four, let's plan to pick up Highway 8 south of the city and follow it west."

Click. Click.

Matt and I knew what he intended: follow Highway 8 until it merged with Highway 1 several miles to the west of the city. Fully fueled and armed, we did quick weapons checks north of Jalibah. The guns were good, and we had all systems armed. We made the turn west, and there was no mistaking what loomed.

Matt instantly spotted the storm. "Four-three, I know you see that."

Click. Click.

Matt and I quickly discussed. Then, he spoke again to Buss. "How about I call and see if we can get an overhead time for mother?"

Click. Click.

The time came for us to make plans to head back to *Saipan*. The weather grew much darker and thicker in a matter of only five minutes. We hit the intersection of Highway 8 and Highway 1 and turned north. The highway looked empty, as did the desert. No lights, no nothing.

I could feel Matt adding power and could see Buss accelerating and descending. It was going to be a race. I liked the plan and thought the same thing that Buss and Rosie did. Run as far as we can as fast as we can, then head for *Saipan* before we get caught by this storm.

Based on our last takeoff time, I had a pretty good idea but asked Matt anyway. "Matt, what do we have for gas? I'm gonna run a fuel ladder to Safwan and then back to the ship."

The gauge was located just a few inches above and to the left of the master arm switch and was a part of any pilot's scan. "We got 1,500 pounds."

Click. Click.

Time for some math.

"I'm going head down for a few," I said.

Click. Click.

A simple statement letting Matt know I was not looking at anything outside of the cockpit was an important detail and a critical part of effective crew coordination. While I did high math on my kneeboard, I was neither looking at anything outside with my eyeballs nor using the FLIR.

The two General Electric T-701 401C engines burned about 450 pounds of gas per hour each. That meant a maximum of thirty minutes with LAR. We hadn't planned for the weather to push this fast, and I didn't want to go back to Riverfront. Safwan was at least one hundred miles away and increasing. I preferred for us to fly back to at least Nasiriyah and then southeast to Safwan. Flying open desert to the north offered nothing appealing with that weather. It wasn't the time to blaze a shortcut.

Buss had made the plan. "Highlander, Deadly 43 is going to push about forty kicks to the north and then RTB. This weather is closing us in."

Highlander sounded moderately interested in our plan. "Thanks, we copy. Pass along anything you see up there."

Click. Click.

That made sense. Buss intended to go at maximum speed and cover the twenty-five miles quickly, then push back southeast. We owed those Marines our best efforts, but we also couldn't turn ourselves into a rescue mission, especially not with that storm coming.

Buss called for our clearance. "Tower, Deadly 43 and 44 for the break."

It was the boss who seemed like he never left the tower. "Deadly 43 and flight cleared to break, report abeam. Expect spots two and four."

The deck of Saipan already revealed signs of the storm. A light coating of sand had settled onto the flight deck, in the ladder wells, and on the superstructure. A windblown browning of the ship. Many of the remaining helicopters were getting covered, and others waited to be brought down into the large hangar bay. It would get much worse.

Matt landed us in spot four. The discipline of the ship reassured us. It wasn't like that afternoon when me and Rosie had performed all the ground crew duties—much better to witness great professionals at work. Red shirts, blue shirts, green shirts, and yellow shirts. White shirts watching, and purple shirts waiting. Within a few minutes, we had shut down and towed into the "slash" on the front and right side of the boat. It would be my last time on the flight deck for several days.

The sandstorm that hit coalition forces on the evening of the 25th would rage for nearly three days. This storm would halt nearly all military operations in their tracks. The heavy winds carried hundreds of tons of sand and debris. The sand penetrated every tank main gun; every artillery and mortar tube; every rifle and pistol barrel; every crack, crevasse, and opening of man and machine alike. Miserable.

It's known as a *turab,* a powerful storm that blows out of the south. Its more famous brother, the *shamal*, brings chaos from the north. Definitions and specifics aside, this was a wicked storm, only increasing in speed and intensity. Blowing winds from the southeast should have been an advantage, hitting the backs of the advancing Marine formations while throwing sand in the faces of the Iraqi defenders. However, the storm generated such poor forward visibility that drivers couldn't see another vehicle ten feet in front of them. Heavy rains like those from a science fiction movie followed. The raindrops became saturated with the blowing sand to create flying mud. To those watching from afar, it appeared apocalyptic.

That low pressure cyclonic storm did give US fixed-wing aviation a window. With all US and allied helicopter and ground forces awaiting a break in the weather, US commanders executed an impromptu air campaign on the larger Iraqi armored units, particularly the Republican Guard and Special Republican Guard divisions.

That would allow tactical fixed-wing aircraft such as US Navy F/A-18s and F-14s, Marine F/A 18s and AV-8s, and USAF B-1s, B-52s, F-15s, F-16s, and A-10s to operate with near impunity. Along with a host of other attack platforms operated by the US and the coalition, they would strike and paralyze Iraqi armored formations already suffering the debilitating effects of the weather.

All the major networks had embedded reporters. Most didn't have full film crews, but the major networks did. Their reporting was spectacular, and the canvas they displayed to the world had only one possible artist.

By the morning of the 26th, the Ghost was a headliner, even though she had long been on my mental marquee. The opening night attacks on Safwan Hill had given her a starring role as the Lady of Death, and now she could add the Lady of Chaos to her list of titles. Still hiding in the storm, obscured by the fog, the Lady of Chaos bought her new Iraqi apprentice some much needed time.

I could hear her soundtrack, ironically written and recorded in America by America. "Ain't it foggy outside. All the planes have been grounded… I understand you've been running from the man that goes by the name of the Sandman." Well, maybe we were running from the Sandman, but every storm will pass.

CHAPTER 21

Location: USS *Saipan*, Persian Gulf
Date: 26MAR03
Time: 0735L

Nervous energy can sometimes cause fatigue, yet Howdy and I paced in our stateroom. It had only been one night, but knowing we were not going ashore today was frustrating. The morning droned on endlessly.

Normally, I relished the routine on shipboard deployments. I'd wake up early for a workout and then go to 0700 breakfast. That would be followed by the morning maintenance and other routine morning meetings. From there, I'd walk through the ship to see how our Marines were doing. I'd follow that with a quick Marine officer resting period (MORP), an essential and traditional time of deep reflection. Then, I'd squeeze in another trip about the ship's spaces, a midday workout, and maybe a trip to the ship's store. If my name appeared on the flight schedule, I'd prepare for that mission, brief, fly, and debrief. Upon return, I'd prepare for another workout, MORP, or meal. Alas, the never-ending life at sea.

The unscheduled break gave me some time to attain a complete update on the aircraft, follow up with the status of critical parts, and review the final details of our debarkation plan. Once the storm ended, we would fly the bulk of the squadron's Marines and gear ashore to Riverfront. I had sent most of my personal gear ashore a few days earlier and needed to remember to find it.

I had just made myself a small clearing on the corner of the desk I shared with Monty when we heard the news. It came from a voice at the maintenance control counter, and I asked him to repeat his message. It was my worst nightmare coming to me in midmorning.

"Sir, I was just told that we had a helicopter go down somewhere ashore. Nothing else."

What, when, where, and how had we lost a helicopter? The news was delivered more as a notice than a statement of fact.

"Hey, Monty, can we reconfirm the exact BUNOs and tail numbers of all the aircraft ashore? I am going to take a walk to the ready room," I instructed, but I already knew Monty was on it.

I needed to get some solid data points if we were indeed missing an aircraft. Our operations department would also have a complete list of the aircrew assigned to each aircraft ashore. I had no direct way of communicating with the XO, Lieutenant Colonel Doug "Spike" Hardison, who was stranded ashore along with a half-dozen or so UH-1Ns and AH-1Ws at Riverfront. I had limited email with Spike, and our primary means of communication came from *Saipan's* operation center via radio to the small MAG 29 operations department at Riverfront.

I had just confirmed, again, the exact tail numbers and crews ashore when the CO walked into the ready room. I could tell from his pensive expression that we had a situation.

He kicked it off with, "Listen up, gents. We have a Huey down somewhere north of Nasiriyah. I just talked with the XO at Riverfront. There's not much else we know."

As he looked at me, I knew we were going to have to put together a reclamation team and have them fully briefed, kitted out with proper gear, and ready to fly ashore whenever possible. I also knew we needed to have whatever department heads we had still on *Saipan*, or their representatives, gather to begin the series of processes that were required for any aviation mishap.

I was running through a mental checklist of the possibilities. Had the aircraft been shot down? Had it crashed? Were the aircrews alive? Injured? Dead? Captured? Missing? I knew better than to request more details. The CO was already asking himself the same questions and had likely asked Spike those questions as well. Knowing

Spike, he was doing everything in his power to get more information and organize a response from Riverfront.

I took this as an opportunity. "CO, we will get a team together. If it's a Huey, then it's either Andy Dyer and Len or Fridge and Cap. I'll get the crew chiefs confirmed from flight line. Ops confirmed they were both supporting the division."

Satisfied with the answers, the CO turned to head to the landing force operations center (LFOC) where the most capable communications were located.

Meanwhile, I needed a plan for the maintenance response—a practical and unemotional response. Callous as it sounded, I didn't need to waste effort on ideas for how to rescue the downed Huey and crews. By now, the MEF commander had been briefed, and so had the MAW commander. The CO hadn't mentioned a rescue plan, but we had standing tactical recovery of aircraft and personnel (TRAP) plans. The trouble was finding the right mix of aircraft and personnel, along with favorable weather, to execute a TRAP plan.

The likely option was a ground rescue, but that only opened the door for more unanswerable questions, especially with the weather still worsening. There was no way MAG 29 had the assets to execute a recovery. This was going to be a mission from the MEF. Only they had the assets and ability to design, build, brief, and control a ground recovery.

The crash site was north of Nasiriyah as advertised. The UH-1N, BUNO 160444, callsign Mongoose 22, piloted by Captain Brent "Fridge" Reifer and Captain Matt Capodanno, had impacted the ground nearly "wings level." The force of the impact had ripped the entire tail boom from the fuselage and crushed both skids. The 1960s seats, for the pilots and two crew chiefs, would have done little to absorb the excessive G-force upon impact.

The crew had been assigned to support the 1st MARDIV. Using their Swiss army knife abilities over the past four days, their engines had slowly ingested pounds of sand and debris. Most engines are manufactured with technology that removes debris as it simultaneously takes in fresh air. The fresh air is then fed into each of the UH-1N's two engines. The air contributes to cooling and combustion inside the engine's combustion chamber. In this case, the engine couldn't handle all the sand and debris, and with more sand and less air to that engine, it had simply failed.

The day had started out promisingly for the flight of two. Even as the weather continued to worsen, the section of Hueys conducted armed reconnaissance for the division. The flight lead, Captain Andy Dyer, Mongoose 21, had just overflown a burning Iraqi vehicle when they'd begun a turn away from their wingman, Mongoose 22.

Both crews were fighting the weather and flying low but were headed back to land after an hours-long flight. Rolling out of his turn, he asked his crew chiefs if they had their wingman in sight. Nothing.

Andy made a radio call to Fridge and Matt. Nothing. Where were they? With a sense of dread, he turned their Huey back to the last place they'd seen Fridge. The crew chief spotted it first. Mongoose 22 had impacted the ground. It was upright, and there were no signs of a fire—both good omens. But there was no movement from anyone in the cabin.

Had Mongoose 22 gotten shot down? Was Mongoose 21 flying back into a kill zone?

They flew over the top of 22 and looked. Nothing. They made a call to Sky Chief and to the 1st MARDIV headquarters with the five W's: who, what, when, where, and why. Two-one had started the recovery process.

The crew of Mongoose 22 had had little time to react to the engine's failure. The UH-1N, notoriously underpowered, couldn't fly on one engine. As Huey crews were fond of saying, "The second engine just flies you to the crash site." In this case, 160444 was in pieces across an open part of desert that was also heavily mined by the

Iraqis. Inside, two were critically injured: Captain Matt Capodanno, the copilot, and Sergeant Dave Oravecz, one of the two crew chiefs.

Andy Dyer and his copilot, Captain Len Walker, were compelled to make an unenviable choice. Either leave while there was still time and land back at the 1st MARDIV's command post (CP) or turn back and try to rescue their squadron mates. In weather that was only growing more treacherous, the entire crew chose to stay.

Andy lined up the Huey and made a sliding landing twenty yards from their wingman. Then, he and his two crew chiefs made the dash to 22. This dash, they would only learn later, was through a minefield.

When they arrived at the fallen Huey, it was clear everyone was conscious, but everyone was not okay. Matt was injured the worst, so they pulled him out of the collapsed cabin and carried him back to their still turning Huey. After a quick talk to Fridge and the crew chiefs of 22, they made the decision to get Matt to the 1st MARDIV trauma unit. They left the other three, now out of their seats, with weapons in hand. Andy had no other choice. The Huey was already close to maximum weight, and loading everyone into 21 would have been disastrous. Plus, the storm was continuing to degrade visibility, and the climb out of the zone only increased the loss of visual cues.

Andy leveled out at fifty feet and turned to the GPS point that was the 1st MARDIV CP. He was an air force of one, the only thing flying under twenty-five thousand feet that day.

Upon landing, he immediately called for clearance to return to the crash site. By this time, a ground convoy had been formed and was beginning the trek to 22, but Andy and his crew were not convinced and took off. Beating the convoy to the site, they carried Sergeant Dave Oravecz onto 21 and took off for the 1st MARDIV CP. Once again, the injured aircrew of 22 was carried off Dyer's helicopter by the trauma team made up of doctors and Navy corpsmen.

While the crew of Mongoose 21 sat turning, Sky Chief pushed an immediate CASEVAC mission to Andy and his crew. This was not to the crash site but to a 5th Marines unit. These Marines had been in a firefight and had two critically wounded. With Sky Chief confirming that the remaining crew of Mongoose 22 had been rescued, Andy was cleared to take off for yet another mission. Beating the odds was one thing, but flying at fifty feet and less than one hundred knots into unmapped locations was really tempting fate. He ordered all unnecessary gear out of the Huey. They were going to find the two wounded Marines.

The thirty-minute flight probably felt like it had lasted hours, but as 21 touched down for the last time with the two injured Marines in tow, Andy and his crew had done the unimaginable. They had danced very close to the Ghost, had seen her work and stared into her face and never flinched. The war had a new hero. An unassuming twenty-nine-year-old from Clay City, Indiana, had, with the help of his crew, saved not only squadron mates but the lives of two other Marines in indescribable conditions.

On *Saipan*, the 26th was a series of highs and lows. The information that the crew of Mongoose 22 had survived was a tremendous relief. Knowing that a convoy, supported by the 1st MARDIV, had immediately been dispatched to retrieve the crew was reflective of the commitment that Marines were making on the ground. Though the crash had injured three and destroyed one Huey, we considered ourselves very fortunate.

The weather was predicted to lift by the 28th, and we were all anxious to get back to the war. The once comfortable life aboard ship hung around our necks like a yoke. We all wanted off, and we all wanted off now. There was an entire MEF ashore, with thousands of Marines and sailors waiting to get back on the move, and we were ready to help them get back on their feet.

CHAPTER 22

Location: USS *Saipan*, Persian Gulf
Date: 28MAR03
Time: 1305L

The morning of the 28th brought an end to the worst of the weather, and we were scheduled for a 1300L launch from *Saipan*. Since I'd sent my sea bag ashore, Matt and I would carry the remaining supplies in the tail boom.

Today was a day to reclaim our mojo, to get back some of the swag and confidence that was so critical to our morale. We were also overjoyed to finally get off the ship.

Matt, Buss, Rosie, and I had briefed what would be a day-into-night mission. Then, we all made a last sweep of our staterooms since we were not coming back for a while. I passed through maintenance to check on the lineup. It was a full schedule. We were flying everything off minus our three spare helicopters and a small detachment of maintenance Marines.

It felt good to have my body armor back on, pistol strapped to my web vest, M4 carbine fitted into the back, and NVGs and spare batteries stored behind my seat, along with water and abundant 9mm and 5.56mm ammunition. The superfluous ammunition was a feel-good move. Not sure Matt and I would ever need the nearly four hundred extra rounds, but better safe than sorry.

I felt even better being back on the flight deck of *Saipan*. The familiar sights and sounds were medicine for the sickness we had felt the past three days. The comforting faces, smiles, and routines cured what had ailed me and my section. Howdy and Flash, Berger and

Bull, and several others would all soon head ashore. It was the last time we would see *Saipan* for the foreseeable future.

After nearly three days of wind and sands, the flight deck looked like a giant sugar donut. A brown and yellow hue with accents of red covered the entire superstructure, with sailors working feverishly to restore the natural grays so expected from a naval ship.

The boss was back in his perch. "Deadly 21 and 22, winds are down the bow at five. Cleared for takeoff."

The launch sequence from *Saipan* was now SOP. I pulled into a five-foot hover and checked the power. Matt, back in the front seat, saluted the landing signalman as I slid left and then pulled 100 percent power. Every aircraft in naval aviation has a specific identification number called a BUNO or bureau number. This AH-1W, BUNO 160113 was smooth. The main and tail rotor blades were balanced perfectly. All weapons systems were operational. I had asked the maintenance control chief for this particular Cobra; it was the same Cobra I had flown the previous two missions, and I was growing attached.

Even mass-produced aircraft with precision tooling and advanced production processes have differences. Every aircraft flies differently, just slightly and with subtle clues. These differences could be caused by any of the thousands of processes they endure or by the hands of the aviation artisans who built these machines. I am also convinced that even a slight variation in materials or assembly can cause these nuances. That was certainly true for the Cobra.

This AH-1W provided a smooth ride. The main rotor blades had been tracked and balanced to perfection. That was the art of ensuring each main rotor blade had the near equal weight of the other, along with having the trim tabs properly adjusted. If that happened, the angle of the blades was consistent. The maintenance flight crews would do nearly the same with the two tail rotor blades. The massive forty-eight-foot blades were actually wings, and the more efficiently they could be adjusted, the smoother the helicopter flew. Those reductions of vibrations went a long way to improve both the flight characteristics and the speed of every UH-1N and AH-1W. There was a science to this procedure, but it was normally up to a captain and sergeant, both flying the maintenance flights, to turn a procedure into a fully mission-capable helicopter.

I was headed northwest, finally away from the constraints of *Saipan* and the air defense ship Green Crown. This was the last we would see of the three spires of the Kuwait Towers that dominated the Kuwaiti skyline.

When we were cleared to change frequencies, I checked us in with a familiar call. "Sky Chief, Deadly 21. Feet dry for tasking."

We had passed to the west of Safwan and were headed toward Nasiriyah when we got our response. Sky Chief had work for us, and it appeared urgent. "Deadly 21, contact Cybil on magenta."

Cybil was another FAC embedded with Task Force Tarawa, and magenta represented the tactical air direction (TAD) frequency, a discrete frequency the FAC used to control one or more flights of aircraft. Our routine was to check in with the FAC, conduct CAS or reconnaissance missions, and then check back in with Sky Chief and pass any BDAs to them. The BDA report was formal, but we essentially passed our location, enemy location, units supported, and targets engaged.

I checked in and somehow wanted to reflect our façade of patience and calm. "Cybil, Deadly 21, flight of two, up as fragged with one plus one five of playtime."

There was already a slight familiarity felt with the FACs. Our once very formal check-ins gave way to a coolness and some intentional flippancy, building confidence in all of us. With that check-in, Cybil knew we were armed per the flight schedules, which they all had copies of, and for how long we could stay until we needed gas—in that case, one hour and fifteen minutes.

Cybil was on his game. "Deadly 21, I want you to push north of the Saddam Canal and get eyes on anything moving south on Highway 1, then screen east of the city. Let me know immediately if you see any movement."

I got it and knew he was driving the fight. "Deadly 21 copies."

We were finally back, and thankfully, the trip from *Saipan* was almost routine. The countryside looked the same as it had three days ago, but somehow, the towns had aged in dog years. The roads and buildings looked caked in dust and mud. Without much traffic, the streets looked less like interstate highways and more like country roads. Spotting anything moving in any direction would be easy. Follow the dust trail.

I felt a bolt of confidence surge through me. Honestly, it was more like a bolt of "fake it until you make it," but it was a bolt nonetheless. Those same bolts of confidence had gotten me through multiple seasons of varsity hockey and lacrosse—wins, losses, good teams, bad teams, good coaches, great coaches, and forgettable coaches. They had carried me through my first and only NCAA lacrosse season and through Officer Candidate School at the ripe old age of nineteen. And now, by some combination of magic, luck, fortune, and a little bit of grind, I was leading a section of Marine attack helicopters back into combat.

I punched the radio. "Two-two, I think we need to push north first and then head out east of Highway 1."

Click. Click.

I heard Buss's response and continued. "Matt, intel briefed that the Iraqis had requested reinforcements and supplies from the north. There's one main road from Baghdad to Nasiriyah."

Click. Click.

Matt stayed heads down in the FLIR, already looking to the north and west.

Portions of the Iraqi 3rd Corps and 11th Mechanized Division remained holed up somewhere in the city. We had no updates on the location and condition of the surviving soldiers of the 507th or the crew of a US Army AH-64 Apache that had been shot down on the 24th.

Assessing the strength and fighting capabilities of the remaining forces was not up to us. We had no way of telling how many had slipped out of their uniforms and into the population or into the surrounding areas.

I could see well enough, but I needed Matt to be my eyes. "Matt, let's keep an eye on the outskirts of the city, and Buss and Rosie, look north."

Matt was still looking into the targeting camera. I didn't expect him to have the answers to the questions in my head, but he was way ahead of me. "Copy. There's nothing moving inside the city. Nothing seems to have changed since Tuesday."

Tuesday? What the hell was Matt talking about? My sense of time had long passed, and every day seemed like a Monday. But if Matt was right, that meant today was a Friday. Prayer Friday. How could I have not known that? Fridays are an important gathering day in the Muslim world, a day to listen to the Imam or other religious people and to pray. Maybe that would give us a quiet day.

The FLIR scans continued, as did the constant chatter with Buss and Rosie. The mission turned us north and then east into the desert, but there was nothing out there. Perhaps there were forces to the northeast, but we weren't seeing anything. We flew into our fourth hour and third sortie for Cybil.

He broke the long silence. "Deadly 21, reports of gunfire by the train station."

I only had one response. "Deadly copies. We are headed that way." They knew my next call, but I still needed to let them know. "Two-one's coming hard right."

I had not even started my turn when Rosie responded, "22."

I turned hard to the south, pulling to 100 percent power, and pushed the nose down. We went back at two hundred feet and 145 knots; 160113 flew smoothly.

The train station was to the south of the city and on the other side of the Euphrates River and Highway 8. What looked like commercial and industrial businesses surrounded the station. Second Battalion 8th Marines, attached to the 2nd Marine Regiment, had also pushed into the area.

We were in no rush, but we still balanced impatience with frustration and agitation. I was getting amped up. "Matt, let me know when you see the station."

Click. Click.

I needed to hear from the FAC. "Cybil, this is Deadly 21. You got anything else?"

"Stand by one," came his response. "Two-one, nothing. Just reports of gunfire."

Another dry well, and after fifteen minutes of using our optics to look at the train station, we called off station for the third time and made the quick trip south to Riverfront. Something seemed weird about the city. Yes, it was Friday, but where were the hundreds of thousands of residents, the 11th Mechanized Division, and the Fedayeen?

With a bitter pill in my mouth, I called us off station. "Sky Chief, Deadly 21, visual reconnaissance of Nasiriyah complete. Nothing to report."

"Copy 21. You're cleared for the switch."

It was time to go to Riverfront and see what the place looked like after several days. We made an arcing approach to the west and south, then headed north to our LZ. Across the east-west runways, I could see a dozen Cobras and Hueys on our flight line. Monty and the Marines had done a great job. They had effectively marked the flight line with sandbags every few feet, and plane captains were ready to taxi us into our spot. We touched down with only a light dusting of the chalky Iraqi sand.

All four of us made it to the newly constructed squadron ready room, complete with dirt floor, one large whiteboard, and a duty desk. There was also a MAG 29 operations tent where we found the group intelligence detachment. I started to feel more normal. After a short debrief with the intelligence team, we headed back to the ready room. We didn't find a formal flight schedule; instead, sections of UH-1Ns and AH-1Ws were assigned to specific missions or areas to support.

We had become very familiar with the city of Nasiriyah and took an hour break before we headed back. Reports continued to show all was quiet. With the city encircled by Task Force Tarawa and other selected units from the 1st MARDIV, we played a waiting game.

They scheduled us for a 1900L launch, another reconnaissance mission for Task Force Tarawa. It felt good to get back on more of a routine. The squadron duty officer had the aircraft lineups, ordnance loads, astronomical data, an intelligence update, and other standard briefing items, all helping create a sense of normalcy.

The intelligence briefs almost sounded comical, a near copy of what we had briefed the MAG intelligence team only hours before. At least the information was being collected and analyzed and was effectively making it from the group to the squadron level.

It was also good to be back on NVGs, having spent the last six or so sorties flying during the daytime. The grainy green hue that was the view through the NVGs brought a welcome sight.

Our startup, check-in, and arming followed the SOP. We had been cleared for takeoff directly from our parking spots. That type of takeoff had risks, but it also had us flying into open desert. While it was not perfect, it reduced the pivoting and turning of Cobras on the flight line. We were always looking for ways to improve safety.

In fact, as fast as we could validate another ad hoc safety procedure, we implemented it. We championed a very iterative process, always seeing risks and making reasonable and executable procedures to remove or mitigate them. Any deviation or acceptance of additional risk was on the aircrews, and only they knew when to push harder and when to pull back.

We were up and out, headed back into the city. "Sky Chief, 21 for the switch."

Sky Chief was waiting. "Deadly 21, contact Cybil on plum."

I knew the routing and saw the pattern. "Two-two, we are going to start west near Talil and then run south over the train station."

Click. Click.

Talil Air Base was a now abandoned Iraqi Air Force base but an easy landmark. Its ten-thousand-foot dual runways were easily identified from nearly any altitude.

I still felt a thrill of confidence. "Cybil, Deadly 21, mission number 7244, up as fragged, one plus three zero time on station."

Cybil was also up. "Copy all, 21. Need you to press up the east side to the Saddam Canal."

That was simple. I responded, "21 copies."

The night was dark and moonless, but the stars were out, and the winds had calmed. The NVGs really liked starlight and were beginning to earn their keep. It was about time I could be a more active crewmember.

Cybil called, "Deadly 21, we have reports of movement from the government building. Multiple MAMs moving north."

It was now more of a conversation. "Deadly 21 copies. We are in the vicinity of the train station. We are going east to take a look."

I had no clue what the government building was, but we were going to find out. We took down the eight-digit grid.

"Matt, where is that?" I wondered aloud. "And any chance we can get eyes on?"

He was in the FLIR and on the map. "Stand by. Let me see where that is."

I took a look down. There were few lights on in the city, and nothing was moving. Man, it was only eight o'clock at night, and the town was buttoned up.

Matt was back. "Okay, it's just off Highway 7 in what looks like the Iridu District. Maybe an intersection with a side street and the main loop road. I think it's called Eridu Street." He paused again and then continued. "Looks like that street continues around to the north. It is the border road, maybe the loop road we have seen just south of the Saddam Canal."

I was trying to take what he was saying and overlay it on the city, but it was not making sense yet. I started a roll out to the north, headed to the canal with Buss on my left in a one-hundred-meter trail position. I was sure Rosie was looking into the city, trying to identify the point Cybil had passed to us. I was focused on providing a stable platform as Matt was heads down trying to see any signs of the MAMs. The calm was temporary.

"Two-one, AAA, break right, break right!"

Holy shit. Who and what the fuck was that? I could only see tracers passing over the left of the cockpit—not too close, but there was a clear adrenaline kick. I immediately pulled power and rolled into a hard 70-degree angle of bank turn, staring into the HUD to stay level. In that moment, I had no time to talk to Matt or answer Buss. I just kept the turn in, extending out to the east.

Matt was now my answer man. "Matt, how are we doing?"

"I'm good. I didn't see where it came from; I was heads down."

I asked Buss, "22, can you mark that position?"

Pause. Pause. Pause. "Nope. We saw it, called it, and turned to follow you. Rosie is guessing it's about where it was plotted. Maybe a few hundred meters to the south."

We understood better now. "Two-one copies. Let's extend east and then north."

It was time to talk to the FAC. "Cybil, Deadly 21 and flight took some AAA fire in the vicinity of the grid you passed. You have eyes on anything?"

Cybil came back. "Stand by, 21."

We had the majority of the friendly positions marked and had assumed Task Force Tarawa had pushed or requested some type of reconnaissance closer into the city, maybe even on rooftops. The Marine Corps had a wide range of options for those types of operations. They could use Force Reconnaissance units, "standard" reconnaissance units, or scout/sniper teams. Any or a combination of any could be possible, but we were unaware of how much intelligence they had on the previous target. We turned north and remained clear of the city while the FAC did some research up and down several chains of command and with adjacent units.

I looked down. We were at seven hundred pounds of fuel. "Cybil, 21's bingo. We will be back in about an hour."

Click. Click. Then, Cybil said, "And I'll have an update on that position once you check back on station."

My turn: *Click. Click.*

Some of the familiarity had turned into passive contempt. It was natural. His job was hard, our job was hard, and we wanted to be more engaged. We would be back soon to solve problems—his, mine, and hers.

The simplicity of the trip back to Riverfront was becoming a welcome routine. We checked in and then out with Sky Chief, passed on the location we had caught the fire, and then continued on to Riverfront. Even though the sky was nearly pitch black, there was a growing confidence. It was really good to be back out on NVGs.

There were a few other Cobras getting gas and rearming after supporting the UK in Basra, a couple of Hueys returning from supporting the regiments, and a few Phrogs doing supply runs and standing by for potential CASEVACs. We also noticed some unmanned aircraft setting up operations and the approach of the airfield. I didn't think much of that, but I also hoped they were looped into our procedures.

The night ended with more fizzle than a flash. We were anxious to get some sleep and welcome a new day.

CHAPTER 23

Location: An-Nasiriyah, Iraq
Date: 29MAR03
Time: 1645L

"Deadly 45, do you see the bridge crossing the Euphrates? It's the southern Highway 7 bridge. Call contact." The FAC was walking our eyes onto the target.

I called it: "Contact." That meant I saw the bridge and was ready for more information.

The FAC was Kool-Aid. He continued, "From that bridge, look west to a row of buildings facing directly to the Euphrates. Call contact."

I saw the buildings. "Contact."

"Follow that road west until the block ends. There is a two-story building four buildings from the corner building. Call contact." Kool-Aid was good.

It was hard to see the specific structure; Matt was trying to pick it out among the rows of buildings. I couldn't be sure. "Deadly has contact on the corner building but can't pick out the fourth one in."

Kool-Aid continued. "Deadly, we have been taking sniper fire from the second floor. That's your target. Call wings level."

I still couldn't see it, but Matt likely had a better angle. "Matt, you see what he's talking about?"

Matt was heads down in the FLIR. More accurately, he was using the daytime camera, and he let me know that he needed more time. "I'm looking. You need to reset to the south and give me a longer run-in."

Click. Click.

Buss and Rosie were now off our right side and slightly behind us. "Four-six, you see which building he is talking about?"

Buss was up. "I definitely see the bridge and the corner building, but it's hard to tell."

It was time to tell 46 our plan. It wasn't sexy, but it was simple and in their faces. "Four-five flight, let's reset to the south. Run-in looks about 010. I'll climb to about four hundred feet and 120 knots. Let's plan for a right pull and then set up a holding track near the train station."

Click. Click.

Time for the FAC to get read into our plan. "Kool-Aid, 45's in from the south. Need a laser on there or a mark."

Pause. Pause. Nothing.

Even though we had a good idea of which building was the correct one, we were about to unleash TOW missiles into the city and would be covering our pull-off with 20mm HE rounds. I needed that mark.

I rolled out of an easy left turn. Surprisingly, I could see the Marines of 2/8 below us. They were covering the southern entry and exit to the city. I peered below and to my left. At two hundred feet, I could see faces. It looked like they were smiling. If not, they would be soon.

I came out of the turn and headed 010 degrees with Buss and Rosie in "combat spread," now off about seventy-five meters to my left. I could only imagine what they were talking about.

I was ready to get this started. "Matt, master arm is going to arm. You lead with TOW. I'll follow with rockets, and you cover the pull with the gun."

Matt was still in the FLIR, but he kept a constant stream of his observations coming. "Okay. I think I am tracking the fourth building in but not 100 percent."

I called the FAC again. "Kool-Aid, 45's inbound. Confirm the mark?"

Nothing. Nothing.

Then, Kool-Aid said what we all hate to hear: "Stand by one."

The silence was almost immediately broken by a third voice. "Deadly, we got your mark."

I had time to spy a single LAV-25, the dust trail making his position obvious. He broke cover from his protected position on our side of the Euphrates River. Coming to a NASCAR-like slide into his firing position, the 25mm Bushmaster began churning out rounds, which immediately impacted the suspected building.

Chunks of cement and plaster looked like they were exploding off the building. Windows and frames collapsed under the weight of the volume of fire. Sparks told us the fate of whatever rebar or metal had been used during construction.

The LAV and the crew had a clear view of the building, but at five hundred meters to the target, the enemy had a clear view of them as well. It was not long before the enemy began to shoot back. It was an amazing act of heroism, an effective display of marking a target and a highly appreciated suppression for our run.

I quickly replied, "45's got the target in sight. Wings level."

Kool-Aid was now seeing a new picture. "Deadly 45, you are cleared hot."

Matt was heads down and had a TOW missile selected. This was going to be about a 1,200-meter shot. The TOW 2 missiles that we used were effective out to 3,750 meters, so this was a relatively close shot. There are no layups with attack helicopter missile delivery, particularly with the TOW. This was a mid-range jump shot.

Matt would need to center his sight on the target, pull the trigger, and then stay focused on the target, not the missile. Again, sounds simple, but the missile is in the camera's field of view the entire time. He would have to guide or hand fly the missile all the way to target impact. This was close quarters, and we would see the missile all the way to impact, and we'd also see anything near the target area. Remaining heads down all the while, Matt would call corrections to my rocket shots, then take over with the 20mm cannon. In that case, he would either continue to suppress the initial target or switch to a new threat. We would likely not be off the target until inside three hundred meters.

Matt reported quietly on the ICS, "I'm going trigger down on the TOW."

I picked out the LAV-25 just to my left. They were still hammering away at the target, but I could also see rounds impacting around them. No doubt the LAV-25 was taking direct hits as well. This was going to get a bit spicy.

Location: Riverfront
Date: 29MAR03
Timc: 0205L

The final fight last night had put us back at Riverfront a little after two in the morning. Besides the random rounds fired at us, there was nothing to report, nothing to debrief, nothing new to plan for. There was a growing sense of frustration, not only for me but for everyone.

We'd spent more than forty hours flying in and around the city. We had every friendly and as many suspected and anticipated enemy positions plotted. We had friendly artillery and mortar units prepared to fire and had developed multiple scenarios to execute FAC(A) missions with fixed-wing aircraft.

Following last night's mission, I went through my post-flight routine including a debriefing with the intelligence Marines. That was followed by popping a "no-go" pill. I finally fell asleep sometime after three thirty.

We had been authorized to take pills that gave an adrenaline rush and then caffeine-like endurance as well as other pills to put us to sleep. I was initially opposed to the meds and didn't believe it was either needed or a good idea for my long-term health. However, like so many other compromises, this one was necessary. I had experienced extreme fatigue, almost to the point of falling asleep in the cockpit, while flying from two to five in the morning. So, I made the decision to take the "go" pills. It was the right decision.

Boomer had taken his medical officer's advice seriously and, after considering the risks, had only authorized the night crews of 269 to take the pills. He'd also implemented strict rules on where the no-go pills were stored. Basically, he did not want any of us to inadvertently take a no-go when we needed a go—smart idea.

As anyone who has worked night shifts can attest, it's nearly impossible to gain and maintain a night routine without serious side effects. The body naturally wants to sleep in darkness and be awake during daylight hours. Your circadian rhythm, or twenty-four-hour internal clock, ensures you go through this natural process.

Last night, we had essentially pulled another of many all-nighters. We needed something to keep us on our game in those late night and early morning hours. We couldn't do it with Diet Cokes and coffee. First off, we didn't have any Diet Cokes, and I didn't drink coffee. The answer came with Modafinil and Zolpidem or whatever generic version was shipped to Navy medicine. These sure worked.

A while later, I woke up to Monty giving my boot a gentle kick. "Hey, sir. You got some time?"

I opened my eyes groggily. The sun sent me a strong message: It's time to get up. Hot, disoriented, and still tired, I was lying on a cot with my boots and flight suit on but had my flight suit top tied about my waist. I was staring into the baking morning sun. Monty leaned over and handed me a plastic thirty-two-ounce bottle of water, one of the seemingly millions of palletized water bottles. I stood up slowly and started to walk with Monty. As usual, he was way ahead of me and ran down the entire aircraft lineup. We had no major issues.

The idea of keeping three fresh aircraft on *Saipan* was already paying dividends. Every time we sent a helicopter to the ship for maintenance, we could also load it with broken parts that needed repairs. Then, the returning and fully repaired helicopter would come back laden with parts and other important things like chewing tobacco and cigarettes from the ship's store.

I was not a dipper or much of a smoker, but we began making small "care" packages. We had 269 Marines embedded in each of the traveling FARP teams, and we tracked them. Once we confirmed the location of a FARP with 269 Marines, we would put socks, dip, and a few packs of smokes in their mail…something out of the movies, but it worked and was an easy way to show Marines we cared.

I listened to Monty's update, popped my first of several "go" pills of the day, and headed for the operations tent. I knew I was on the schedule today, and I already knew where we were going. The message from Task Force Tarawa was more subtle, but the intelligence team's brief said it more directly: We were "taking the gloves off." We could expect the remaining battalions to begin entering the city from several directions, and Cobras and Hueys would be on station 24/7 until operations were complete.

Location: An-Nasiriyah, Iraq
Date: 29MAR03
Time: 1650L

Whoosh. Tick. Tick. Tick.

The missile's launch motor made a distinct noise when separating from the hardened tube. That was followed by the sounds of the fins moving—hundreds of adjustments to Matt's every change in the missile's path.

I saw the missile first, coming off the right weapons pylon with a small plume of white smoke. It immediately began a rotation before it stabilized about two hundred meters in front of the aircraft. I was nose on to the target and scanning for anything near the second floor.

Matt was tracking the missile. I couldn't see what he saw, and I was not about to ask him any questions. This was his missile.

He wasn't quiet for long. "I have a good capture, and tracking the second floor, I'm aiming about two feet below the center window."

"Copy."

The explosion was anticipated, but the destruction wasn't. The TOW ripped open the entire second floor, leaving a gaping hole. The debris accelerated outward in all directions as a steady smoke cloud began to form over the top of the building. Any Iraqi sniper team in that building was, at a minimum, no longer combat effective.

Buss was about thirty seconds behind us. "Kool-Aid, Deadly 46 is wings level."

I could see Buss off to the left. It was time for Rosie to put another missile into the second floor.

"Deadly 46, hit leads hit, cleared hot!" There was a sense of relief in the FAC's voice.

Once our missile hit the target, I was too close to shoot rockets. Matt took that as a cue to open with the gun. The gun is bore sighted to ensure the reticle in the targeting camera is where the rounds impact. This is an imperfect process, so Matt would sometimes have to walk his rounds onto the target. "Walking the rounds" was a technique that required Matt to pull the trigger and, regardless of where the sight pointed, physically push or pull the joystick until the rounds hit the target.

Matt continued to fire until the gun hit its lateral and mechanical limit. At that point, I called us off the target. "Four-five's off safe, rolling out one hundred."

Our cannon automatically stopped firing as it hit its mechanical limit to the left. There was a moment of silence, then the sound of another explosion. I turned to look over my left shoulder in time to see the second floor encased in smoke. Rosie had nailed it—looked like he'd aimed below the remaining window ledge. The force of the explosion could be heard above the chatter of the FAC. I was still at a 60-degree angle of bank turn to the east, staring through the HUD.

Kool-Aid chimed in, "Those were good hits, 45 and 46. You are cleared for an immediate reattack."

"Kool-Aid, confirm you want to hit the same building?" I was waiting for a response, but I suspected he was getting an update from the spotter or was up looking at the damage himself. In either case, there was no way anyone on that floor was alive.

We gave Buss a quick reminder. "Four-six, we are extending to the east and then coming right for another run at the same target. I am going to set us up for a longer shot and be off target prior to crossing the water."

Buss was catching up to us. He had cut inside our turn and come back into position on the right side. "Four-five, Rosie thinks he saw several MAMs with weapons one building to the left."

Before we could continue the discussion, Kool-Aid was back with an update. "Four-five and flight, it looks like the remaining shooters have moved between buildings, and we are taking fire from the third building from the corner. Do you copy?"

"Four-five copies. We will be running in from the southeast this time and will call wings level." The "wings level" call or "In" call was required for our attack and all attack aircraft. It let the FAC know we were pointed at the target, clear of friendlies, and ready to deliver ordnance.

I had enough time to squint through the HUD and confirm I was in a level right-hand turn at about three hundred feet and closing in on 130 knots. I was pulling more power than I needed. Although I didn't feel anything strange on the run-in, I could feel my heartbeat accelerating. I had the brief realization that we were going back to the same target from the same general direction. Wasn't sure how smart this was.

It was time to share the plan with Buss. "Four-six, we are going to run in from the southeast about 340. Once we see the target, we are calling wings level."

Click. Click.

Matt had his dog whistle ears on and realized I had repeated myself. "Sir, they got it. Keep coming hard right. Roll out 330."

What the hell was Matt saying? I felt a ping of frustration. I wanted to say, "No shit, Matt, but it's my fucking job to make sure he's got no doubt about what we are doing." However, I swallowed that thought.

"Okay," was all I could muster. I was amped up, needing to calm down and focus, and Matt was just doing his job. I continued to turn right. Bam, there it was—330. We had a nice, long final attack run-in.

"Kool-Aid, 45's in from the south. Four-six, right pull again." I waited for anyone's response.

Click. Click.

I started to get that pinch in my stomach. There was no damn way the Iraqis were going to let us pound them again with the same tactic. They were going to make us pay. I could almost feel my head shaking left to right, an involuntary "no," but my hands and legs were pushing us inbound, 330 degrees, 140 knots at two hundred feet. The buildings felt close enough to touch.

I called Kool-Aid. "Four-five's wings level. Matt, master arm's going to arm."

Kool-Aid wanted this target now. "Four-five's cleared hot."

I could tell that Matt had the building in sight. He pulled the trigger on the laser. It showed 2,300 meters and closing. He didn't need to tell me when he was pulling the trigger; my job was a stable platform.

Whoosh.

The familiar sound let me know the missile had fired. I saw the brief trail of white smoke and then the corkscrewing missile. A TOW missile on the wire, headed for the second story of someone's former business, apartment, or café on the Euphrates River. Almost surreal.

The time of flight (TOF) showed in the HUD. I tracked the missile launch. It quickly fell out of sight and was on a stabilized path to the target. Except for the routine noise of the engines and rotors, the cockpit was silent as Matt tracked the missile.

There was a flash and then an explosion of plaster, cement, and metal. The damage was harder to see this time due to the added distance, but as I pressed in for rockets, it came into focus. Matt's missile had created a hole that was cleaner than the first but that had still caused irreversible damage. I had the rocket symbol in the HUD, and I'd selected my left pod of 2.75-inch HE rockets and pressed the trigger. A nearly simultaneous release.

If you have ever been to a NASCAR race, you know the sound that's generated when the cars are tight on the straightaway, going by you at two hundred miles per hour. It's a staccato rush of wind, barely distinguishing each car traveling in a tight pack. A similar sound is created by fast-moving rockets in close proximity to each other. I had just sent seven of those rockets directly into the second floor. Matt followed with 20mm.

Buss was next. "Four-six is wings level from the south."

Kool-Aid was ready. "Four-six, hit leads hits."

That sounded simple enough, but the target was now slightly obscured by the aftermath of one TOW, seven rockets, and about fifty rounds of 20mm. We slowed down on the turn, enough to see Rosie put another TOW into building number three. I was off the target with a hard turn to the east, and Buss was in hot pursuit. I couldn't tell, but it looked like Buss and Rosie had covered their pull-off with some rockets and 20mm of their own.

Kool-Aid was back. "Nice work, 45 and 46. We've got reports of a mortar team one block north of the intersection. Call contact."

I was 180 degrees out and headed south. "Four-five's pushing south. Stand by one."

I wanted Kool-Aid to realize that we were almost two miles from that intersection and would need to come in from the east to get eyes on the target. I eased the stick back and got some distance between me and the desert, always the desert.

"Four-five flight, check." This was my call for both aircraft to "check" themselves. It was my open-ended and informal request for an update from Buss and Rosie—a status check. It was also a chance for Buss to assess fuel, ordnance, and time on station as well as do a self-assessment. Plus, it was an opportunity for Buss or Rosie to verbalize anything that was on their minds and get a vote before we accepted the next 9-line.

To my knowledge, there were no Marine ground units in direct contact with the Iraqis at the time. We seemed to be the only show in town. It was good for Kool-Aid but also made us Iraqi public enemy number one. Kool-Aid was doing his job very well. He used us to pick and eat his low-hanging fruit, giving us as much opportunity as possible to engage targets before the Marines of Task Force Tarawa and the 1st MARDIV were sent back into Nasiriyah.

Those military or paramilitary forces had clearly become impatient or ordered to take some type of action. We were 2-0 and I wanted us to go 3-0, but our presence here was obvious. I remembered the RPG or SA-7 shot from the other day, I did not want a repeat performance, and we were becoming predictable. I needed to change our tactics.

Buss and Rosie had time to assess. "Four-six has got about thirty minutes of playtime and plenty of ordnance."

We had the same amount of fuel and ordnance, so I keyed the mic. "Copy."

Kool-Aid was back on the frequency. "Deadly 45 and flight, I'm pushing you to Hawk on TAD-5."

I called out, "45 copies. Flight switch to magenta."

Click. Click.

We began another check-in with a new FAC. "Hawk, 45 and 46 with you. We got thirty minutes on station for your work."

There was a slight pause followed by a confident and clear response. "Four-five, we are taking sporadic mortar fire to the east. I have a 9-line. Advise when ready to copy."

This was moving fast. I didn't like the idea of going deeper into the city to find the suspected mortar position, but *here we go*. "Hawk, 45's ready to copy."

I was still flying to the southeast when Hawk began passing the 9-line brief to Matt. The target was deeper into the city, flying parallel to the river, and one block north of the last targets. There was no easy way to get where we needed to go. No way we were going to fly from south to north again.

We were limited in our approaches to the reported mortar position. The first option was a low-level approach from the east along Habobi Street, an east-west road that led into the intersection of Highway 7, which ran north-south through the city. The target was another three hundred meters to the west and described as two sandbagged mortar tubes with six to eight armed MAMs.

We had several options, but any plan with us flying inbound from the west or north had us firing toward friendly positions and put us over the city for nearly two minutes.

Firing toward friendly positions sounds more daring than it is, especially during the day. It would require us to deliver rockets and cannon fire from a shallow dive angle. Whenever we planned to shoot rockets, we reviewed several tactics and training manuals. As the dive angle of the Cobras increased, the surface danger zone decreased. The smaller the danger zone, the less distance the parts and pieces of a rocket warhead or 20mm HE can travel. This reduced the chances of us sending shrapnel or any effects into friendly forces.

With friendly forces more than two thousand meters to the east and to the north, we were confident about not impacting friendly positions. What we were not confident about was flying over the city at two hundred feet, executing a pop maneuver or immediate climb to about five hundred feet, and then pushing the nose over into a 10- or 15-degree dive.

If we came in from the east, we limited our exposure to three or four blocks and avoided flying directly over the entire city. It didn't take a tactical genius to realize low-level daytime helicopter operations exposed us to nearly every weapon the Iraqis had. We needed to minimize our exposure time while ensuring we could do this in one pass.

I had an idea, but I was going to wait to hear what Matt had plotted and what the plan from Hawk looked like. It didn't take long to see we were expected to run in from the southeast and would need to nearly overfly the target before we could see based on the elevation of the buildings and our preferred low altitude tactics.

The sun was beating down mercilessly, even with the air conditioning turned to maximum. The canopy gave us great visibility but also acted as a greenhouse. It had been more than an hour on station with both FACs, and we had about eight hundred pounds of gas remaining. I had emptied my CamelBak, the sole water source in the cockpit, so I needed a break soon. With the fuel on board, it would be enough to take one or two shots at the mortar position.

Matt had been looking at the map and the 9-line, and it seemed he had a plan. "Okay, we can come at about a 300-degree heading and track on about a 45-degree angle from the river. The target is three hundred meters from the river in the road intersection."

I thought about that. "Okay, this is going to be guns from you. I am not sure I can get a dive angle, and we are too close for TOW."

Time for Buss and Rosie to get the plan. "Four-six, go trail. Expect a left pull and guns only."

Click. Click.

The trail position meant to simply follow behind me, not on either the left or right. I thought that would allow us to make quick corrections once we saw the target. It was a crapshoot; it was not doctrine, but it was the only idea I had based on the environment.

Hawk was back with us. "Four-five, you are cleared for an immediate attack. Report wings level." There would be no mark and no suppression.

"Four-five's inbound."

I waited after the call and then heard Hawk respond, "Continue," which meant he saw us and was waiting for our wings level call to clear us hot into the target. I pulled 100 percent power, pushed the nose down from five hundred feet to two hundred feet, and rolled out 300 degrees. I saw the Marines from 2/8 to our left. We still had M1A1 tanks off the nose and then the Euphrates River. On the other side of the intersection was our target, still about 1,500 meters out. It was like waiting for the dentist to drill. I just wanted it to start so it could stop.

The buildings began to zip by us, 140 knots, two hundred feet.

Matt said, "Put the master arm to arm."

I paused. "Hawk, 45's wings level."

Nothing.

Every second he didn't respond felt like ten. We were now only five hundred meters east of the two still smoldering buildings we'd previously hit and running out of runway—or at least running out of time to put these rounds on target.

"Four-five's wings level." This time, I spoke with a little more volume, a little more projection, a little more clarity, a little more attitude of, "Hey, fucko, we are hanging it all out up here. I need you to be quicker."

Hawk keyed the radio. "Four-five and 46, you are cleared hot."

What was up with the late clearance? I could feel my blood starting to boil and knew I was working myself up for no good reason. Hawk was fine. I was the impatient one, and it was beginning to affect me. I could feel my pulse beating in my hands, in my arms, and in my feet. My head was developing an ache, and I started to feel trapped, claustrophobic.

I took a deep breath, held, and then exhaled. With a mighty effort, I snapped back into reality and checked the heading. We were now two blocks over the city, cutting across streets on a diagonal path. We purposefully avoided going down the long axis of any roads to reduce weapons tracking time of Iraqis forces. Hawk had just cleared us both hot. It certainly made it easier to clear the flight versus one aircraft at a time. More on that later.

"Matt, are you seeing anything?"

The tracking angle, or the amount of time from block to block, was just too fast. Matt was trying to compare what he was seeing in the targeting camera to the map, but there was no time.

When we passed the fourth block, the buildings gave way to a large two-lane road. It was Highway 7. As we cleared the last building, we had a perfect view of the intersection.

There they were. Two clearly fortified mortar pits and a dozen or so Iraqi soldier and armed paramilitary forces looking right at us. I could see their faces, and they appeared surprised. We passed them as fast as we saw them.

We needed to warn Buss. "Four-six, in the middle of the intersection, just off our left wing—that's your target!"

I was in a hard left turn. I could see the Iraqi teams staring at me, and they likely didn't have time to think about Buss and Rosie. As we continued a left turn to the south, I was struck by an idea.

"Four-six is off, no shoot." I could hear Buss's frustration. I had dragged them into the city center again only to be a forty-eight-foot flying target.

Time to put my idea to work. "Hawk, 45 and 46 request an immediate reattack from the east."

Pause. Pause.

Hawk wanted a little more from us. "Deadly, confirm you have the target in sight?"

We did. "That's affirmative, Hawk. We have the target in sight but need a better run-in."

Hawk didn't waste any time. "Deadly 45 and flight, you are cleared for an immediate reattack. You'll be in from the east."

The plan would bring us in from the east, but I needed to share it quickly with 46 and then execute it. What we saw were a dozen or so armed MAMs. They were arrayed at the intersection we had just flown over. If we could come in from the east on the street that flowed directly into their positions, we would have more time to acquire and engage them.

I was about to sell a plan with a profile that I had rejected as too dangerous only minutes earlier. I was already making excuses for my impatience.

"Four-six, we are going to reset to the east and then fly directly down what looks like Habobi Street. It's a two-thousand-meter run. Let's do this in trail. The mortar position will be the second main intersection. How copy?"

Click. Click.

Matt was next. "Matt, you got anything? Once you can get eyes on the target, open with the gun. I will put a pod of rockets into the mortars, and you got the gun on pull-off."

It was a question, a statement, and a course of action. I got the sense we were all holding our breaths and were all a little unsure about the plan, but this would be the last pass on this target.

Matt was already looking through the camera as I came east of Nasiriyah and tried to line up on the street. I thought we were on the right one, but it was hard to tell. I was doing this starting at five hundred feet with a planned acceleration down to three hundred feet.

I passed over the caked mud flats that were on the east and south of the city. Then, we passed over the main road that circled the city and lined up on what we hoped was the right street.

I keyed the radio again. "Hawk, 45 and 46 wings level."

Hawk was prepared, and I'm sure he heard the inflection in my voice this time. "Deadly 45 and 46, you are cleared hot."

I was ready. "Matt, master arm is going to arm. Let me know when you see any…"

Chug. Chug. Chug. Chug.

The three barrels began spitting out 20mm rounds. Though I couldn't see the target, I knew Matt could because the rounds kept coming out. He had the trigger down for a solid eight or nine seconds; that was nearly one hundred rounds of 20mm.

The buildings were getting bigger on each side of us, a clear sign I was still descending. I pulled gently back on the stick and leveled out the descent as the intersection opened about four hundred meters ahead. The pandemonium in the intersection reminded me of the misfortunes of the Iraqi defenders on Safwan, everyone scrambling in all directions. I could see Matt's 20mm rounds had devastated the two positions.

I had a single pod of 2.75 inch HE rockets selected. I put the rocket reticle in the HUD on the first position and smashed the trigger.

Whoosh.

Seven rockets on their way, each carrying two pounds of high explosives. They impacted almost as soon as they left the rocket pod. I was too close to miss. They struck the closest mortar position, destroying anything remaining while sending shrapnel and debris into the other position just meters to the west.

I could picture Buss and Rosie just ten seconds in trail. "Four-six, leads off. Hit the westernmost position."

I knew Buss and Rosie were concentrating. Buss was maybe a hundred feet above the buildings that flanked his left and right. It must have felt like they were flying down into the street.

I rolled hard to the left as Matt got off the last few rounds of 20mm. I craned my neck to the left to see where Buss was. He was just flying through the intersection. In my head, I was repeating to myself, *Come on, come on, come on, get off target…* Silence. Nothing for one, two, three.

Finally, Buss announced, "46 is off to the south. Good effects on target."

I breathed a slight sigh of relief, but I didn't like the position I had put them in. I'd pressed us too hard, too close. I rolled out south and started an easy left turn to allow Buss and Rosie to join up.

We were done. It was time to go for fuel. "Hawk, 45 and 46 are checking off station. BDA to follow."

Matt and I did a quick assessment. "Four-six, I'm passing two mortar positions destroyed and two sniper positions. Do you have anything else?"

Buss and Rosie were likely comparing notes. "No, that's what we got, but I think we took some rounds on that pass."

Four-six certainly had, and we knew it would not be the last time.

I quickly reminded them it was over for now. "We are turning direct to Camden Yards."

Click. Click.

CHAPTER 24

Location: Camden Yards, South of An-Nasiriyah
Date: 29MAR03
Time: 1735L

Camden Yards was yet another FARP, but fortunately, it was located just a few miles south of Nasiriyah. It consisted of fuel trucks, an ammunition truck, several other support vehicles, and about fifteen Marines. They had established fuel hoses and had marked landing spots. We made an uneventful landing on the dirt road, which was only several hundred meters from Highway 8. This was not a "gas and go." We were going to shut down and talk for a bit. We also needed to reload the TOW as well as the 20mm and 2.75-inch rockets.

Matt and I didn't have much to say on the way to Camden. It was the normal checkout with Sky Chief. Buss and Rosie made those calls and passed the BDA. Meanwhile, Matt and I ran through our prelanding checklists and made calls to the FARP team indicating we were inbound. As this was going on, I experienced that sinking feeling again—the feeling I had somehow let Buss, Rosie, and Matt down. My frustration and anger were hiding a growing sense of disappointment in my own decision-making.

I preached team effort, I said everyone got a vote, but then I'd thrown caution to the wind and made what could only be described as an emotional decision. I'd really wanted to destroy that position. The Marines in Nasiriyah had needed us to hit that mortar position, right? We had seen the manned positions, and there was no way we could have left them intact, but had there been a better way? Had there been other assets? Better geometry? Should we have climbed really high and lobbed Hellfires from five thousand meters? Would we have seen it from that far out? Would we have been an obvious SAM or RPG target at one thousand or 1,500 feet? No answers—only more questions.

That perceived need to always accept the 9-line or find a way to get positioned to shoot had polluted my risk versus reward meter and clouded my judgment. How else could I validate a two-hundred-foot gun and rocket attack essentially down a side street, straight into and over an enemy position? Maybe I'd been taunting the Ghost. Maybe I'd thought we were beyond her reach. Maybe I'd believed her newly adopted allies were no match for us, and I needed to prove it.

Matt and I completed the shutdown and popped open the canopies as the blades slowed to a halt. The sand we had stirred still hung in the air. What hit me first was the heat; it was at least a 30-degree change in the temperature. A dry and throat-stinging blast of desert air. I needed water, and I needed to get out of the cockpit for a while.

Buss and Rosie were shutting down and climbing out as well. The refuelers and ordnance teams were meandering up to us, doing a mental count of what we needed. I looked to see Buss and Rosie take a walk around their Cobra. It was normal to do post-flight inspections, but this was different. I knew what they were doing. They were looking for evidence like cops at a crime scene, and I was the accessory to the crime. I could see Buss pointing at several places. He and Rosie turned to me as I moved toward them. Both wore inquisitive expressions.

I was ready for an honest discussion, but their questioning look shifted to become an almost Robert De Niro smirk and shoulder shrug. It said without saying, "Whatta ya gonna do, huh? It is what it is."

I took the brief opening as an opportunity. "Hey, guys, that's on me. We are not going to do that again."

Rosie nodded, and Buss added, "Copy that. We took a few rounds on that last run."

I followed them around their Cobra and spotted several more scars. The wingman or last aircraft over the target area always seemed to be the most vulnerable. Vulnerable because the enemy was now aware of an attack and could focus on the last aircraft, especially when pulling off the target.

There was another hour or so until sunset. We had a hard scheduled or planned escort of several CH-53Es to do a resupply just before midnight, so we still had a long day ahead of us. The refuel, reload, and return to the outskirts of Nasiriyah happened too quickly. We had all taken some time to relax with a bottle of water and enjoy the select contents of an MRE. If nothing else, we were hydrating and getting plenty of natural vitamin D.

Buss had been coordinating with the CH-53E squadron, and I was passing him the tactical lead of the section starting immediately. After an uneventful departure from Camden, we were back to working with a new FAC to the south of the Euphrates. I was enjoying the relative peace of flying as a wingman. I, like Howdy, had a wingman who was a fully qualified flight lead. It gave us tremendous flexibility, redundancy, and capability.

Sky Chief had work for us. "Deadly 45 and flight, contact Vino on plum." That was the last call from Sky Chief for a while. I was now 46, and Buss took the 45 callsign.

"Vino, Deadly 45 checking in. One plus three zero, ready for your work."

We were in a "combat spread" formation, which gave me the freedom to roam each side of Buss in about a 210-degree bubble. It kept me close enough to watch his "six" and far enough away to look for anything else in the area.

"Deadly 45, stand by for 9-line." That was quick. They must have had this teed up for us.

Matt took down the 9-line. It was very similar to the last one: a reported mortar position but another four hundred meters east and in a main intersection. If we were plotting it correctly, it was the first intersection we'd flown over a few hours before. I got the feeling that we were being dared to come back over the city.

But before we could plan to do that, Vino came back. "Deadly flight, we got sniper fire coming from two buildings facing south on the river."

Buss turned us back to the south and to the east over dried mud flats.

"Deadly flight, from the southern bridge, look north until you see a gold domed building. Call contact."

Buss had the radios. "Deadly 45, contact."

Vino continued his talk-on. "From that building, go one block northwest and call the westernmost corner building."

"Deadly 45, contact."

"Deadly 45 and flight, that is your target. Call in from the south."

"Four-five copies." Buss turned hard to the right and was setting us up for a long run into the target area. "Four-six, we are going to put TOWs into that building. We are going bottom floor; you hit the top floor with a left pull."

Click. Click.

We were out of the turn and could see the entirety of the city in front of us. It was amazing to have a few extra seconds to absorb even snippets of what we were doing. This was a major metropolitan city. I assumed it was inhabited by mothers and fathers trying to live their best lives but surrounded by a combination of zealots and understandably confused conscripted and professional soldiers. What a dilemma.

We were accelerating. To my right was the now infamous southern bridge. Directly ahead were restaurants, shops, apartments, and who knew what else.

Buss called the flight. "Vino, 45 and flight wings level."

Vino, also known as Major Marc Weintraub, was a native New Yorker and a semi-distinguished alumnus of Hobart College, class of '91. Vino, prior to the start of the war, had been "drafted." He'd already served a FAC tour with 3rd Battalion 1st Marines several years earlier, and the Marine Corps needed as many FACs as possible in the fight. His former squadron from Marine Corps Air Station Yuma, Arizona, would not go to Iraq on this deployment, but Vino would.

Assigned to the 2nd Marine Regiment prior to the invasion, Vino found himself job seeking. As a major, he was too senior to be a company FAC and too junior in rank to be the regimental or brigade air officer. So, he had milled around Task Force Tarawa looking for work. Luckily, work had found him, and he'd been assigned to the remaining LAR company attached to Task Force Tarawa. An experienced AV-8B Harrier pilot, he knew CAS, he knew how to coordinate fires, and he knew the value of coordinated fires. From the macro perspective, he was overeducated and underemployed, but that's exactly where Deadly 45 needed him.

As I pulled wings level, I heard Vino. "Deadly 45 and flight, you are cleared hot."

I saw the flash of the launch motor as it fired. The TOW leapt off the right wing stub of 45 and headed toward the building at three hundred meters per second. The late afternoon sun was causing some glare, but I could still see Buss. Matt quickly followed with his own TOW missile aimed at the second story. We had more than two thousand meters of direct line of sight to the target. We were just crossing the southern bridge over the river when Rosie's missile impacted, and the TOW flown by Matt impacted seconds later. The building seemed to vibrate and then became engulfed in the explosion. Debris, smoke, dust, and whatever else was inside the structure succumbed to the thirteen pounds of HEs carried in the missile.

A new voice pierced the radio. "Vino, Blackjack 71 flight of two, angels fifteen." There was a slight pause and then, "Ah, thirty minutes time on station."

The sound of forced oxygen, heavy breathing, and a slightly muffled or muted radio transmission was a dead giveaway. We now had fixed-wing CAS on station. It was a welcome sound and our first chance to work with Marine Harriers.

The Harrier is a remarkably capable CAS platform, particularly with its LITENING targeting pods. I had previously deployed with Harriers to Somalia and to the former Yugoslavia. These are jets that take off from amphibious ships like a traditional jet but that must land vertically like a helicopter. Today, there were two Harriers, and both were the AV-8B II Plus, with a mix of five-hundred-pound bombs and their 25mm cannon.

The cannon was the GAU-12, another genius design from General Dynamics that pushed out the three hundred rounds of 25mm ammunition via a five-barrel Gatling-inspired cannon at a rate of 3,600 rounds per minute. It was a beast, the same type of cannon used on AC-130 Spectre gunships. With the 25mm round leaving the barrel at a velocity of one thousand meters per second, by the time anyone saw the muzzle flash, it was simply too late.

Their timing, along with the ordnance they carried today, was perfect. We were in a position to run them from the south onto the new mortar position.

Buss was way ahead of me. "Four-six, you have Harriers. I'll coordinate with Vino, and let's get after the mortar positions."

Click. Click.

Based on Vino's limited ability to see both the target and the Harriers, he pushed control of them to us. During our check-in with FACs, we would often provide a statement that we were FAC(A) capable. Our ability to control and observe all the Harriers' fires allowed Vino to track the mission and respond to other requests, making the most of the assets he had on station.

I was busy in the back seat, and Matt was busy pushing the 9-line brief to Blackjack. We all agreed on the TOT, and though we couldn't guarantee a mark, we could try. We planned to have a 2.75-inch rocket mark the target for the Harrier and then put additional rockets in close proximity to cover their pull-off. The initial point (IP) was the location to begin their final attack run. For the Harriers, the IP was well south of the city. The two Harriers said they planned for a low-altitude delivery, but no one in our flight was expecting what we got.

"Blackjack 71 is wings level. We have the target in sight."

I looked off my left shoulder for the lead, but there was no way I would see him. My job was to fly, and Matt's job was to find and then clear the lead "hot" onto the mortar team. It was Matt who had to see them coming in the dive from fifteen thousand feet. I was the FAC(A), and those would be my bombs, but I trusted Matt to ensure they found the right home. The five-hundred-pound bombs' new home would be at the intersection of two unknown streets in an otherwise unremarkable southern Iraqi provincial capital. Iraq's fourth largest city was about to get a much bigger taste of Marine aviation.

Matt was well up to the task. "Seven-one, continue. Negative mark." That told the Harrier pilots to keep flying the same course. Once Matt judged they were clear of friendlies, he would provide the clearance to drop. It also meant that we were unable to toss a single 2.75-inch rocket onto the target as a mark.

I do mean a toss. Firing a 2.75 inch unguided rocket from any distance over six or seven hundred meters was a Cobra pilot's worst nightmare. It was like the naked dreams you had as a kid where you had nowhere to hide, and everyone was watching you. That was the cold, hard truth of shooting a 2.75-inch unguided rocket with the MK 66 motor. For every good dream you had about shooting rockets, there were ninety-nine nightmares about being exposed. It simply was what it was.

If only we had the ability to make that one-in-a-hundred shot. If we could, we would have given immediate directions from the rocket's impact to the target, literally talking the pilot's eyes onto the target.

With the LITENING pod, the pilot had long entered Matt's 9-line into his targeting system. He had likely slewed the targeting pod to the grid and confirmed visually what we had told him.

One. Two. Three. Four. The silence was nails on a chalkboard.

Finally, Matt saw the Harrier. "Seven-one, you are cleared hot."

That was followed immediately by an audible *beep*. I knew the sound, and it meant a bomb was on the way. We were both over the river, no more than eight hundred meters from the target.

The explosion was immediate and terrifying, discharging debris two hundred feet into the air. The blast seemed to ripple through our cockpit.

Matt saw this. "Seven-one, good hits. Seven-two, hit lead hits."

Matt was heads down in the camera for all of this and trying to make the most out of 72's bomb run. Even more impressive than the accuracy of 71 was his pullout below one thousand feet with a stream of orange flares tracking his left turn to the west. There are things, both natural and unnatural, that make you stop everything and watch. It's unexplainable. A Harrier pushing five hundred miles an hour and then making what I guessed was a six G nearly vertical climb with flares filling the skies like daytime stars is one of those things. It was impressive.

For context, six Gs meant the pilot was feeling six times their body weight press them into their ejections seats. A two-hundred-pound pilot would feel twelve hundred pounds of weight on their chest.

Seven-one didn't say anything. He didn't have to—his profile and pull-off said it all. It was a personal message to every Marine in that city. I spoke aviator, so I understood he was saying, "Hey, boys, apologies for the delay, but we are here, and we ain't afraid of gettin' dirty."

I watched, mesmerized. It took the impact of 72's five-hundred-pound bomb to snap me out of my daze. Seven-two's work was as impressive as 71's. The entire intersection was a white and gray cloud of dust and debris and only God knew what else.

I hardly noticed Matt on the radio. "Seven-one and 72, cleared for an immediate reattack."

Well damn, that was a great idea. While I was busy following Buss in a turn back to the east, I could also see both jets. They were still in an aggressive climb and in a tight turn to the south.

The radio cracked with the muffled and strained breathing of a pilot clearly fighting the forces of gravity. "Seven-one's in from the south, guns."

Matt was quick with the clearance. "Seven-one, continue. Same target. Negative mark."

Buss was rolling us out facing north, and we were in a perfect position to see the Harriers. I was looking "three fingers" above the horizon but caught a glimpse off my left shoulder. Son of a bitch, they were low—really low. They were already in a shallow dive.

I called out, "Matt, you got 'em? They are left at eight o'clock just above the horizon." Matt had long seen them. "Seven-one, cleared hot."

It was that same NASCAR style drive-by, but they were going close to five hundred miles an hour with a flame coming out of the left side of the fuselage. They reinforced the point they had made on the first pass. "Seven-one's off."

I was still heading north. Matt was on the sensor looking at 71's hits. "Seven-two, west fifty, cleared hot."

The second Harrier was in the same profile. I couldn't see him, but I could picture the scene. I could visualize him in the dive, hand gripping the stick, 25mm cannon selected, peering through his own HUD reticle, looking for 71's hits, likely listening to his radar altimeter telling him to "pull up, pull up."

"Seven-two's in hot." Then, 72 was there. I mean, *right* there. Holy shit, he was low! The flame coming for the GAU-12 was visible but gone in a flash, as was the jet. I guessed he'd bottomed out around five hundred feet but had gone immediately into a nearly vertical climb with a hard pull to the west. I was so impressed again with the profile that I wasn't looking at the target.

"Seven-two, good hits. BDA to follow."

The Harrier section lead, in his climb to an altitude sanctuary, checked off station. "Blackjack 71's RTB. Thanks for the work."

Matt passed the two positions destroyed to the Harriers and did the same to Sky Chief. We also checked off station and headed toward Riverfront. I was starting to feel the effects of the day, not as overwhelming as sandstorms and extended night operations but just an unsettled feeling. It was more like a mental tick, like I had missed something. The adrenaline fog had long lifted, and I suspected the same was true for the entire section. Buss was in the lead, and I had closed into a tighter formation. As we flew, not much was said.

I was already anticipating my next few hours. We needed to have the plane captains do a good walk around and start getting ready for the anticipated four or five hours of NVG ops. It had been a long day already. I was not exactly sure of the escort plan for the CH-53Es. Buss had been working on that, but I also needed to take an active role in the final planning.

"Hey, Monty. How are we doing?"

Monty was sitting on a camp stool, or small foldout chair, writing on a small field desk. He was wearing desert camouflage pants, boots, a green T-shirt, a desert "boonie hat," and his classic tinted glasses.

"Sir, we are looking good. Got a couple with battle damage, including Buss's aircraft. Nothing critical. So far, the rounds look to be hitting at angles and skipping off. The few that have penetrated have done nothing serious yet."

I grabbed another thirty-two-ounce water bottle off the stack. Nothing like some hot water, but I needed it. I could see the condition and functioning of the flight line was improving. We also had ground support equipment arriving. This included tractors, forklifts, power carts, and a couple of Humvees.

We also had spaces designated for all the maintenance functions. This included a place for our flight line, ordnance, airframes, avionics, quality assurance, and other teams critical to the success of the squadron.

I could see Warrant Officer Luke Crouson, Top (aka Jim Quirk), and our "Iron" gunnery sergeants, Gauthier and Cafarella, walking the flight line, talking to Marines, and generally leading by being seen. Suffering and smiling through the same heat and sun and dust as the private. These were good signs.

CHAPTER 25

Location: Riverfront – Jalibah, Iraq
Date: 30MAR03
Time: 1100L

We walked from the operations and intelligence tents, getting a few briefs and updates. It was dry and hot, and the sand always seemed to blow at a constant ten knots. The foot traffic had begun to pick up. There were now four MAG 29 squadrons at Riverfront, but they were almost transparent to us. Our concern was today's missions.

We grabbed a corner spot in the 269 ready room and went over the general plan for the day. The ready room was coming along nicely. It had a small desk and chair for the duty officer, along with maps of Iraq taped onto plywood and then hung with parachute cord. With cases of water and MREs everywhere, it looked like we were digging in for a long stay.

On those maps were enemy and friendly dispositions and their general routes of march. The direction of travel for the MEF, even with minor detours east and west, was north. The jewel in the crown had to be Baghdad with Saddam Hussein's hometown of Tikrit a symbolic second. The famous Prussian military strategist Carl von Clausewitz talked of a center of gravity or perhaps centers of gravity. They represented the power hub or hubs of nations. The seizure of capitals was historically deemed critical and symbolic of an enemy's defeat. Seize the capital, and you break the will of the people and the armies. Once the army and population quit, the government and political leaders should soon follow—at least, that's the plan.

Baghdad, though only two hundred miles from Nasiriyah, seemed like an impossible destination from our corner briefing table in the 269 ready room. We were not going that far today but far enough.

As we briefed, other 269 crews and sections flowed in and out. With only a quick wave, joke, or light chat, they came and went. Gone were the formal, focused, and almost sterile mission briefs expected of the WTIs and flight leads. Now, it was SOPs, a quick review of lessons learned, and a shared understanding that we can't repeat mistakes. There was no room for inflexibility; we were learning how to operate in an environment dominated by ambiguity. It was controlled chaos.

It had been a few days since I had seen my XO, and today, the XO was making the rounds. Spike would be heading out about the same time as me but was being tasked further north as units of the 1st MARDIV were pushing toward Al-Kut and Al-Hay. Places we would all get to know very well in the not-so-distant future but not today.

Spike, the quintessential Texan and Baylor University graduate, had spent his first few years in the Marine Corps as a combat engineer before heading to Pensacola for flight training. He was also a WTI and had cherry picked his front seat, 1st Lieutenant Jeremy Hester. Hester had enlisted in the Marine Corps directly from high school and had been selected for officer training. He'd been sent to college to earn a degree and then his commission. Hester and Spike made a great team and were complemented by their wingman, Major Chris "Cut" Patton and his front-seater, Captain Alan "Chief" Merrell.

Spike's section, along with a few other unfortunate aircrews and maintainers, had been stranded at Riverfront during the two-day sandstorm. Spike, like most others, was showing the strain of the first ten days. He looked tired, like he'd dropped a pound a day, but appeared even more focused. He was quietly developing a reputation as a fearless and innovative flight lead. This was not the norm; it was as if he had stepped into the fountain of youth. The forty-one-year-old lieutenant colonel was acting more like a twenty-six-year-old captain, and his team had already racked up a significant number of tank, armor, and artillery kills.

Location: FOB Riverfront, Iraq
Date: 30MAR03
Time: 1225L

We were taking off in less than an hour. It was already a blistering 110 degrees. Even though it had been almost 0230L by the time we'd finally de-armed and shut down earlier this morning, I felt like I had just closed the throttles. It didn't matter. We were walking back to preflight. *Was that only yesterday…or early this morning?* That didn't matter either, but I knew I was beginning to feel the impact of the heat, the lack of sleep, and likely dehydration.

Today was expected to be another yesterday, another ten plus hours in the cockpit. We were living on MREs, bottled water, and a few liberated items from *Saipan*. Everything needed to be flown or trucked into Riverfront. There were no showers, and there was little electricity. On the other hand, the toilet facilities were an engineering marvel. Toilet design began with a backhoe digging a large hole in the ground. That was followed by a line of hastily constructed benches parked precariously over the hole. Put into square shape, they would accommodate sixteen. Finally, holes were cut into the plywood. Bam! There was your toilet—just you, your thoughts, and fifteen of your closest friends with another twenty-five or so staring at you, waiting their turn.

Late last night, or more accurately, earlier this morning, Buss and I had run through the debrief with the intelligence shop after we'd done a section debrief. I don't believe any of us understood the impact of yesterday's events, but with a scheduled 1330L launch, it meant we would be briefing in under eight hours.

The feeling I had leaving Nasiriyah yesterday was back. It was a sickness akin to a migraine—a pain that quietly but methodically consumed me but almost unrecognizably disappeared. Or maybe like a deep cut. You remember the shock, the pain, the bleeding, the scab, but strangely, you don't or can't exactly remember when it healed or when the pain stopped. In any event, the onset was real. The sense of dread had returned. Regardless of what I was feeling, we were walking to launch. I had done this before, and I sure as hell could do it again.

The brief for the section was SOP, and with a full ordnance loadout, we were quickly at five hundred feet and gaining speed with Riverfront in my rearview mirror. We headed north back to Nasiriyah. Our intelligence briefs showed Task Force Tarawa's plans to push further into the city and begin the end for the encircled 11th Mechanized Division, the Fedayeen Saddam, and anyone else with malicious intentions.

Today was going to be another prize fight with whatever and whomever remained in Nasiriyah, and Task Force Tarawa was going to be throwing the first punches. I was back to formally leading the section, though I had appreciated the support and leadership that Buss and Rosie had shown yesterday. We were expecting more fixed-wing CAS on station today, and Buss and Rosie were already preparing for the likely A-10 and AV-8 sorties.

It was a new day, and after the lessons learned yesterday, we were better today. Buss checked us in with Sky Chief, and we made the familiar push from Riverfront back to the south of the city. It was already well over 100 degrees. This was our first real daytime only mission, and we were expecting it to be busy.

I called Vino. "Deadly 15 and 16, one plus three zero for your work."

We could immediately sense a change. There was a buzz, movement of Marine ground units east, south, and north of the city. Task Force Tarawa was tightening the noose. As we checked in with Vino, we could also hear fixed-wing and other aircraft checking in.

Vino was ready for us. "Deadly 15, stand by for 9-line."

Today, Buss and Rosie would be handling the FAC(A) responsibilities. We—more accurately, Matt—would be coordinating any other supporting arms, such as 81mm mortars for a fixed-wing mark or for suppression prior to fixed-wing CAS aircraft attacking.

The 9-line from Vino was inputted into both Cobras' navigation systems and plotted on our paper map. We were all familiar with the city, and finding the new targets was easy. The grid for the target in the 9-line was four blocks to the west along the Euphrates. It seemed as though the Iraqis had reestablished both mortar and sniper positions in and around the buildings facing south to the river.

In Vino's remarks, there was a laundry list of suspected targets along the same riverfront-facing buildings. This included an ammunition storage site on the ground floor of the corner building. We had been limiting ourselves to TOW missiles, but it was time to use Hellfire. It was a clear and hot spring day, and we had a direct line of sight to the first target from more than three thousand meters away.

The laser-guided Hellfire was capable of hitting targets well past the effective observation range of our FLIR or camera. It also came in several flavors of warheads designed to be either overtly or subtly destructive. For example, some warheads were intended for armored targets, while others limited the effects to the desired building or floor. Today, we only had one option—the overtly destructive kind—and we had four per Cobra.

It was time again. Even though we were still ten miles to the south with the city just coming into focus, I got that now familiar and persistent sick feeling. I added power and made the right turn to the southeast. The attack headings were going to be to the northwest. This would allow both Cobras to fire from a sanctuary created by the ground units positioned to the south. It also meant we needed to clear them before engaging positions across the river—or, at least, that was the plan.

I turned to see Buss and Rosie to our right in combat cruise. "One-six, we are going to make our first run from the east of the train station. We will take the most eastern building. Be prepared to hit that again or adjust."

Buss was back quickly. "Copy that. You going with TOW? And do you see the friendly positions to the north?"

I saw the Marines organized in clusters. A few light armored vehicles here, a few AAVs there, and individual Marines everywhere.

We were going to have to fire over the tops of their heads; there was no way around it. The sun was baking the buildings, and we could already see the heat radiating from the metal roofs. We were closing in on the city fast, and the TOT from Vino was less than two minutes away. As much as I wanted to use Hellfire, TOW missiles seemed to be the weapon of choice for this attack.

I immediately responded to Buss. "Yes, we are going to lead with TOW and then press no further than the southern bank of the river."

Click. Click.

Matt was already heads down, scanning the three miles or so into the target area. "Matt, how are we looking?"

"I can see the building. White two story. I'm ready."

I called it. "Vino, Deadly 15 and 16 wings level."

We were now about two miles out and closing in on a two-thousand-meter TOW shot. I was too far to see anything in front of me except the city. I was getting close. Suddenly, I felt something odd—something new. My right foot began to involuntarily twitch, almost like a nervous knee bouncing but different. What was this all about?

Vino was ready for us. "Deadly 15, you are cleared hot. It's that fourth building to the east from the corner. Take out the top floor, and 16, hit the building's first floor."

I had the call to Vino. "Vino, 15 and 16 copies, in hot."

I continued flying straight ahead, the nose pointed at the target as the master arm went to arm. I could see Marines looking up at us. I could see faces, fine details. Matt pulled the trigger, and a TOW leapt off the right wing stub in a white cloud of smoke. It started to make its characteristic rotation, but after less than one hundred meters, it careened straight down, impacting less than fifty feet from a Humvee.

I could only muster a, "What the hell was that?"

The model of TOW we'd fired needed about two hundred meters to arm the warhead. Fortunately for everyone, the missile had slammed harmlessly into the ground, but it could have been disastrous. The likely cause was that the wire that provided all the tracking data from Matt to the TOW had simply snapped, a situation where the missile had no guidance. It was rare, but it had just happened. Not a big confidence builder.

The Marines next to the Humvee didn't seem to flinch. I would have sworn the 2/8 XO, Major Dale Alford, was glancing up at me and muttering to the Marines next to him, "Damn pilots." They seemed to nod and then look back toward the target building, almost saying, "Hey, fellas, the target is over there." Point taken.

Before I could get a response from Matt, another TOW popped off the rail. This one began its normal rotation. I took a deep breath. So far, so good. After about four hundred meters, it stabilized. I had slowed to one hundred knots, and the missile tracked toward the number four building. It was going to be about a fifteen-second TOF until the TOW impacted the second floor. The TOF data popped into my HUD and was also repeated in Matt's targeting camera. Once the master arm went to arm, everything Matt saw in the camera was captured on the VHS system.

Matt was tracking the missile, and I was tracking our closure rate to the target. We were inside one thousand meters and within a couple of seconds of the missile impact. Vino was seeing more than he could tell us but not for long.

The radio crackled. It was Vino. "One-five, we've got eyes on several shooters on that second floor. One-six, can you put another missile in there?"

Before Buss could answer, the building's second floor erupted. Plaster, glass, and flames shot a hundred feet into the air. That was followed by another explosion, this one grander and accented with orange and white flames. The blast hurled debris towards the Euphrates River. I couldn't tell if that was a second missile, if it was Rosie's missile, or if Matt had hit an Iraqi ammunition or explosives store. I didn't care.

I pulled the Cobra hard to the right. As I rolled, I craned my neck to the left. I could see Buss and Rosie still putting 20mm into the building, slowly chewing it to pieces. I could see there was nothing left of the top floor, and Deadly 16's rounds were slowly collapsing the walls on the first floor. It was not instantaneous. The 20mm rounds were determined, like a heavyweight boxer who delivered repeated blows to his opponent. Eventually, the doomed fighter, like these walls, would crumble. It was surreal.

I made our call. "Deadly 15 is off, extending to the southeast."

I had long started a steady cold sweat. I felt ill and unnerved. It wasn't the missiles, the 20mm, or the explosions. It was something else. I didn't have much time to reflect or analyze. Maybe the Ghost was here, maybe she was directing the fight, maybe she was bringing us in closer. Maybe we had been here too long. We were tempting fate.

We had been in Nasiriyah for nearly three days and nights. I couldn't shake the feeling that we were being watched, not just by the Iraqis, which was obvious, but by her. My right boot had not stopped its involuntary tic. Something was definitely wrong with me.

"Vino, Judson 11, mission number 6373, checking in as fragged with about thirty minutes time on station." The distinct sound of forced oxygen and of a pilot breathing and talking through a mask was unmistakable. It was a section of A-10s from the 75th Fighter Squadron based at the Ahmad al-Jaber Air Base in Kuwait. We had expected them, but we also knew priorities could change, so we were not counting on them.

Buss had pulled off the target and was now following a hundred meters in trail. Matt was recoding the Hellfire missiles, along with preparing to listen to the 9-line that Buss would be passing to the A-10s. Buss was the FAC(A) for today, and this was our first chance to work with A-10s.

In the two minutes it took for us to pull off to the south, Vino had time to assess the damage from our first run and gameplan for the use of the A-10s. It didn't take him long. Vino was concerned with the estimated fifteen Iraqis who were moving into previously vacated positions in the corner building. So, he provided us with continuous updates. We were more than three miles from the target, but we all knew the building, and both Matt and Rosie had confirmed the location on their maps.

Vino was pushing the A-10s to us. "Deadly 15, I'm passing you Judson 11."

Buss was ready. "Vino, Deadly copies. Judson 11, this is Deadly 15. Stand by for a 9-line."

So it began.

Buss and Rosie were ready. The A-10s digested the 9-line and reaffirmed their run-in heading and the location of friendlies. The heading was given in degrees magnetic from the IP to the target, sometimes in a basket or range. In this case, the heading for the A-10s was 350 degrees, but we gave them 330-010 degrees, providing them some flexibility to maneuver. The A-10s were also getting a mark from Buss with a 2.75-inch HE rocket. Even with the smoking shell that was building number four as a great reference point, the corner building was going to get a mark.

The sound of forced breathing was our audible cue. "Judson 11 is IP inbound with 12 thirty seconds in trail."

Buss replied, "Continue."

I was expecting to see the A-10s at any moment. I had pushed us from the southeast, moving closer to 320 degrees. The heading would put the A-10s arriving over our left shoulder, giving Buss a few more seconds to clear the lead hot and make corrections for the wingman.

Buss had slowed down, and I was pushing forward to get the rocket onto the corner building. It would have been much easier to do this from a hover, but we were still carrying a heavy load of fuel and ordnance. Add that weight with a two-hundred-foot hover in high heat—not a good idea.

The plan called for Matt and me to sprint ahead and deliver the mark about thirty seconds prior to the A-10s' TOT. I would pull off to the right while Buss was still a thousand meters to our six o'clock position. That would allow him to make immediate corrections for Judson 11 and then adjust the wingman's rounds accordingly. Yup, it was going to be a gun run.

The A-10 Thunderbolts gun, the GAU-8 Avenger, was a thing of legend. It fired a much larger round than the Cobra or the Harrier. The larger 30mm rounds were delivered through a seven-barrel Gatling-style gun, which could fire up to four thousand rounds per minute with the 30mm shell measuring nearly a foot long. The explosive warhead weighed almost a pound and, like most cannons, traveled at a thousand meters per second. If there were a list of aircraft built around a single weapon, the A-10 built around the GAU-8 Avenger would be close to the top.

We heard the lead's strain from a high G pull-up. "Judson 11's in the pop."

Buss gave an immediate, "Continue."

We were late. I had misjudged the time we needed to get into position to deliver the mark. "Shit, Matt, you see the building yet? I'm going master arm to arm. Once you get the laser on it, let me know."

Matt was looking. Having your head buried into a rubber mount that forces one eye to view the world through the targeting camera or FLIR is disorienting. It also takes a few seconds to expand the field of view, find the buildings, and then identify the actual target. Once he had the target building locked via the auto-tracking function, he switched to higher magnification to confirm it was the correct target.

This is where the coordination and trust between Matt and me became critical. I trusted him to select and confirm the correct target. He pulled the laser, and that laser energy reflected an exact ten-digit grid of the target building. I didn't have the time or inclination to look at the grid and compare it to the target location we'd given in the 9-line. That was Matt's flight pay to earn. The laser hit the target. Depending on what gave him the best awareness, the map or the laser, he would clear this flight "hot," but I needed the laser to get this rocket close.

I pulled 100 percent torque, maybe a few more than that, but I wanted the mark on or close to the building within thirty seconds of the A-10s' TOT. The Cobra strained and protested under the weight, heat, and new demands I put on the engines and transmission. The river was in sight, and I could see the new target building. So did Matt.

"Laser on," he said.

I had one of the 2.75-inch rocket pods selected and could see the rocket reticle adjust to Matt's laser "spot." I needed to get a little higher so I could put the Cobra into a shallow dive before firing. The dive would build airspeed and provide a more stabilized rocket shot. Both the climb and the dive would take time and drive us closer to the river. I pulled back on the stick, paused, and then pushed the nose over. We could feel a brief lightness in the seat, not a good feeling to have flying a two-bladed helicopter. With the reticle on the target, I mashed the thumb trigger once.

Whoosh!

We knew immediately the mark was good enough. It impacted at the base of the target building. We had released the rocket less than eight hundred meters away with the help of the laser spot and the HUD software. I wrenched the Cobra to the right, and we both craned our heads in time to see the A-10s.

The sound of exhaled oxygen over the radio was followed by, "Judson 11's wings level."

Buss had seen the mark. He noted that the A-10s were pointed at the target and that we were out of the way. "Judson 11, hit the mark. You are cleared hot."

Matt and I were now headed south but had a perfect view of the lead A-10. He was in a shallow dive and descending through a thousand feet. This guy was in the "don't fire until you see the whites of their eyes" club. He was closing at more than three hundred knots. I saw the white smoke coming from under the chin of the aircraft. He was firing the 30mm GAU-8.

These rounds came in a very distinct sequence. First, the smoke. Then, a slight pause followed by the sound of a heavy zipper being pulled down quickly. Next, 30mm round impacts. Oh my god, the impacts were devastating. We could hear the sound of the gun in our cockpit; it had been less than a three-second trigger pull. Three seconds meant almost two hundred rounds of either armor-piercing or HE warheads impacting the target. I looked up in time to see the rounds had torn off what was left of the roof.

We were refocused by his wingman's call. "Judson 12's wings level."

Buss was ready for the correction. "Judson 12, you are cleared hot from leads hits. Shift down to the first floor."

As we rolled out, there he was. Judson 12 was close enough that I could see the pilot's helmet. We were headed due south and had a perfect view of Judson 12 in his dive, an even better perspective than we'd had with his flight lead. Judson 11 was sky-lined over 12; it would have made an amazing portrait. A scene with two A-10s, Judson 11 in a dive at less than a thousand feet and Judson 12 silhouetted just above him in a picturesque arching climb. The A-10 looked smooth and steady as it pitched skyward. He was resetting to the south for the obligatory "immediate reattack."

Judson heard Buss's correction. "One-two copies, in hot."

The cannon of Judson 12 repeated the sequence we had just seen and heard from his lead. First, the smoke cloud under the chin followed by the heavy zipping sound. Pause. Pause. Then, the chaos of two hundred 30mm rounds impacting the first floor. That was more than 150 pounds of high explosives impacting the building just milliseconds apart. The result was more devastating than ever.

"Judson 12's off, resetting to the south."

Buss was in a slow sixty-knot and fifty-foot pattern. It gave him the advantage of pivoting 365 degrees in any direction. He was positioned east of the train station and well inside the perimeter established by Task Force Tarawa. I was still headed south and started a turn to make the join-up.

Buss was not done with the A-10s. "Judson 11 and flight, stand by one. Hold south angels twelve for further tasking. BDA to follow."

It was now Rosie's turn. "Judson 11, one sniper position destroyed and one fighting position destroyed. We have a 9-line to follow."

Buss and Rosie were firing on all cylinders; we could hear it in their voices. There was a refreshingly vocal swagger, a confident cadence that accented a clear sense of purpose. Maybe not to the casual listener, but it was obvious to me. Matt heard every word too.

Buss and Rosie, with the self-assurance of a red shirt senior, pushed the A-10s to twelve thousand feet and had them ready to prosecute another target. Those were Buss and Rosie's A-10s now. Sometimes, it's hard to recognize the exact moment when a player goes from walk-on to scholarship starter. The transition is often subtle with once unknown players suddenly having breakout plays or unexpectedly fantastic performances. Other times, it's almost an unnoticeable maturation. Today was a combination of both. Buss and Rosie had always been starters, but today was their breakout all-American performance.

I had almost forgotten the obvious—the Iraqi 3rd Corps. On each pass, Judson had reported taking small arms fire, and we had seen multiple MAMs on the top floor. Fortunately, that floor and the entire building was now rubble.

Just then, the A-10s called us back. "Sorry, gents, Judson 11 and flight is bingo. We are RTB. Great work down there. So long."

Another FAC joined in on the TAD frequency. Mouth said that they had been taking mortar fire from three hundred meters to the north of the last target. He also observed that twenty to thirty enemy fighters were congregating another two hundred meters north at the Fedayeen Saddam headquarters. Without the A-10s, it was back to the Buss and Ferris show, and no one in this flight wanted to see a rerun.

I asked Matt, "Where is that position, and do you think we can either get a 2.75-inch mark on it or tap it with a Hellfire?"

Matt started to respond. I could tell because once you even breathe hard into a voice-activated microphone, it drowns out the other radios. He hesitated, then spoke. "That's north of where we made the gun run yesterday. It's just that much deeper over the city."

He'd cleverly avoided the question, but I received the message. Getting to that target would expose us and put us over the city. There was no way I'd repeat that mistake. Had I heard correctly? The Fedayeen Saddam headquarters? They had an actual building with a sign? If so, why hadn't we hit that immediately? I visualized a cartoon version of a Lions Club or Rotary Club meeting with all the men hunkered down, feverishly devising plans. It ended with someone throwing out an idea of grabbing RPGs and AK-47s to attack the American helicopters. I got an immediate flashback to Somalia, and that was anything but comical.

We pushed back to the south and began to plot both the Fedayeen Saddam headquarters and the Ba'ath Party building. The latter presented a new twist. It was a tempting title of a target and reported to be located in the same general area.

We had clearly become Vino's best asset. He needed us as his eyes and ears, but we also needed to avoid being drawn deeper into the city. We enjoyed the relative sanctuary and freedom of movement to the south. I had a tactical "no-go" line of the Euphrates River located to the south of the city and the Saddam Canal that bordered the city to the north. It meant that today, Deadly 15 and 16 would not fly north past the river or attack any further south than the canal if engaging from the north. Well, unless we had a really good reason.

Vino passed a new 9-line that definitely had a more challenging geometry. Both buildings sat in the southern half of the city but several blocks deeper than we had flown previously. Time also presented a problem. Judson had just checked off station to hit an aerial tanker, and we needed to do the same.

I made the early call. "Vino, Deadly 15 is checking off station. We will be back in about forty-five minutes."

"One-five, we copy. That should work for timing. Will have another section of A-10s checking in at the top of the hour." Vino sounded calm and confident, and we could tell he looked forward to us being back on station at 1500L.

The trip to Camden Yards had become almost routine. We would have time to shut down, refuel, and rearm. It would also give us time to grab some water and an MRE. Buss had already checked us out with Sky Chief, and I had made the call for us to land at Camden Yards.

The brief respite also gave the four of us a needed opportunity to talk about what we could expect from the impending afternoon missions. It had been a good start to the day. The coordination and timing for the A-10s hadn't been perfect but had certainly been effective. I'd been late for the 2.75-inch marks, but we'd still managed to get the mark on the target and on time. The 75th's A-10 crews had impressed us and made a statement. We looked forward to having another section on station.

CHAPTER 26

Location: Camden Yards FARP, South of Nasiriyah
Date: 30MAR03
Time: 1510L

We had coordinated and executed our attack runs well, and minus the errant TOW, the missile shots we'd taken had all arrived on target. The daytime operations were also an added benefit. The squadron had been challenged with several cases of the crud or whatever else they called it. Sections had lost pilots necessitating the swapping of wingmen to support the ever-growing flight schedule. Until today, we'd had only one scheduled day op. Before walking, I had checked the flight schedule for tomorrow. It showed us back on nights, and I was told to expect us to stay on nights indefinitely. I knew it was where we needed to be.

The conditions for night operations were expected to improve. The moon offered one positive aspect of going back to nights. It was finally scheduled to make its appearance over the next few days, a game changer for us. Even a little slice of the moon drastically enhanced the efficacy of our NVGs. It made everything less complicated. Takeoffs, landings, obstacle avoidance, formation flight, target identification, and engagement all became significantly less demanding. For example, if I could see an unlit building at one mile under no moon conditions, I could probably see it, and likely any vehicles parked around it, at two miles with the moon. It made attack helicopter operations much safer and more effective.

It was time to start back up and make the short flight back to Nasiriyah.

Buss and Rosie had just heard the flight of two A-10s check in with Vino. “Owl 33, this is Deadly 15. We have your 9-line. Advise when ready to copy.”

The familiar sound of a voice being projected into an oxygen mask came back. “Deadly, Owl 33’s ready to copy.”

The afternoon would clearly give us a different approach compared to earlier. We had a target deeper into the city, and the section carried MK-82s. These were five-hundred-pound bombs, and our weapons to target match said they gave us the best option on the two reported headquarters.

We’d find the building only another four hundred meters north into the city, and even though we had it in sight, no way would we try a two-thousand-meter rocket shot to mark the target. So, we decided to climb and maintain a five-hundred-foot and one-hundred-knot pattern. This was more southeastern than the morning missions had been. It gave us a sanctuary over Marine positions, and it also put a lot of open space between us and the southernmost corner of the city. The position made us more visible and predictable but gave us more standoff range and the altitude needed to see down into more parts of the city. We constantly had tradeoffs.

“Owl 33’s wings level.”

I couldn’t see them as they flew in a dive coming out of eight thousand feet, but apparently Buss could. “Owl 33, you are cleared hot.”

This attack showed that we could execute old school CAS when needed. This could have been an F4U Corsair in Korea or an F-4 Phantom in Vietnam. The basics were timeless. In this case, no visual mark and no laser mark was needed. The A-10s’ crews used their eyes and the eight-digit grid coordinate inputted into their targeting system. With the help of Buss’s continuous corrections, they had the right target.

I had just come back to the right and faced the city when the first of two MK-82s hit the Fedayeen Saddam building. Since it had been pummeled with almost two hundred pounds of composite explosives, the devastation was immediate. The second bomb impacted in the blink of an eye after the first. Now, the building was on fire and in ruins.

"Owl 34 wings level," came from the second A-10.

Three-three was off and headed north, then south, while 34 was visible off our left shoulder, about four fingers above the horizon.

"Owl 34, hit leads hit," came the call from Buss.

The power of the sun pushed straight through my canopy and into my skin. Relentless. I felt the fatigue sapping my energy and baking what was left of my brainpower. I strained to see the A-10. *Where is he, and why is he taking his sweet ass time from the IP?* It really didn't matter.

The explosions of bombs, missiles, rockets, and cannon fire seemed like the only things that would snap me back into focus. I could see the immediate plume form. I should have been impressed, but the second pair of MK-82 bombs almost seemed routine.

The A-10 pulled hard right and made another picture-perfect ascent to the east. I could see the fifty-seven-foot wingspan arch gracefully into a near vertical climb. Smart move. They knew if the Iraqis could muster AAA fire or an effective SAM against them, it would be now. They also made sure their pull-off would be pointed toward friendly lines. They had to know that Marines would sacrifice nearly anything to ensure a crippled A-10 or their crew was never alone. Never.

The next forty-five minutes passed by in a blink. We had been more effective than anticipated. The city seemed as calm as a punch-drunk bully. If the Iraqi defenders were talking tough, no words were heard. If they wanted another fight, they had better stand back up first. We'd had a good day, and it only got better.

We had thanked the Owl flight and passed along our own version of, "Good hustle out there. See you in the locker room!" The truth was simpler and more direct. The A-10s had acquitted themselves and set a new standard for CAS. The legacy of USAF A-10s in Nasiriyah remained open for debate. The reported friendly fire incidents on the 23rd of March were still being investigated, as was the mission on the 28th in Basra while supporting the United Kingdom. In the CAS world, there are only expectations.

I calculated my version of winning, or the illusion of winning, in inches. Inches leave little room for error or debate. If any of my decisions ever led to a friendly fire incident, whether through omission or through a random 20mm round skipping into a Marine position, others would second-guess everything I had done or failed to do. It would be expected and should be demanded.

Any investigation into an aviation mishap or into errant bombs or rockets was an unenviable task. A skilled investigator could undoubtedly find mistakes and faults somewhere in my decision matrix on any attack and on nearly every mission. We were all human, and we all accepted commanders asking or demanding us to make decisions with imperfect information and within an unrealistic decision loop.

Being a CAS pilot was different. Rarely were we called when things were going well; instead, we were usually called after things had become a complete shitshow. Ground commanders not only asked us to join a knife fight but expected us to jump right in. Trust me, I loved it, and it was exactly what we'd all signed up for. We had no illusions about who we were and what we were, but after days like that day, it began to wear more and more on my patience and physical endurance.

"Deadly 15, contact Vino on plum." The expected call came from Sky Chief.

We made an SOP frequency switch, and the flight back to Nasiriyah provided a welcome change from the one-hour scalding we had endured in the late afternoon sun. Vino, ready for us, had found another set of active targets. Amazingly, they sat in a section of southeastern-facing buildings just to the north of the Euphrates.

It included what looked like a mosque, and we didn't have a specific playbook for the place of worship. We universally considered any religious house of prayer as off limits. It was a respected refuge, a safe harbor for those who sought the calm seas of a sanctuary.

Unfortunately, so many of our enemies would test our moral resolve and use those same sanctuaries as fighting positions. They would use mosques and minarets to protect themselves and their weapons. They were the opposite of everything they claimed to be. They were not warriors; they were cowards, cravens, and caitiffs purporting to save the same people they were exploiting. They would eventually find those same mosques and minarets as a final resting place. From those locations as snipers and missileers, they would bait and then wait on us.

We began the final mission of the afternoon. As we pushed into our fifth hour of flight time, we realized a weather front was moving in from the west.

"Deadly 15, we have shooters. Stand by for a 9-line." Vino was again calling us from the relative comfort of his LAV-25, and we were prepared to check as many of his boxes as possible.

"Matt, let me know what you have, but it looks like the two buildings to the west of the temple." I was sure I had it in sight and wanted Matt to know.

These targets were almost too easy. They were open shots into prey that seemed built for Hellfire missiles. The time had come for us to punch out a few Hellfires. We had become tired of carrying so many long-range weapons for such a close-range fight. The Hellfire was amazing, but we had only fired a few. That would soon change.

"Deadly 15, call wings level."

Vino had us running to the northwest, and we had put a laser spot to designate the target. The mark ensured the laser headed to the target Vino had chosen. Matt had coded the missile to the requested laser frequency. He had also put the correct four-digit pulse repetition frequency (PRF) into our embedded laser. Our Hellfire missiles could talk to—or, more accurately, listen to—the laser code Matt had inputted.

It only took a few seconds for our Hellfire's computer to find the proper code. We were understandably excited. I wanted to see our most favored players get some game time. I looked to my left at the Hellfire rails. The missile's electronic seeker was located at the front of each Hellfire, and they were all spinning wildly. They were caged lions waiting to be let loose on their lambs.

"Vino, 15's wings level." Matt had the calls and the missile release responsibility.

"Deadly 15 and 16, you are cleared hot." Vino wasted no time.

Matt had selected a lock-on-before-launch mode, meaning the Hellfire's seeker had seen and recognized the correct laser code before it launched and was ready to go to the target. The missile would fly a direct path to the building. The shot would be measured less than two thousand meters. Unlike the TOW missiles, Hellfire flew twice as fast and nearly three times as far. With multiple warheads available, they could effectively destroy everything from sophisticated armored vehicles to buildings and reinforced bunkers.

We had slowed to about ninety knots and flew in a three-hundred-foot glide toward the target. "Buss, we are taking the one on the right, and I've got the corner building."

Click. Click.

We felt the power of the launch motor immediately as it sent a quick flash of light and a small smoke cloud trailing behind us. The missile was on its way. At nearly 950 miles an hour, the missile quickly accelerated, started to climb, and began an immediate track for the westernmost corner building. With nearly twenty pounds of composite explosives, the impact was less than six seconds away.

The impacts looked near simultaneous, with Matt's Hellfire hitting the corner building and Rosie's "shacking" the neighboring structure. The term "shack" was a WWII phrase used when a bomber hit the bullseye on a bombing range. It was both too late for WWII quotes and too late for that building. Its reaction to our missiles was immediate. Plumes of smoke poured out and continued to rise from Rosie's impact. We had a few seconds to press in closer and observe the destruction.

Vino expressed his satisfaction. "Deadly 15, those were good hits. The corner building was also a reported weapons storage house. Looks like we have secondary explosions. That's about all we have for you."

I was ready to head back to Riverfront. "Vino, Deadly 15 copies, and we will push BDA to Sky Chief. That was really good work. Might see you later."

After a pause, we all heard a keying of the radio, but no one spoke. It seemed as though someone was talking to Vino, and he was trying to listen and get us checked out at the same time.

Finally, Vino said, "Hey, 15, I got a request from one of the air officers you just flew over. They have another target on the river and want to know if you would have the time to engage. If you can, call KoKo on plum."

That seemed to be about the vaguest request yet, but with a little over nine hundred pounds of gas left in the tank, we had some time.

I needed to check with Matt and then with Buss. "One-five and flight, you got gas for another fifteen minutes or so?"

Click. Click.

Matt didn't say anything, so I took that as a yes.

"Deadly 15 and flight, switch plum. Vino, we will see you later." It was time to see what they needed.

"KoKo, Deadly 15 with you on plum. Standing by for tasking." His turn now.

KoKo was waiting for us. "Deadly, we have a single target just south of your last target. It's a non-standard target and stands alone facing south. Call contact."

"Matt, you see what he's talking about?" I was curious.

I was waiting for Matt to respond when I heard Buss. "You're not gonna believe this."

Matt was on the camera. "It's a large bronze or metal statue of Saddam Hussein. He's striking one of the Stalin poses with his right hand in the air."

I could not believe it. He wanted us to blow up a statue?

We needed confirmation. "KoKo, say again the threat?"

A short pause. "Hey, Deadly, it's a real threat to morale, and it has been taunting us all week. We have tried to neutralize it with 25mm and .50 cal, but no luck. Any chance you can hit it with a TOW?"

Well, it sounded reasonable enough—in a remarkably unreasonable way.

Time for a few more TOWs to go down range. "KoKo, we are coming in from the southeast. Will call wings level." Then, I spoke to Buss. "Buss, we are going to hit that target. Recommend you go trail. It'll be a right pull and then one more pass if needed." I left it as simple as that.

I asked Matt, "You think you can hit it center mass, maybe at the base?"

Matt chuckled lightly. "Well, you're the weapons expert. I'll aim for the head."

The following five minutes involved possibly the most egregious unprosecuted case of fraud, waste, and abuse in United States military history. We made two passes, expending about one hundred rounds of 20mm armor-piercing incendiary rounds and three TOW missiles. We all could hear the cheering over the radio as KoKo cleared us for the last reattack. It seemed like the bully was finally getting his due, but the victory was short lived. As we came off "target" for the last time, and as the smoke cleared, we realized Saddam remained standing. His twenty-five-foot monument to himself stood chipped, pockmarked, and listing about 10 degrees to port, but it had survived. We'd have a next time.

I rolled the Cobra hard to the south and checked out with both KoKo and Sky Chief. We may have omitted the last target set. The sun began to dip below the horizon as we flew southwest to Riverfront. We had another quiet ride back, and we all looked forward to a few hours off.

We found the flight line in great shape. From my vantage point at three hundred feet approaching Jalibah, the once mighty Iraqi MiG-25 base appeared to be thriving. It had been revived with the help of MAG 29 and the massive logistical trains continuously rolling through. New GP tents, antennas, air conditioners, portable showers, and better food would soon arrive.

The flight line had matured. Monty, Luke, and Jim Quirk ensured we had a well-established parking spot and landing program. It now was capable of handling forty or more arriving and departing Hueys and Cobras.

Matt had flown us back. I appreciated the break. Plus, it was always good to exercise the muscle memory of flying from the front seat. Buss and Rosie touched down to our left, and after we had de-armed the Cobra, we shut down and began the trek to maintenance.

I counted fourteen helicopters on the flight line, and a quick walk up and down revealed a few from our brothers and sisters from MAG 39. Despite the limited number of parts and supplies, I'd asked Monty to treat all visiting aircrew and aircraft like our own. It was a risk, and I left the level of support up to Monty, but no way would we leave any crews stranded. With three on *Saipan* for maintenance and 160444 destroyed, we had eleven aircraft out flying.

Monty and every 269 Marine and sailor had been contributing to make Jalibah a highly functional air base. Riverfront had more than two hundred tents, hundreds of support vehicles, thousands of pieces of equipment, and more than three thousand inhabitants. I took some time to soak in the environment. It amazed me that we had come so far so quickly, and Boomer had done it all with almost an "I told you we could" mentality.

Buss, Rosie, Matt, and I had finally debriefed the missions to our intelligence department. We knew we had another day and night of flying tomorrow, so I told them I planned to head to maintenance. From there, they walked back to one of the officer tents to unwind while I made my way to the flight line where I sat with Monty and listened to the details of the 269 fleet.

Despite the rising number of aircraft being struck by Iraqi gunfire, we were lucky. The recent damage had been exclusively caused by small arms fire—enemy bullets fired from an AK-47 assault rifle or smaller machine guns. Though nearly every crew had been fired upon by larger heavy machine guns, RPGs, and SAMS, we had avoided any direct hits. We all knew it was only a matter of time before some of those larger rounds would find their mark.

Boooom.

"What the hell was that?" came a random voice from outside our office.

I paused. Then, we all heard it.

Boom. Boom.

The rapid sound was more muffled, like distant thunder. It left as fast as it came. We had no clouds in the sky and no friendly artillery units close enough. We were thirty-five miles from Nasiriyah. So, any sounds of enemy artillery or mortar fire would have been swallowed by the desert before making it as far as Jalibah.

There are no coincidences. There are no flukes when you are deployed. There are no sounds that pass without investigation. So, we took nothing for granted, and this was clearly something that needed to be checked out. We all stood there, waiting, listening, and holding our breath. Each of us quietly wondered how secure our air base was. Had we become complacent or vulnerable to Iraqi special forces or to a desperate and impoverished populace? Riverfront sat in the wide open, and we didn't have any perimeter security. Should we have expected to be impervious to a crafty enemy? No way.

Shouts and the cacophony of vehicles starting promptly followed the sounds of explosions. Something had happened, and I needed to get to our operations tent to know what. Monty and I had an immediate sense that events had spiraled out of control. The façade of safety had left us. I walked out of maintenance, turned on my flashlight, and made my way to operations.

When I arrived, the operations tent was standing room only. A helicopter had gone down. That's all I heard. We still had multiple sections of Cobras out flying, including our CO's section. We also had several Hueys out with the regiments, but they operated well north and wouldn't have flown in or out of Jalibah. Who was it? What had happened?

Countless aircraft flew in and out of Jalibah every day. Besides MAG 29's fleet of more than sixty, we had helicopters from MAG

16, MAG 39, and the 15th MEU as well as untold numbers of US Army and coalition helicopters transiting through Jalibah.

There was no way for Monty or me to know what helicopter had gone down, but if we could get a callsign, it would be a start. The most likely person to know that information was the senior Marine manning the air traffic control tower. Known as the tower chief, they would have cleared the helicopter to take off or land. That tower chief knew the callsign. If we got the callsign, we could match it to the ATO and would likely have the unit, type of helicopter, and names of the crew.

Before we had a chance to ask, the callsign came from the tower, and then we knew. The crash and fire rescue Marines had made their way west of the Jalibah runways to find the wreckage. Not only had a helicopter gone down, but the rescuers knew, even in the dark of night, that they'd walked into a tragedy. They immediately realized it was unlikely that anyone could have survived. The Marine UH-1N, BUNO 160620, assigned to HMLA 169 from MAG 39, had been destroyed. It was gone, as were three of the four crew. The surviving copilot would quickly be whisked to a trauma unit and then flown far away from this patch of no name desert.

Another black horizonless and moonless night. They had launched for HMLA 169's headquarters in Kuwait after refueling. The crew and their squadron mates had spent another long day flying combat missions to the north. Their Huey had barely gotten airborne when she'd reached up from her hiding place. After several days of stalking, the Ghost had chosen them, and there was no escaping her clutch. The Ghost had just raised another trophy and claimed another Pyrrhic victory.

BOOK THREE

A Thousand Miles from Nowhere

I pray for no more youth to perish before its prime;
That Revenge and iron-heated War may fade with all that has gone before into the night of time.

— *Aeschylus (Greek Philosopher and Orator) 435 BC*

CHAPTER 27

Location: 40 Miles North of Riverfront – Al-Shatrah, Iraq
Date: 01APR03
Time: 1815L

We had a mixed blessing on the 31st of March. The sandstorms that had pushed into Riverfront had limited air operations. Our flight of two had picked and poked our way through the weather, but after taking off a second time, we'd returned. The desert and the impenetrable weather had been a testimonial of the relentlessness of the Ghost. It was as though she knew we had slipped past her again but reminded us that she remained in control. The tragic loss of the HMLA 169 crew on the night of the 30th had given clear evidence of her dominance. Though she had only slightly faded from our memories, we knew she would continue to watch and wait until we became more vulnerable.

Somehow, we stumbled into April. I can only describe the experiences of the four previous days and nights as a souvenir but not one I wanted to put on my shelf. I recognized a new month and then had a brief respite.

I spent a few minutes reflecting about my own family some six thousand miles and seven time zones away. My daughter Katherine was still nine. She'd been born in August of 1993 while I was deployed on the USS *Wasp* somewhere off the coast of Mogadishu, Somalia. My second daughter was Cassandra. I could almost visualize her chasing her sisters and brother in our backyard in North Carolina.

She'd been born three days before I had left on my fourth major deployment in 1995, also on *Wasp*. She was seven, and both she and her older sister had been looking after their four-year-old brother, Eric, and their two-year-old sister, Caroline. My son had had only one request as I'd flown away in January: "Be home for my birthday." At the time, I knew he had more to say, but I needed to keep my choices simple and my promises realistic. Caroline had been born a week before 9/11. She was our baby, and she would never know a world not at war.

Life was clearly more complicated for my family than I could have ever imagined. It was chaotic for families at Camp Lejeune, Camp Pendleton, Fort Bragg, Fort Benning, Fort Hood, Moody and Seymour Johnson Air Force Bases—any base, station, or fort across the globe. It was a time filled with listless days and nights, fearful weeks and months.

My son had asked me to be home in June. June was Pluto to my Earth. It was an almost unfathomable distance in the future—a future I could only hope to be alive in. I quietly prayed for him and his sisters.

I had refocused after a light day on the 31st of March. I was learning to have selective recall. My memories of each mission had become a hazy or deferred reality and recollection. I forced myself to take detailed notes whenever possible, typically while getting fuel and rearming or during our often quick debriefs. The lessons were being harvested yet blurred into one collective truth. I was counting on my new aggregated yet biased reality and experience.

Today, we had a change of venue, and as much as we had turned our fight with the Iraqis in Nasiriyah into a crosstown rivalry, tonight was definitely going to be an away game. The 1st MARDIV pushed north, and we planned to fly in support. Speed and tempo fueled their commanding general's intent, and with that came a need for twenty-four-hour CAS.

Specifically, we headed to support the 1st Marine regiment, also referred to as RCT-1. Each of the regiments were task organized and had more than infantry units assigned. In RCT-1's case, they also had LAR, tanks, artillery, supply, intelligence, communication, and ground reconnaissance units all unified under the leadership of the RCT's CO. Tonight, we headed to Al-Hay, a city about eighty-five miles north of Nasiriyah, due north on Highway 7.

Over the past four days, we had logged nearly thirty hours in the air, and more than half of those had been at night. With that, we had expended twenty one TOW missiles, four Hellfire missiles, more than 150 2.75-inch rockets, and another 1,200 rounds of 20mm. By any quantifiable measure, no one could call us rookies, but those metrics didn't matter because we all knew tonight would be different. We had no sense of success; nothing and no one said we were "winning." We only had expectations that we would need to find a new way to succeed.

Even with all the unprocessed emotions of angst, trepidation, and fear, I believed we had become better. We had survived a sundry mix of engagements, near misses, and close calls. I could see the harmony within the section with zero personal tension. I believed Matt and I, and Buss and Rosie, had finally gotten into a sustainable rhythm. Tonight, we'd have another test.

The moon stayed on my shitlist. Every mission had been a dark, moonless dance with the Ghost, and we'd have to wait several more nights before the moon would show itself again. No moon meant our NVGs remained a great asset but were working nowhere near their potential. Fortunately, in an almost bizarre but ironic alliance, the ambient city lights of Nasiriyah had helped us.

As we passed to the west of Nasiriyah, in some warped view of our new reality, I believed we all wanted to stay close to the Marines that trusted us, stay close to a city we knew well, and stay close to some glimmer of normalcy. I silently hoped the next three days would become as predictable as the last three.

We took off from Riverfront just after sunset.

"Sky Chief, Deadly 23 and 24, mission number 7244, one plus two zero time on station."

I was tired of our callsign. Deadly was pretentious. I enjoyed the previous anonymity of a daily changing callsign. I wished for it, but we were stuck with Deadly.

Matt tried to confirm the location of RCT-1 forward elements. The lead element was likely "Godfather," or 1st Reconnaissance Battalion. The RCT pushed north along Highway 7 and was expected to cross over the Shaṭṭ al-Gharrāf, or the Hai river, a canal that connects the Tigris to the Euphrates, into Al-Hay or Al-Hai.

The connection with RCT-1 didn't go as planned. We were passed to several FACs and finally assigned an innocuous mission of "screening to the northeast." With less than a half hour on station, I called us off to head to Fenway Park, a new FARP. I wanted to ensure we had time to find it with fuel to spare.

Location: Nasiriyah, Iraq
Date: 01APR03 – Joint Special Operations Task Force
Time: 2355L

Even as we engaged Iraqi Army and Fedayeen units in Nasiriyah, we were keenly aware that captured US servicemembers could still be in the city. Unbeknownst to us, US commanders chose that night to pool together the forces required to reclaim those Americans.

This would be no easy task and would test the planning and execution capabilities of our special operations and conventional forces. After days of planning, the US Army's 160th Special Operations Aviation Regiment (SOAR), or the "Night Stalkers," along with elements of the US Army's Delta Force and Rangers, the US Navy's SEAL Team 6, USAF Pararescue, and aviation elements of multiple services, would move to rescue US Army Private Jessica Lynch and recover the bodies of fallen American servicemembers. Lynch, a member of the 507th Maintenance Company, which had had the misfortune of driving into the city on the 23rd of March, was reportedly alive and being held in a hospital in Nasiriyah.

One of the two Marine squadrons assigned to carry US Army Rangers of the task force was HMM 165, the White Knights, commanded by Lieutenant Colonel Gregg "Sweet Pea" Sturdevant. Sweet Pea was another one of my flight instructors from Pensacola and a squadron mate from my 1994 deployment with HMM 365.

Gregg and his seven Phrogs, six of which would fly the mission, positioned themselves and awaited the final "go" to load the Ranger security force. Another Marine squadron, Marine Heavy Helicopter Squadron (HMH) 465, supported the mission. It provided three CH-53E heavy lift helicopters to help deliver the Ranger security force.

The target was the grounds just outside the Saddam Hospital in Nasiriyah. The Rangers had the mission to establish a security perimeter and isolate the hospital—no one in, and no one out. US special operators, delivered in helicopters of the 160th SOAR, would breach the hospital itself.

The mission had a laundry list of nearly thirty aircraft playing a lead or supporting role. Those other aircraft included a US Navy EA-6B Prowler for electronic warfare, USAF AC-130 Spectre gunships for additional fire support, US Army MH-60s for command and control and delivery of special operators, and US Army M/AH-6 "Little Birds," as well as USAF A-10 Thunderbolts, USMC AH-1Ws, and USMC AV-8Bs for CAS. This would be a massive effort and a mission that would garner global visibility, and we had absolutely no knowledge that it would take place.

Ultimately, the mission proved to be a success. As three Marine battalions executed diversionary attacks in Nasiriyah, the task force moved into action at the Saddam Hospital. We defined that success as the rescue of one and recovery of eight American servicemembers who'd been swept up in the chaos of combat. Unfortunately, we'd need more than one rescue and recovery mission in the war.

Location: 60 Miles North of An-Nasiriyah
Date: 01APR03
Time: 1845L

My flight had no idea that a rescue operation was being planned, and by the time it was executed, we were a hundred miles to the north. Matt and I spent the next half hour attempting to negotiate the weather into Fenway Park. The sun had long faded, and the darkness enveloped us like a blanket. We had an empty and black sky with only the green hue of the HUD for any reference to altitude, speed, and heading. The trip to Fenway went quickly but gave us a growing sense of apprehension.

"Fenway, this is Deadly 23, flight of two, entering from the west." Nothing.

Eventually, the FARP team found the radio. "Last calling Fenway, the winds are out of the west. There are two fuel trucks located midfield on the north side of the east-west runway. They are marked with chem lights. They can take you both at the same time."

I thought that sounded reasonable. "Deadly 23 and flight copy. We are going to circle to the east. Should be on deck in two minutes."

The chem lights consisted of eight-inch-long thin plastic tubes, which, when bent, produced a chemical reaction that caused them to turn several colors. Red, blue, and green were the most common, with red being the easiest to see on NVGs, but we didn't see much. As we approached a mile, we started to recognize the outline of the airfield, and Matt identified the heat signatures of several vehicles on the FLIR.

I wanted to come in slowly. "Two-four, go trail. Think we have the fuel trucks at midfield. We will plan to land facing west."

Buss had heard us. *Click. Click.*

Behind us, as we made the left-hand turn, I could see Buss had reduced power and slid back into a trail position. We wanted enough distance between the two aircraft to allow time for us to find the spot, identify the taxi director, land, and let our sand clear before Buss repeated our steps.

I lost sight of Buss as we looked for the fuel trucks. I needed Matt on the FLIR to find their heat signatures. "Matt, keep an eye out to the right for the fuel trucks. I am going to keep a high hover until I see them and plan to come straight down."

From the tone of his voice, I knew Matt was on the FLIR. "Okay, I see the two fuel trucks about fifty yards to the right. Keep coming forward, and you can slide right about twenty feet."

I continued forward and began to see the outline of the fuel truck and the chem lights of the Marine refueler. As they came into sight, the plume of white powder cut visibility to about fifty yards. Matt had the FLIR locked into a fixed straight position so he could judge our left and right drift. We had already taken Buss's advice and covered our left red position light with duct tape. We'd cut a small slit into the tape so a portion of the red overt light could escape. That tiny glow was enough to allow the NVGs to perform significantly better.

Matt could see off to the right where the fuel trucks were parked with his NVGs and used the FLIR to stop my drift. I looked through the HUD to adjust my heading and altitude while also looking down to my left to catch any relative motion as the dust blew away. I caught sight of the pavement, focused on a single piece, and lowered the collective.

Matt concentrated on the fuel trucks. "Stop. No, more to the right. Come straight down."

Thump. Thump. Slide.

The Cobra touched the ground with the left skid, then the right skid, and with a little forward momentum, we ground to a stop. Not a pretty landing, but we'd come down, and the dust had cleared out.

"Two-four," I called to Buss and Rosie, "23's down, spot one. It's really dusty, but it cleared out."

Click. Click.

I kept the rotor spinning until Buss touched down and then reduced the throttles to idle. Matt hopped out and quickly walked about the aircraft, de-arming all the weapons. I saw him step to the right, looking for the fuel hose. It was like a scene from *Field of Dreams*, but instead of Shoeless Joe Jackson who disappeared into a cornfield, it was Matt who melted into a cloud of gray and then disappeared. I had lost sight of him just outside of the rotor arch. A few seconds later, he returned with the fuel hose. He attached the pressure port on the left side of the aircraft, and we took on another nine hundred pounds of fuel. We had to make this a quick turnaround.

Then, the radio cracked with news no one wanted to hear. "Two-three, we are down," said Buss. "I can't get the number one engine started. I think the starter-generator went."

Bell Helicopter made a very durable and rugged attack helicopter, but we found some of the parts notoriously unreliable, including the combined starter-generator. Each engine had one. If it went bad, we had no way to use the other engine's starter. With Buss stuck, we had some decisions to make.

After I called Sky Chief and the FARP team confirmed they had communications with the aviation supply detachment, we hatched a plan. We could get the part from Riverfront to Fenway, but Buss would need to shut down at Fenway and wait for a Huey or Phrog to drop it. Our maintenance team, embedded with the Fenway FARP team, had a Marine qualified to do the remove and replace of the starter-generator. Unfortunately, we had no timeline on the part's arrival, and there was no telling whether Deadly 24 had bigger issues than just the starter-generator.

The next decision was more difficult. We still had a mission, and we needed to stay in the fight. The FARP had a security detachment. They had MREs, water, and communications with Riverfront and Sky Chief. I decided that we would leave Buss and Rosie and try to link up with our XO, Spike, and his wingman, Cut. They were reportedly getting fuel at another FARP to the west, Coors Field.

We were fully refueled, armed, and, with both cockpit canopies closed, ready to take off for Coors Field. There were no lights; there was no moon. Even with NVGs, I couldn't see very far ahead of us, maybe seventy-five yards, but beyond that, there was only darkness. I planned to come into a low hover while simultaneously pushing my nose forward. It would take a few seconds of acceleration before we entered "translational lift." Once through that, we would have the energy we needed. I would pull back on the stick and trade the airspeed for altitude. That was the plan, but plans change.

Once Matt was secured in the cockpit, I spoke. "I talked to Sky Chief. We have Spike and Cut at Coors Field. Plan is to leave Buss and Rosie here, fly to Coors Field, and brief up with Spike. Looks like they are on tap for a mission supporting 1st Marines in Al-Hay."

Click. Click.

The steady beat of the rotors increased, as did the pitch of both engines as I rolled the throttles up to 100 percent. We armed the aircraft and completed the after-arming checks. I made one last look around us and then signaled the FARP Marine with a quick flash of our landing light. As I began to pull in power, the dust immediately started to swirl. I concentrated on the HUD and down and to the left while Matt looked right and through the FLIR.

Matt already saw more than I could. "Keep coming up and hold the hover for a few more seconds."

We agreed that a three-foot hover would blow out some of the sand. So, I pulled more power but still had very little to reference outside of the HUD and a small patch of pavement.

Matt's voice quickly broke in. "Come forward and left. You are drifting right."

Having lost any sensation of relative motion, I pushed the stick further forward and pulled to maximum power. The Cobra begrudgingly moved forward, and I anticipated the natural "settling" toward the ground before we entered into translational life.

We had lifted no more than five feet in the air and maybe accelerated through twenty knots when I heard it.

"There's something in front of us," Matt stated sharply.

Options came into my head at a pace I was unprepared for. Like a multiple choice test, but the answers all seem blurred. I chose E, none of the above. It had only been a second, but if I could just hold that power setting and nose attitude, we could be airborne in another three, maybe five, seconds.

There are things that you can practice, and then there are things you can only read about. I had taken off at close to maximum gross weight in the past, but in those instances, I'd had windsocks and weather reports to give me wind direction and wind speed, both important data points. Tonight, the winds were a swag—serious wild ass guess. I was low, slow, and about to demand every ounce of power from these engines. We were at a gross weight that required more speed, more time, more wind, and less weight. I'd never demanded this much power so quickly. It was not something I had tried in a simulator, and it wasn't something I'd practiced in the helicopter.

Matt kept up the dialogue. "Okay. Ahh… Keep coming forward."

He tried to look out in front, doing his best to get more from the FLIR. "There's something ahead. I can't tell how far… Oh shit, it's a truck about fifty yards off the nose. We gotta climb now. Power, power!"

In a tandem seat aircraft, voice inflection tells its own story, and Matt's was telling me it was going to be close. I pulled more power. The HUD showed us at fifteen feet with the airspeed building slowly and torque nearing 110 percent. With a full ordnance loadout and full fuel tank. We needed more runway, but we didn't have more.

I focused my NVGs through the HUD. My brain processed bits of information on airspeed, heading, power, and altitude. As I continued mulling over Matt's last words, I reflected that I couldn't see anything outside the cloud of dust and debris. It had formed a bubble around us, and there was no light and nothing to see. I pulled more power.

The nose suddenly pulled to the left and then dipped. I countered that motion with more right rudder and pulled back on the stick. In fact, I pushed the right rudder to its maximum deflection. I had simply pulled more torque than the tail rotor could counter. I felt it coming, and there was nothing I could do. Well, that's not actually true—I could have taken out power and attempted to fly out of it but only if there'd been an open runway in front of us and more time. We had neither. It was too late.

The initial tuck to the left was followed by the entire tail of the Cobra coming over my right shoulder as we lost tail rotor authority. We entered a left spin at twenty feet and about forty knots. I focused on the altimeter in the HUD. We began climbing. The nose came back into the relative wind—a wind created by our direction of travel. That would normally allow enough air flow to let us fully transition to forward flight, but not that night. A self-generated sandstorm had simultaneously trapped us. Zero visibility.

"Keep wings level, keep wings level… Take out some power." Matt's tone came across as matter of fact, but I could tell he wanted out of this spin.

No way I would take out power, so I continued to pull more. It solved one problem—altitude—but created another. The G forces built as we went into another full rotation. The correct procedure was to lower the collective or reduce power and push the nose over to gain airspeed. I would try that as soon as we moved above the brownout and away from the truck—a truck I never saw.

I was in the fight of my life. Not just my life but Matt's. I fought a fifteen-thousand-pound beast who refused to obey my commands. There were, in hindsight, a few brief moments of clarity but not enough to make the connection between what was happening and what could very well be the end of us.

We continued in a spastic, out-of-control spin. We were climbing and remained wings level. So, we had some control in our uncontrollable situation. Sun Tzu supposedly said, "In the midst of chaos, there is also opportunity." I looked for any opportunity to change our current state. The nose pitched left a third and then a fourth time. Each time the tail whipped over my right shoulder, it had the G-force of a carnival ride.

"Matt," I almost yelled, "once we are at fifty feet, I'll take out power."

Matt replied, "Push the nose over. Take some power out!" But he had quickly changed his tone.

How do you make decisions inside of a completely irrational and foreign world? We'd never discussed this specific situation. Never read about this. Never trained for this. I needed to find a crumb of familiarity. From that known point, I could assess and make a logical next step. It never came.

The concern was real, and even through the chaos, I realized that our aircraft flew, and we continued to climb. We finally got over the brownout so we could now make an adjustment. After the final spin, I lowered the collective and pushed the nose over. I felt as though I had taken out more than enough power, and the airspeed built up through sixty knots. The Cobra almost shuddered as we stabilized about 90 degrees off our original heading, having completed five 360-degree rotations.

From the ground, in the cockpit of 24, Buss and Rosie sat with their jaws dropped. They had witnessed everything. Almost everything. They had seen the attempted takeoff. They'd watched as our aircraft had spun into the cloud of dust. Later, they would both admit that, as we went out of sight, they had held their breath and waited for the fireball.

Matt and I didn't say anything for a few minutes. I immediately felt that familiar sense of dread and failure as we climbed to five hundred feet and accelerated to cruise speed. We had survived a confusing, disturbing, and wickedly dangerous situation. I didn't have time to talk about it or even think about it. The entire event needed to be choked back for now. I had to compose myself. Plus, I needed to check in with Sky Chief, get the grid coordinate that led to Coors Field, and quickly recover my wits.

"Sky Chief, this is Deadly 23. Do not, I repeat, do not close and move Coors Field. Additionally, Fenway can't be used for helicopter ops. You need to request tankers to spray the sand and debris on the runways." There was a long and anticipated pause.

As I said the words, I began to relive what had just happened. My right foot began to frantically bounce off the rudder pedal. That uncontrolled tic was back. My brain was doing its own thing, as were my heartbeat, my hands, and my feet. The spoken words were uttered from someone—I guess it was me. I needed to breathe.

Sky Chief came back, and from the tone of his voice, I suspected it was one of the colonels who acted as the battle captain riding in the back of KC-130. The battle captain was the designated decisionmaker for the commanding general, and this was clearly the voice of someone in charge. "Aircraft last calling Sky Chief, say again?"

Here it went. "Sky Chief, this is Deadly 23. We had a near mishap coming out of Fenway. There is too much dust and sand on the runways and on the taxiways for safe operations. We will need water trucks in the morning. In the meantime, we need to keep Coors Field open. It's our only fuel and ordnance. I am headed there now and then north to support 1st Marines."

Another significant pause as though he'd written it all down and was thinking of his response. Finally, Sky Chief came back. "Copy that, Deadly. Appreciate the update, and I'll push those changes."

That had gone better than I'd imagined, so I took the opportunity. "Sky Chief, my wingman, Deadly 24, is down for maintenance at Fenway. Can you also push that 24 is an AH-1W and needs a starter-generator for his number one engine?"

After a slight pause, Sky Chief responded. "Deadly 23, I copy 24 is down at Fenway, and I copy your request. I'll push it."

All good news. Coors Field was only another twenty minutes out and would likely stay open. Once the chatter had subsided, I had some time to reflect on my non-standard takeoff. More unnerving was not having Buss and Rosie on our wing.

At ten miles out from Coors Field, I made the call, hoping the FARP team had gotten the message to remain in place and were still there. "Coors Field, Deadly 23 is five minutes out."

We waited. Then, the FARP radio responded. "Last calling Coors Field, winds are from the east. You will be landing to the north of two Cobras currently shut down." I heard the winds from the east. That made more sense.

My voice felt tired. It faltered, and I suspected it sounded almost defeated. I could not shake that uneasy feeling that had followed me from Fenway. Resilience was one thing, but I had come so close to crashing an otherwise perfectly good Cobra. My internal cynical and sometimes overconfident monologue tossed those ideas aside. I could fly a Cobra—could actually fly the hell out of a Cobra—and had done it for nearly my entire adult life. Maybe I could blame the unrelenting weather, the endless sand, the misplacement of a random vehicle, or even the Ghost.

Truth was, there was no one to blame but myself. I should have walked the four or five hundred meters in front of me at Fenway or had Matt walk it. I should not have taken a full load of fuel. I could have done a lot more than accept the hand the mission had dealt me. I had become complacent, and complacency would kill us faster than any Iraqi gunner and more effectively than any ghost. I needed to get better fast.

I called Coors again when nearly over the top of the FARP. "Coors, Deadly 23's a single coming in from the east for landing."

The radio crackled again. "Deadly, the road runs north-south. You can land pointed to the east. There are two Cobras that will be on your right."

"Deadly 23 copies." I let them know we were inbound but then circled wide to the west to set up for an easterly landing.

Coors was not an airport but simply a piece of the now unused highway. It had an overpass about eight hundred meters to the south and some rising terrain to the west. Coors also had unlit power lines and phone lines, which we had not yet seen, draped to the west of the road.

These temporary FARPs were sometimes highways; other times, they were side roads or even open fields. The FARP teams did little to improve them since they were only likely to be there a few days or maybe even a few hours.

Since we had a more confined area in which to land, I passed the controls to Matt in the front seat. He had the best visibility, and I could clear the area to the left and the right as we landed.

"Matt, you have the controls." Matt's turn to fly.

He responded with the required three-way transfer of the primary flight controls in most multi-piloted aircraft. "Roger, I have the controls."

I followed with a simple, "You have the controls." Then, I tapped gently on the canopy, letting him know my hands no longer touched the flight controls.

If Matt had passed the controls to me, he would have completed the three-way transfer by quickly putting his hands into the air to show me that he no longer flew. Unfortunately, naval aviation history is littered with tragic examples of aircrews crashing, believing the other pilot was flying when, in fact, no one was flying.

Matt flew us about five hundred feet and eighty knots, half a mile from the intended landing spot. I noted a cable stanchion to the right and traced an invisible line to another stanchion to our left. That meant we had a wire somewhere in front of us.

"Matt, I don't see the power lines, but there are towers on each side. Let's stay high until we see it." More a comment than a request.

Click. Click.

I could feel and hear that he'd added power, and the pull of power arrested our rate of descent. Front seat flying was more art than science. I had the HUD, which made airspeed, heading, and power information readily available. The front seat had no HUD, and the primary instruments were half the size of the rear seats and stuffed out of the way to make room for the FLIR, trigger grip, hand controller, and camera system.

"Got 'em off the nose. You see them?" Matt said cheerfully.

Click. Click.

I saw them. We cleared the wires, but damn, they were big and a significant obstacle. The FARP team needed to know about these power lines and needed to brief every arriving helicopter. It was certainly no dig on the FARP team because they likely couldn't see them. Matt got to the other side and began to execute a textbook steep approach into the spot. We could see the outline of a lineman. We came into a five-foot hover and then landed.

Out of the darkness came an ordnance crew, a welcome sight. Matt and I immediately went through our de-arming checklist. Within a few minutes, they'd de-armed us, and we were ready to shut down.

I watched a pilot walk to the parked Cobra, open the canopy, and plug in his helmet. It was Spike, our XO.

The radio came alive. "Hey, Ferris. Is that you, buddy?"

It was good to hear his voice.

I owed him a quick update. "XO, how's it going? Buss and Rosie blew a starter and are stuck at Fenway. Fenway's a shitshow, but we had a frag to support 1st Marines later tonight. Mind if we tag along with you?"

Spike keyed the mic. "Yeah, that sounds like a plan. We are not scheduled—"

Flash. Boom. Flash. Boom. Boom.

The noises had interrupted him. "What the hell was that?"

I looked up in time to see a series of brilliant flashes of light one hundred meters to the south of Spike's position. *What the hell was that?* exactly mirrored my own thoughts. I looked down the highway as I flicked our searchlight on and off. I needed the ordnance teams back now! Those were mortar rounds.

I reached for the throttles and ran them up while telling Matt, "I have the controls."

I looked back to where Spike stood. He was still there. In prototypical Spike fashion, he had not moved an inch. Gazing past the nose of his Cobra, I saw one more explosion and then a scene that burnt itself into my memory. As the last round landed, I heard the final muffled explosion. Nearly simultaneously, I saw a figure stumble maybe another fifty meters from Spike's position. From where and how the figure had stood, I guessed it was a refueler or aviation maintenance Marine. The silhouette righted itself, standing almost frozen in an upright position, and then rolled to the ground.

Precious seconds ticked by as the ordnance team came running back to our aircraft. We armed quickly. I was naively waiting for an update, but from whom? The FARP team knew less than we did. It was only couple of minutes before we were ready to launch.

"Matt, you ready?" A rhetorical question—more a preparatory comment before I pulled power and took off straight ahead.

Click. Click.

"Deadly 23, this is Coors. We are taking mortar fire, and I have no idea where it's coming from. We have one Marine wounded. CASEVAC has been requested."

I responded quickly as we formulated a plan. "Copy that, Coors. We are going to run a perimeter sweep, and we will let you know."

Coors came back. "Okay, Deadly, appreciate that."

"Hey, Ferris, you good?" Spike asked on the FARP frequency. "Do you want me or Cut to join you? They are getting the Marine stabilized. Think we have a CASEVAC Phrog on the way."

Spike had certainly taken everything in stride. I had never experienced a FARP motoring before. Matt and I wanted to find those guys and collect some debts. We went through a quick logic drill based on the accuracy of the mortars.

We didn't think they'd been 120mm mortars based on their minimum ranges, weight, and need for extremely accurate coordinates. Also, the explosions had seemed smallish, likely the result of older British three-inch mortars that were part of the Iraqi inventory. The kind that the enemy could hide in a car's truck, fire by hand, or simply use with very little coordination. Based on their maximum range, the Iraqi shooters had likely worked from within 1,500 meters and had an escape plan. We didn't expect to catch them. It would be nice, but we planned to fly low and fast enough to let them know we were out there hunting them.

I was already frustrated, and this just added to it. I wanted to find the shooter and talk to them. I wanted to ask them the obvious question: "Where is your Ghost now? She can't save you. You are alone, and you're going to die alone!" It sounded tough, but we needed to find them first.

Matt got back on the FLIR and picked up a new scent. "Come right. We've got several buildings and vehicles to the south."

We had completed a close search, and now we headed further south to an area with several buildings—more like a cluster of houses. A dirt road connected those houses to a highway, as was the case with most every other building. Anything hot would show up to Matt, but he found nothing. We also knew that if anything happened to us, we had no mutual support.

After nearly forty-five minutes, we headed back to Coors, checked out with Sky Chief, and began our approach to land.

I passed the controls to Matt, and he made the call. "Coors, Deadly 23 inbound."

Not finding the shooters was disappointing, but we knew they'd likely had a plan. It was an unexpected place to be hit with mortars. Maybe that was the biggest lesson: expect the unexpected, anticipate the unanticipated, take nothing for granted.

CHAPTER 28

Location: MAG 29 Operations Tent, Riverfront
Date: 01APR03
Time: 1945L

Fuzzy, the HMM 162 CO, had been up for more than fifteen hours and had logged nearly eleven in the cockpit when the call came in. A long day would soon turn into an even longer night.

Availability of aircraft and personnel restricted the typical Phrog squadron. Yes, they could run twenty-four-hour operations, but with only twelve CH-46Es and a limited number of fully qualified crews, they had to maintain a delicate balance. For every Phrog scheduled to fly, they needed four in the crew. Sometimes the crew chiefs also filled another critical billet in the maintenance department. Unlike the pilots who served the maintenance department, the aircrew both flew and did actual work on the aircraft.

Sky Chief had passed the CASEVAC request to the 3rd MAW operations center located in Kuwait. They'd immediately processed the request and then sent it to MAG 29. After all, MAG 29 was already in Iraq and more than one hundred miles closer to Fenway than any units stationed in Kuwait.

The secure computer system used by all Marine forces had sent a "chat" message tasking MAG 29 with the CASEVAC mission, something they couldn't refuse—nor did anyone want to. However, matching the requirement with the right capability wouldn't be easy. HMLA 269's Hueys would have been a good choice, but the squadron had tasked them as CAS platforms or attached them to the RCTs in their "Swiss army knife" mission. The CH-53s of HMH

464 were heavy lift platforms, and they didn't routinely conduct CASEVAC missions.

This left HMM 162 or the undermanned HMM 365. HMM 162 got the nod, even though their crews were either already tasked or out of crew day. The standard crew day was twelve hours with no pilot allowed to fly more than eight hours a day. Boomer had already been pushed to relax a few of those restrictions. After all, those were peacetime standards but long-standing ones nonetheless. Those rules, whether in our SOPs, in our tactics manuals, or in our standardization manuals, had been established over years and only after countless accidents. Those lessons or best practices came routinely at the expense of aircraft and lives; to break or modify those created another one of Blackjack Matthews's slippery slopes.

Fuzzy got the message that MAG 29 had tasked 162 to send a single Phrog ninety-seven miles one way to retrieve the wounded Marine at Coors Field. It was a point-of-injury CASEVAC. That meant the injured Marine was being picked up where he had been wounded, which implied a more dangerous mission. He didn't have any more information. Who was the Marine? Were they still under attack? Was the wounded Marine from an infantry unit? Had 162 just been tasked with flying into an active firefight?

Fuzzy was fine with any part of the reality on the ground. He didn't focus on the obvious risk but rather on mitigating risk wherever possible. He wanted to have more background before he assigned a crew that would include a full medical team. Like any good commander, he wanted the crew to have as much information as possible, but with that information unavailable and time potentially running out on that Marine, he needed to act now. First, he needed to talk to Boomer.

The operations tent was dimly lit with stagnant air, the smell of dank rubber, and the constant hum of a generator and laptops. Fuzzy had walked into a beehive of activity. The buzzing was about the impending CASEVAC mission assigned to 162.

When Fuzzy found Boomer, he said, "Hey, sir, we are down to our last crew for this, and there's no intel. Are we the only option for this mission?"

Boomer had been up all day and would likely stay up through the night. Boomer looked back at Fuzzy. "This is our mission. This is your mission. We need to get that Marine. He's with one of our FARP teams. That's all we know. I need you to go and go now."

He had little room for negotiation, but Fuzzy needed to advocate for his crew. "Sir, I'm the last crew, and I've already flown way out of crew day."

Boomer turned. "Well, Bob, looks like it's you! I'll see you when you get back."

Location: 6 Miles South of Coors
Date: 01APR03
Time: 2035L

Matt was on short final into Coors and on the radios. "Coors, Deadly 23 inbound. We cleared the areas. We didn't see anything, and there were no vehicles on the highway headed toward you. We are coming in to shut down and top off fuel."

The Coors FARP radio confirmed. "Thanks, 23. You are cleared to land at the same location you departed from."

Click. Click.

I saw the wires again. "Hey, Matt, you see those?"

"Yup, I got them. What's the plan after we shut down? I think the frag for the 1st Marines mission was for 2200L."

We started our approach once we passed over the power lines. The Cobra flew on a near 45-degree flight path to our landing spot. At sixty knots, Matt established a comfortable eight-hundred-feet-per-minute descent. We came into a hover and then touched down with a light thump. The ordnance crews returned, and we began the shutdown process again.

I had taken back the controls and, with the engines at idle, was preparing to close the throttles when the radios chirped again. It was a familiar voice.

"Coors, this is Legion 57, inbound for CASEVAC."

The FARP radioman had a plan. "Copy that, 57. Recommend you land from west to east closest to the southern parked Cobra."

I recognized the voice. "Five-seven copies," Fuzzy said.

Was I hearing Coors correctly? Was he telling them to fly the same route we had? It made no sense. I could see the Phrog turning to the west. He'd lined up to do a steep approach, but did he see the wires?

"Matt, you see the Phrog?" I asked.

Before he could answer, I saw the Phrog descending. We still had no moon. Only the starlight helped the Phrog crew see with their NVGs. The Phrog didn't have a FLIR or any type of navigation sensor to search for obstacles or hazards in their flight path. They flew as old school as it got. I had no idea what they did or didn't see, but I wasn't waiting any longer.

I pushed the transmitter. "Five-seven, you need to wave off. There are unmarked power lines to the west."

Nothing.

I suspected the crew were discussing what they had just heard. *Who was that? What did they see that we didn't?*

The crew of Legion 57, like every crew, tried to build situational awareness before making another decision. Most likely, the pilots were asking the crew chiefs whether they saw any wires. All that communication took time. At one hundred knots, they moved fifty meters every second. If they didn't see the wires, the call had likely confused them. They continued their approach, and they didn't have more time.

I didn't know what they saw, but I was done trying to guess. Following my gut, I pushed the transmit switch again, thinking that being more directive and descriptive may help. "Fuzzy, this is Ferris. Wave off. There are unmarked power lines. Wave off!"

The sound of the twin General Electric T58-GE-16 turboshaft engines was unmistakable. I heard all 1,870 horsepower of each engine as the crew of 57 pulled power. The Phrog pitched up gently and then flew past me to the right at about three hundred feet. I still didn't know whether they saw the wires, but no way I was staying silent, so I continued.

"Five-seven, recommend you extend to the southwest and then land to the north. There is an overpass, and once past that intersection, there's plenty of room before the two parked Cobras."

Click. Click.

Matt and I watched the dust kick off the rotor blades. The crew of 57 landed to our south, no more than three hundred meters from us. I didn't know if I'd helped Fuzzy and his crew or made the night even more challenging, but I sure felt better. I'd already had one brownout landing and one complete loss of tail rotor authority takeoff, and I'd survived my first mortar attack. So, I owed my former flight instructor and squadron mate my unsolicited advice.

I chopped the throttles. The canopies opened, and I sucked in a lungful of the dry and hot Iraqi spring night. The only sounds came from Legion 57's engines and rotor blades. However, that relative quiet didn't last. I heard the Phrog before I saw it. I looked up just in time to see Fuzzy as he flew overhead at one hundred feet and in a climb to the south.

He had landed, secured the wounded Marine, and taken back off. They could not have been on the ground for more than a minute. The world had just gotten a little smaller. On board, they had the crew, a wounded and soon to be recovering Marine, and a full medical team. They likely thought nothing of it, but as I watched them fly off, I had some envy. There they went, alone and unafraid.

I pulled on the rotor brake lever in the rear seat. As our rotor blades stopped, we saw the faces of two 269 Marines walking underneath the blades. Big smiles and finally someone to catch up with. Also, they opened the ammo bay doors located on both sides of the Cobra. These doors exposed the large storage area where we carried the massive 20mm ammunition cans. More importantly, we could now step out of the cockpits and onto the horizontal ledge created by the opened doors. With weapons, body armor, and other kit, jumping the three or four feet onto the ground had become tiresome.

Spike and his wingman, Cut, followed shortly behind the FARP team. Then, we waved in the refueling truck. We had plenty of ordnance but wanted a few more pounds of JP-5 for the next mission.

I opened the talk. "XO, how was that Marine? We didn't have any luck finding the guys who shot those mortars. They could be hiding anywhere."

Spike countered, "He's gonna be good. Looks like shrapnel in his shoulder and maybe in his leg. I agree about the mortars." As I followed Spike and Cut back to their Cobras, he continued. "I've already briefed the section. It's a direct shot from here to Al-Hay. Looks like the 1st Marines are hunkered down south of the river and have 1st Recon and LAR watching the river. There's one main bridge that goes in. Not much else. We will crank up in about fifteen minutes."

That was all we needed to hear. We were "dash last," making us the third Cobra in this trio. We considered flying in the third position, or dash three, a gift. It would let me and Matt maneuver any way we chose. It also gave Spike's wingman more freedom knowing we provided cover for the flight.

The evening of April 1st began like so many we had already experienced. Another moonless night with endless open desert and a light breeze that pushed up just enough sand. It was also unfamiliar territory. That meant unlit radio and cellular towers, unmarked power lines, unknown and potentially previously undetected enemy formations, and a host of other manmade obstacles we needed to consider.

This also became the first time Matt and I would be flying for an extended period as a wingman. We needed our eyes peeled not only for an enemy and obstacles but for Spike and Cut's aircraft. Rule number one for flying off anyone's wing: Do not run into them. Rule number two was very close to rule number one: Do not shoot them. Both fair and reasonable requests, but it takes a change in mindset.

We had another rule with Buss and Rosie. If I called for an attack with a right pull off the target and decided to pull left, they had to be in a position so their rounds were above me. It meant that during any of our previous 2.75-inch rocket and 20mm cannon runs, Buss and Rosie flew an additional fifty to one hundred feet above us. That exposed them more, but their rounds traveled above our flight path, not potentially through it.

Spike and his copilot, 1st Lieutenant Jeremie "Hank" Hester, were a good team. Another in an apparently endless line of Midwesterners, he was a Fighting Illini and a graduate of the University of Illinois. Hank, as we called him, brought a bit more seasoning than the average lieutenant. He also brought an infectious sense of humor but balanced that with a quiet intensity often couched with a smile.

We had several lieutenants flying as copilots, but most others took turns getting their missions. Not Hank, welded into Spike's front seat. The team of Spike and Hank, along with wingman Cut and his copilot, Chief, was formidable. Both Spike and Cut had served as WTIs, and we considered them as capable and fearless as any section we had flying.

The takeoff from Coors and radio switches had become a familiar routine. Simply following and keeping up was a welcome change. Sky Chief was up, and we could hear the chatter with more aircraft flying tonight than I had previously recalled. That made sense. The 1st MARDIV continued its march north.

Sky Chief pushed us to turquoise to contact a FAC whose callsign both Matt and I missed. Spike checked us in. "Deadly 51, flight of three, one plus one five for your work."

There was a slight pause and then the sound of a radio being keyed. The static held for a few seconds. We could all hear voices in the background, but no one spoke. Not a good sign since we all used turquoise, a TAD frequency. If someone had accidentally pressed that button, no one would be able to use the frequency. I was always amazed at how one "hot mic" or one simple act could cause so much friction. However, after another few seconds, it went quiet.

The FAC or more senior air officer got us moving. "Deadly 51, contact Gump on this push. They are our most forward unit along with 1st Recon on the bank of the river."

We flew off of Spike's left wing about a hundred meters away, and Cut cruised off to his right. It was one of my jobs to balance the flight. That meant if Spike turned right, Cut would come across to his left side, and I would fill in once Spike rolled out of his turn on the right. It let Spike maneuver as necessary and gave us all firing lanes. If the weather, the visibility, the light level, or any other situation dictated, Spike could call for us to fly a "welded wing." This concept provided an added measure of safety if the flight leader deemed it necessary. It meant I would be exclusively on one side of the lead aircraft and Cut would be on the other. It limited our agility but also prevented excessive maneuvering of the three aircraft in close proximity to one another.

We pushed to the outskirts of the city. The Marines were positioned on the southwestern side of the Gharraf Canal, which connected the Tigris and the Euphrates rivers. On the Marine side of the canal was RCT-1 with all its supporting elements. They had the job of pushing through the city along Route 7 and continuing to race into Al-Kut—the prize. Al-Kut was many things to the Marine commanders. It held a large Iraqi airfield and a suspected weapons of mass destruction facility as well as suspected Iraqi armored forces and Fedayeen Saddam fighters.

We had approached from the southwest, and when we were ten miles away, we started to see the firestorm that had begun building. Heavy machine gun, small arms, and rocket fire danced from both directions across the river.

"Five-one flight, looks like there is more happening here than we were briefed." Spike stated the obvious in an almost comically rhetorical tone.

Truth be told, we'd received no brief from Sky Chief or from anyone else that effectively described what we saw. The FAC had tried to paint a picture of the plan, but as of right now, they needed help engaging infantry on the east side of the river. As we came in closer, we saw a full-blown firefight between the LAV-25s of LAR, the armed Humvees of 1st Recon, and whoever was dumb enough to expose themselves to their heavy and light machine gun teams. Never mind the firepower of LAR's 25mm Bushmaster guns.

The call from the FAC came immediately. "Deadly 51, follow the river until you see a bridge. Call contact!"

Spike came hard to the right and rolled out, looking at the bridge. "Deadly 51, contact."

"Deadly, from the bridge track back west five hundred meters, there's a small bend in the river. Call contact!" The FAC walked our eyes onto his target.

Spike saw it. "Deadly 51, contact."

"Okay, Deadly, in the tree line three hundred meters east is your target. There are thirty plus personnel on the bank and several moving down the back toward the canal. Call wings level." The FAC had wasted no time.

Spike turned the flight south but set us up to run parallel to the canal in an almost northeast direction. It would give us a good view of friendly positions and allow us to pull off to the right toward friendly lines. Any turn to the north was a no-go. It would have us fly right over the city. I wasn't sure what Spike and Cut had encountered in Nasiriyah, but Matt and I had had enough of overflying population centers.

Spike, two thousand meters out, made the call. "Cut, this is a 45-degree attack with a right pull. Ferris, go trail."

Cut gave a quick, "Two."

I followed with, "Three."

"Deadly 51 is wings level." Spike had pushed his nose over.

The green 40-degree field of view though my NVGs revealed the most coherent and pure picture as far as I could remember. The lights from Al-Hay, the stars, and the flashes from the running gun battle on the ground all helped improve the NVGs' performance.

"Matt, master arm is going to arm," came my all-too-familiar call.

I slid slightly to the left and now trailed both Spike and Cut. Cut flew on the left side of 51. We had dropped back about seventy-five meters or so—now serving as the cleanup hitters. We planned to see what Spike and Cut would do to the target and to adjust from either the FAC's corrections or from Spike or Cut's calls. Or do what a dash three does best—any damn thing we wanted!

"Deadly 51 flight, you are cleared hot," came the muffled clearance.

As we rolled in, bolts of light lit up off our right side. A series of thunderclaps followed. Holy shit. What was that? It took a second to register, but then I realized artillery had started firing. These were likely US Marine 155mm howitzer cannons firing into targets either in Al-Hay or further out. I wished someone had briefed us on those guns. The cannon flashes looked close to us, but they were likely several thousand meters to the south. Al-Kut lay thirty miles further north. The 155mm cannons could shoot a long way, but thirty miles was out of the question.

I looked up to see Spike and Hank going hot on the 20mm. The stream of rounds impacted exactly where the FAC had called targets. We watched and waited. The 20mm being fired from the sky must have been terrorizing. Getting shot at by anything is life-changing, but from the sky had to be a new level.

Cut called, "52's in hot." A courtesy call and less a doctrinal requirement, but it built situational awareness for the FAC, Spike, and us.

We flew low, no more than two hundred feet and 120 knots. I finally started to see the target area and noticed a lot of enemy infantry. I didn't know if it was the noise of their own weapons or those sounds combined with the Marines firing at them no more than three hundred meters away, but the Iraqis held their ground. The 20mm run of Spike and Cut continued with industrial efficiency. It created a nightmarish scene. I eased out the power while simultaneously pulling the stick back, and we slowed. I wanted Matt to have time to identify and then track targets on the FLIR.

I pushed the radio. "Five-three's in hot."

Matt pulled the trigger. I could hear the gears of the M-197 turret engage and move the barrels slightly left and down. A flame and the sounds of three-inch projectiles heading down range followed.

Chug. Chug. Chug. Chug. Chug.

We had a long ten-second run. Matt kept the trigger pulled until we hit the mechanical stop more than 90 degrees off the axis of the Cobra's centerline. Rather than watch his impacts, I looked for 51 or 52. It's common for aircraft to accelerate coming off a target, and I needed to find them fast.

Fortunately, I spotted the glowing strip light on the side of 52 and closed in. We had not heard anything from the FAC. I flew south and prepared for the likely second pass. Anticipating that the run would come from the same general direction, I increased power to reduce the gap between us and Spike.

The FAC had another idea. "Five-one flight, can you see what is on the bridge? Looks like the Iraqis have moved a large box or some other kind of obstacle. We are sending up a tank now. Can you look and provide cover?"

Well, the FAC had accomplished some impressive and immediate mission creep. Had he just asked us to observe a bridge obstacle? Not only that, but he'd also implied we should get close enough to identify the obstacle and also maintain a position to support a single tank. I suspected this had already been a plan, and since we had just arrived, he was trying to work us into the solution.

The 25mm cannon fire from LAR and the .50 caliber fire from 1st Recon across the river had slowed after our pass, but rounds continued to fly in both directions. We had barely come out of our turn when Spike saw it all unfolding.

"Five-one flight, the tank is already on the move. Let's roll out about 050, and I'm slowing down for a better look." Spike had a plan, but I was not sure exactly what it was.

I needed Matt to be my eyes. "Matt, do you see what they are talking about? I am coming up on the left side of 51. Tell me if you need the master arm."

"There is definitely a tank moving to the edge of the bridge, and there's more of a barricade on the north side of the bridge than a box, but it's cold and hard to tell." Matt completed an incomplete thought.

We flew in closer. We were no more than five hundred meters away when the tank opened fire. The M1A1 Abrams was a main battle tank that masterfully mixed agility with speed and firepower with sixty tons of steel and armor. The backbone of any US armored formation, it carried a 120mm main gun, a coaxially fired 7.62mm machine gun, a .50 caliber heavy machine gun, and another spare M240 7.62mm machine gun. It was the undisputed king of battle.

I caught the initial flash as it fired the first of several 120mm rounds into the obstacles. The flash, particularly on a moonless night, was spectacular. The flame shot out nearly thirty feet as the German-designed smoothbore gun launched its fifteen-pound projectile at 1,500 meters per second at its target. The initial flame was followed nearly simultaneously by a vertical and horizontal flame of equal distance. The entire tank rocked back as the stabilized gun fired another round and then another into the target.

That immediately caught the eye of the Iraqi defenders. The volume of enemy fires from across the river slowed and then began to concentrate on the tank. The tank crew was prepared; it opened up with its coaxial 7.62mm and what looked like the .50 caliber machine gun located by the tank commander's hatch. We didn't need to see anything else. We could also anticipate what came next as Spike began a turn to the left. He planned to hit the positions firing on the tank. I guessed correctly and began a hard right turn as we crossed the canal into Al-Hay proper.

"Five-one's wings level on the infantry positions on the north side of the canal. We have friendlies in sight." Spike had already turned.

"Five-one flight cleared hot to engage those positions." The sounds of gunfire outside his vehicle nearly drowned out the FAC's transmission.

"Hey, check that out." Matt was almost talking to himself, but I could follow his gaze.

Several vehicles moved toward the canal from the city. Even with the distance and limitations of the NVGs, I could make out a few minivans, a couple of small buses, a trickle of cars, and some SUVs. If this was the calvary, they needed more horses. If they thought they'd come to save the day, any day but today was the day to save. If they thought they would have a chance against US Marines, they needed to read the yet to be written primer titled, "The pros and cons of a frontal assault against armored vehicles, reconnaissance units, mortars, tanks, and attack helicopters."

Through Matt's FLIR and my NVGs, it seemed obvious that none of these Fedayeen Saddam loyalists, jihadists, zealots, foreign adventurists, or Iraqi nationalists would pen any new ideas soon. Truth was, that would be the last night on earth for most of them.

We had to respect their heroic effort, but it was apparent someone had sent them as fodder or as a diversion. In the Corps, we often say of mistakes, "good initiative, bad judgment."

That particular group of about fifty moved as a mob and had clearly made an unrecoverable mistake in judgment. As the car doors opened, they ejected dozens of armed personnel, all on a slow jog to the edge of the river. Even a casual observer could tell they had no plan. These were likely untrained young men recently handed AK-47s and a promise of glory. The trained forces were likely holed up with ambushes prepared and with mortars and heavy machine guns zeroed onto the city's streets and choke points. These were streets that Marines would soon explore.

Our first pass put us close enough to see more than we needed. This became the first time Matt and I engaged infantry at such close range. It was also our first time flying as a dash three. It gave us time to see the impacts and effects of both 51 and 52. The 20mm rounds were simply devastating. Each was a cold, faceless, uncalculating, and relentless phantom. Under the right trigger finger, the rounds may be best described as a hangman's noose. There was simply no escape. No compassion, no clemency, no charity.

The time between when the rounds left the barrel and when they impacted their targets was measured in milliseconds. The devastation was immediate and irreversible. The human body was never designed to endure, much less recover from, the influence of 20mm rounds. The rockets carried a stronger message.

I could only imagine what Matt was seeing. After 51 and 52 had pulled off target, the twenty plus human heat signatures on his FLIR had become forty—maybe sixty or more. They were splashes of heat painted into his FLIR. As we pressed closer, and in the blink of an eye, those splashes again transformed. Each one became smaller, rapidly extinguishing. Like a dying battery that powered a fading light, except these were lives.

I had previously thought of us as repo men, debt collectors, or sheep dogs, but maybe we should aim a bit higher—spread our wings so to speak. I liked being the hunter instead of the hunted. Maybe it was time for a new title.

"Five-one, you are cleared hot." Was that for me? The crackle of the radio snapped me out of my daydream.

I called to Matt. "Matt, master arm is going to arm. You seeing leads hits?"

I looked at Spike's Cobra flying at my ten o'clock position. The flash from his right wing stub had nearly cleared. He had rippled a full pod of 2.75-inch rockets directly into the formation of the doomed. The first impacts only confirmed what we all knew—Hank was on the FLIR and had opened up with the 20mm cannon. It began to burp a few rounds to the left and then a few more off the nose but then vomited a long and lazy stream of 20mm into the same position.

Never mind the abyss that was our target. The attackers tried to cover their movements in tall grass and shrubbery. Unfortunately for them, their attempts to mask any movement proved pointless.

I waited for Spike to make his turn.

Shit, was he pulling off the target left? Or did he call right pull?

We remained in position to either shoot right or left. As a matter of fact, I couldn't remember which way he had called the attack. Or maybe he hadn't called the pull-off direction at all. In that case, I really liked his style. Knowing that Spike was a cagey and seasoned leader, I believed my second thought was more likely. I felt privileged to have experienced a firsthand and intimate look into the workings of Spike's team.

I pulled the Cobra left to move into position and felt that alarming twinge in my right foot. It began to shake uncontrollably. I tried to flex my leg muscles to tell my errant foot that I was in charge, but it was clearly disobeying my physical and mental commands.

After a slight pause, Spike almost conversationally transmitted, "51's coming off right."

Cut and Chief rolled onto the target next. Matt and I saw the rockets spit out from Cut's right wing. Those rockets headed toward the spot where Spike's rockets had impacted and where Hank, from Spike's front seat, continued delivering 20mm fire.

At the same time, we heard Cut. "Five-two's in hot."

Cut delivered his 2.75-inch rockets into the same position, but it looked like Chief had shifted his fires to the northwest a few meters. I took this as an opportunity to apply more power, gently pull the nose up, and simultaneously add a bit of left rudder with additional left stick. That combination of control inputs allowed me and Matt to climb above both Cobras while essentially sliding from the right side of the formation to the left side, putting us into a position to cover Spike's and Cut's pull to the right and to engage.

"Five-three's in hot," I called as we headed northeast with the canal almost parallel to our run-in.

I had armed the weapons, and with Matt putting a laser onto a second grouping, I selected my nineteen-shot pod of 2.75-inch rockets. I didn't want to ripple those since they were all we had left. So, I selected singles. That meant I had to mash the thumb trigger each time I wanted a rocket to fire. This was time consuming, but at these ranges, I could make immediate corrections. Plus, I wouldn't run out of rockets on only two passes.

Our ability to not only engage the enemy but to remain on station in between engagements had a quality all its own. Whatever axiom you prefer, our availability was now one of our best abilities. Even the sound of Cobras had become a weapon. The distinctive rumble of the AH-1W's main rotors was unmistakable. That sound was its own "it" factor. The deep thump of the main rotors only needed to be associated once with the firepower it carried to terrify any man at any time and in any place.

The distinct two-per-revolution beat of forty-eight feet of rotor blade would conjure images of destruction, evoke feelings of despair or elation, trigger vivid recollections, and revive once dormant memories. Those Marines who saw and heard us deliver 2.75-inch rockets and 20mm cannon fire above their heads knew it. And for those few Iraqis who would survive the night, they would never forget it.

"Come left. Good hit. Up, up… Good hit. I'm going hot." Matt watched my impacts, making corrections, and then started firing the cannon.

Once he started firing, it caused "rocket lockout," meaning an electronic signal sent from the activation of the gun to the main weapons systems stopped me from shooting any more rockets. This provided a safety measure to prevent 20mm rounds from hitting rockets only feet in front of the helicopter.

We had begun our run only a few seconds after Cut had made his right turn to the south, and it felt liberating to fly alone for a few seconds. I had almost forgotten about the Marine LAVs aligned on one side of the canal. Both the Marines from LAR and 1st Recon delivered a continuous stream of 25mm and 7.62mm fire as we engaged the advancing infantry on the other side of the canal.

As we pulled off target, I looked left and was given a clear picture of the enemy's dilemma from across the river. It was more chaotic than I'd imagined. There were plumes of smoke coming from a dozen burning enemy vehicles. There were still other vehicles fully engulfed in flames and buildings smoldering from the telltale signs of a long-running firefight. Whatever Iraqi forces remained had made a run for the city. As Spike called the FAC, he reported our BDA and then checked the flight off station. It was time for a break.

CHAPTER 29

Location: Coors Field, Iraq
Date: 02APR03
Time: 0030L

On our final pass in Al-Hay, we'd fired the remaining 20mm and 2.75-inch rockets into several additional vehicles to the east side of the canal. With six hundred rounds of 20mm and twenty-six rockets expended, we were empty. Well, almost.

We had landed and shut down to debrief the events of the past two hours. Matt and I had whipped BUNO 160822 all the way back into Coors. We had used and abused this helicopter for more than seven hours, and she'd never flinched or faltered.

Coors didn't have aviation ordnance, so we refueled and talked about options with Spike. Combined, we still had twenty-four Hellfire and TOW missiles, so we were more than capable of another sortie or two, but eventually, we needed to get to Riverfront for more ordnance.

Sky Chief didn't have any immediate work for us, so we opened the ammunition bay doors and sat down. I carried a green nylon helmet bag in my tail boom. It contained the standard spare batteries, poncho, extra chem lights, imported Italian salami, crackers, and water. The specialty food was from my dad. What he had sent me was a favorite. We spent the next half hour just bullshitting and sharing some crackers and salami in the Iraqi desert.

The early morning gave way to a final sortie. Spike had reached out to Sky Chief for any possible work. We hadn't seen that before. Our section generally remained well tasked and gainfully employed. When we weren't, we took the time to catch a quick nap or plan for our next mission. This was different. Spike actively looked to push the fight north.

We had heard about several west coast sections pushing way out in front. Referred to as DAS, these missions operated beyond the support of friendly fires or the fire support coordination line (FSCL). We needed to coordinate any fires inside of the FSCL with ground and other aviation units. Fires beyond it didn't require that level of coordination.

Fixed-wing attack aircraft commonly conducted DAS missions, but rotary-wing aircraft rarely flew them. Though we'd planned and executed DAS missions at MAWTS-1, those weapons school missions had focused on a single deep target. That was fundamentally different from asking or trolling for enemy formations. Some of the risks associated with a DAS mission cannot be mitigated. The obvious risks include one or both Cobras being either shot down or forced to land. Lack of fuel and ordnance and lack of airspace awareness were also serious considerations. Other risks were the countless unmarked towers, wires, and antennas throughout the country.

DAS also put the onus on those flight leads to know every—and I mean every—potential friendly unit operating beyond the FSCL. Just as the night's Special Operations Command mission into Nasiriyah remained unknown to most everyone not involved in the operation, US Army and Navy special operators likely conducted deep reconnaissance. Just as likely, Marine Cobra crews operating deep had no idea those units were out there and had no idea what types of vehicles they operated.

The friendly fire incident on the 20th of March and the disgusted feeling I experienced hearing the calls from those on the ground stayed fresh in my mind. The last risk required the inevitable recovery or rescue effort should we be killed or captured operating well beyond friendly lines. That was actually the only risk that concerned me—putting Marines and sailors unnecessarily in harm's way.

Sky Chief had work for Spike and Deadly 51's flight of three. The mission called for us to push north and conduct reconnaissance along Highway 1. It seemed an odd request since we had supported RCT-1 closer to Al-Hay along Highway 7. Sky Chief had to know we had a strong familiarity with that area. This meant new territory for the squadron; we had yet to send aircraft this far north before.

Spike kept the plan simple. We'd push north for thirty minutes, looking and recording anything of value. We would keep Highway 1 to our west and use our three sensors to scan for pretty much anything of interest. The city of Ad Diwaniyah would mark the hard stop point. To the west of Diwaniyah, connected by a twenty-five-mile road, lay the city of Najaf, and then it was only one hundred more miles to Baghdad. Though fixed-wing strike aircraft and heavy bombers had made the flight over those same skies, they'd had the sanctuary of both speed and altitude.

The Cobra and Huey were limited to about three hundred miles of range. We did have the option of mounting an external fuel tank, but that would add significant weight and remove one of the four stations that carried ordnance. The Huey had an internal fuel bladder, and filling that would have the same effect. On the other hand, our fixed-wing brothers and sisters could fly the A-10s and Harriers much further. They could range out to eight or nine hundred miles on a single tank of gas. They also had the ability to aerial refuel or simply stay at a high altitude and fly a fuel-conserving profile.

There were US forces somewhere out here—we just didn't know where. Additionally, the US Army 3rd ID had long begun their run to Baghdad. Though their push had been through the open western desert, their AH-64 Apaches had previously taken a beating over these same skies of Karbala on the 24th of March, even though Karbala was another fifty miles to the north. The ten-thousand-man-strong 2nd Medinah Armored Division, a division of the 1st Republican Guard Corps, protected the city and outlying areas.

If Spike had any concerns, I couldn't tell. We had good weather, or as good as any we'd had to date. We experienced a low scattered layer of clouds, but otherwise, excellent starlight and a defined horizon made flying less fatiguing. The flight of three advanced in a combat spread formation, flying almost three abreast. We covered almost half a mile of open sky with our sensor trained to the east. Spike and Cut focused on the road and anything to the west.

The trip north was uneventful, and like the turnaround point of a road race, we made our turn back to the south as we passed just to the north of Diwaniyah. At 130 knots, we would make the trip to Riverfront in about thirty-five minutes.

By 0300L on the 2nd of April, we had finally touched back down at Riverfront. It hadn't been our longest day, but the nine hours of flight time had seemed endless. We had a lot to digest and still more to plan for.

Buss and Rosie, still stranded at Fenway, were waiting for delivery of their parts and for their Cobra to be repaired. Disappointed, but not discouraged, we expected to have them back later in the day.

Spike and Cut returned to a flight of two. That was my only chance to fly with Spike in combat, but I took away some valuable lessons. Rarely had any of our WTIs and senior flight leaders had an opportunity to fly with our XO or CO. Our instructor pilots and flight leaders needed to fly with our less experienced crews. Truth was, I rarely ever flew with anyone except junior officers who needed a check ride or a new qualification. So, the time with Spike and Cut had provided an unexpected bonus.

In aviation, particularly in attack aviation, we often have too much unhealthy bravado and bullshitting of one another. However, last night's and this morning's flights had reinforced the value of simple and straightforward leadership. Spike kept it simple on every mission. We had no unnecessary communications, no complex attacks, and no inflight micromanagement of anyone or anything. He was all business but led in such a way that never made anyone feel anything but invaluable. I would have flown off his wing any day or any night.

It made me realize just how much talent the squadron had. Matt and I had seen a tightly knit team, as tight as any. It also reminded me how much I needed to get my team back together, but that would have to wait at least another day.

With no wingman, Matt and I became free agents. We were flying again later today, attached to another flight but not as the lead. Anything else would have seemed like the CO or XO had sent us to observe. It would have signaled that the flight lead was somehow deficient.

Matt and I went through our post-flight ritual before heading for our tents for some sleep. However, I took a short detour into maintenance.

Master Sergeant Jim Quirk greeted me. The clock showed five in the morning, and the senior NCO in our maintenance department looked like he had been up for hours. In the past two weeks, Jim had changed from what he had been into something we'd all hoped he would be. That wasn't a value judgment but simply an observation. Now, he was more metered and calmer. He remained the engaged leader he was meant to be, and I think he knew it. He wasn't part of the problem, and he didn't create problems; rather, he solved problems.

"Hey, Top. How's it going this morning?" I may have caught him off guard.

He responded before even turning around. "Major, how was it out there tonight?"

"Easy lift tonight. How are we looking for today's schedule?" I had generally left him alone the past few weeks, but even light chatter was good.

"Today and tonight's another surge schedule, but we are looking good. There is a Shitter coming in later with parts. We are also finding space for the 263 det," he said plainly.

"Thanks. Let me know if I need to talk with anyone about 263. I'm headed for some sleep." With that, I exited the tent and began a trek to operations.

When he'd said "263," he'd been referencing the "Thunder Chickens" of HMM 263 arriving with the 24th MEU aboard the USS *Nassau*. The MEU was scheduled to return home, but after the events in Nasiriyah and other perceived setbacks, more US forces had flowed into the theater.

I knew both the CO, Lieutenant Colonel Jay "Yoda" Kennedy, and his XO, Major Karsten "Hazel" Heckl, of 263. I had deployed with both of them, and it was beginning to feel like an old home week. HMM 263 would add additional Cobras, Hueys, Phrogs, CH-53Es and six AV-8B Harriers to the fight.

The detachment of Cobras and Hueys had originally come from 269 and had been assigned to 263. Both units normally reported to MAG 29 and Boomer. But for the last year, they'd fallen under the command of the 24th MEU. Even with 263 under the umbrella of the MEU, Boomer still had influence. Senior leaders had made the decision to bring the detachment ashore and operate alongside 269. It seemed an easy plan on paper, but things were never easy.

We were doing our best to integrate their flight crews and aircraft into the flight schedules. Our crews had been well established, and no one wanted to give up their seats or any missions, even to old friends and former squadron mates. I had sat down with our CO, Spike, and the 263 detachment officer in charge of the Cobras and Hueys, Major Jim "Jinx" Jenkins, to find an acceptable compromise. We planned for 263 Cobra and Huey crews to fly off the wing of 269 crews. It was not as though we thought the 263 crews were either unprepared or unqualified. On the contrary, they had an exceptional bench full of talent with callsigns like Chet, Fluffer, Opie, K-9, Hairball, 2Bit, and Babs.

The issue revolved around risk. Believe it or not, the past two weeks had given our crews insights and experiences that often took years to develop. We agreed the best and fastest way to assimilate the new crews was to fly them as wingmen. It gave them a chance to watch, listen, and ask questions. We would need everyone and every Cobra soon enough.

Jim went by the callsign of Jinx and was also a Cobra pilot. We had been friends for over ten years. We'd played basketball and hockey together on squadron teams, and I considered him one of the few people in my absolute "circle of trust." The former Cornell University wrestler had the additional stress of being the operations officer for 263. Jinx, as a former MAWTS-1 instructor pilot, came well prepared for the job. He'd already achieved worldwide notoriety while piloting a Cobra in the fall of 1995. The understated and humble Colorado native had flown as the armed escort with the CH-53Es who had rescued downed USAF pilot Scott O'Grady in Bosnia.

Exhausted and bleary eyed, I walked into operations. There, I saw the plan for our launch later that evening. Matt and I would join Howdy and Flash as guest members of their flight. I liked the idea of getting portions of the band back together for at least a one-night show.

The duty lieutenant also let us know that the CASEVAC Phrog from 162, Wombat 57, had made it back to the trauma unit some hours ago, and the wounded Marine from Coors was stable and on his way to Kuwait. Fuzzy and his crew had also done the improbable. I could barely remember that portion of the night; it seemed like days ago.

A bit further north at Tallil Air Base, west of An-Nasiriyah, Sweet Pea and his flight of six Phrogs from HMM 165 had landed. They had successfully supported the insertion and extraction of the US Army Ranger security force. The larger mission to rescue US Army Private Jessica Lynch, along with recovering the remains of other soldiers, had gone almost exactly to plan. The story of the 507th Maintenance Company would continue, but one chapter had officially closed in Nasiriyah. As for the other missing soldiers of the 507th? Their saga continued; they remained in captivity somewhere in the vast Iraqi military network.

We considered the mission of the Special Operations Joint Task Force a success. With the support of Marine aviation units, the mission had been led and executed by the 160th Special Operations Aviation Regiment. The "Night Stalkers" seemed to be everywhere but also nowhere in Iraq. The secretive and ultra-talented helicopter unit had once again done the unthinkable and seemingly impossible.

It would take a few more days to hear more details of the mission, but we only cared that Americans had been rescued or recovered. Airmen, soldiers, Marines, sailors, and other government agencies had pooled their best and brightest planners, leaders, and operators to pull off an amazing feat. If it had been another place or another time, the mission would have garnered more attention, but there were still a thousand Marines and sailors, along with another two hundred thousand soldiers, airmen, and allies, flowing into and up the major highways of Iraq. Their story would have to take place in line.

CHAPTER 30

Location: Al-Kut, Iraq
Date: 03APR03
Time: 0230L

We had just completed our third of three sorties for the night. We'd provided support for the 1st Marines, and the push into Al-Kut was on. We'd stayed well short of the city's outskirts, and we had spent most of the night clearing potential enemy positions.

Howdy rechecked the flight. "Deadly 13, flight check."

Flash and Country were on it. "Two."

Matt responded, "Three."

RCT-1 had pushed through Al-Hay, and the Marines of 1st Reconnaissance Battalion had led the charge. Inside one of the lightly armored Humvees of 1st Recon rode Evan Wright. Evan, on assignment from *Rolling Stone* magazine, numbered one of the nearly eight hundred embedded reporters and photographers with US forces. Evan would record, recount, and recall his crazed and wacky adventures with the heroes and perceived villains of the 1st Reconnaissance Battalion. He highlighted his remarkable experiences and viewpoint in his critically acclaimed work, *Generation Kill*, later turned into a hit HBO mini-series.

Al Hay, by Marine Corps maneuver warfare standards, was a surface and a gap. It was both an enemy strong point and a soft point. The city defenders blocked RCT-1's ability to bypass Al-Hay by denying access to the main bridge.

Choke points like the bridge leading into Al-Hay put the Marine Corps concepts of maneuver warfare to the test. The ideas inherent in maneuver warfare call for bypassing enemy strongholds and, instead, attacking them from the rear or where they are most vulnerable. Very Sun Tzu. Those are great war college debates, but sometimes, you need to go head on into a surface to create the gap. This could be a physical gap between enemy units. It could also be a disruption of the enemy's timing or ability to work together. In the case of Al-Hay, RCT-1 needed to get over the bridge and exploit their speed advantage along Highway 7 into the division's primary target of Al-Kut.

Howdy called it a night. "One-three flight, we are coming right. Nothing here, and nothing more expected from Sky Chief. We are turning south and heading back toward Riverfront."

Click, click came from Flash, and I followed with the same.

We'd had a quiet night, and Matt and I had spent a good deal of time chatting about a lot of nothing, but our confidence had silently risen throughout the entire flight. We had not flown with Howdy in nearly two weeks, and the feeling of absolute dread had finally left. Maybe, in part, the better weather had influenced that. Maybe the slowly improving NVG conditions had helped as well. Perhaps getting another chance to fly wing off Howdy and Flash had made a difference. Maybe the forty plus hours of NVG time over the previous thirteen nights had finally gotten us up to par. I couldn't put a finger on it, but we all could feel a sense of calm and familiarity. That said, we had been lulled into this before. Before the first night. Before Nasiriyah. Before Fenway and Al-Hay.

We put Highway 7 on our nose and headed south. The one-hundred-mile flight took us to the east of Nasiriyah. The few lights had grown. Even since last night, the city showed more signs of normalcy. It was changing, seemingly waking up from what had been a two-week slumber. We had captured the commanding general of the 11th Infantry Division, and Marine infantry patrols continued to root out the remaining Fedayeen.

Location: Riverfront – Jalibah, Iraq
Date: 04APR03
Time: 1230L

Buss and Rosie had finally escaped Fenway and flown back to Riverfront but felt trapped. They had spent the last two days pacing like caged tigers at the zoo. Our section had been kept off the flight schedule yesterday. That had provided us with less than a day off but had given me a chance to do my job as the maintenance officer. It had been good to spend time on the flight line catching up with Marines, with Monty, and with our senior NCOs. It didn't take but a few conversations to take the pulse of the entire maintenance department. It also gave me an opportunity to fly a few maintenance flights.

I had always enjoyed flying maintenance flights aka test hops. As one of several qualified maintenance check pilots, I was responsible for ensuring whatever maintenance had been performed on the Cobra met an exacting standard. Check pilots would fly the aircraft and measure specific performance parameters. I had earned that qualification as a lieutenant and found it to be one of the more rewarding ones. It forced me to become an expert in every system on the Cobra, and it was the same for our Huey maintenance pilots. We considered it both a privilege and a responsibility.

The flight schedule had picked up. We flew an average of eighteen of our remaining twenty-six Cobras and Hueys per day. The speed of the MEF's advance also challenged us. It became clear that Boomer planned to move MAG 29 to a base deeper into Iraq. Even though the other flying air groups still operated from bases in Kuwait, Boomer and his staff were rightly thinking of ways to generate more combat sorties and cut the response time to Marine ground units.

Riverfront had more than doubled in size over the past week. All the 24th MEU's helicopters from HMM 263 now sat somewhere on the flight line, and we had additional aircraft arriving every day. The 15th MEU had also come ashore and had been reassigned to the MEF. The 15th MEU had been initially assigned to the United

Kingdom's 3rd Commando Brigade, and they had participated in combat operations since the opening night. The two-thousand-strong MEU had recently pushed north into Nasiriyah to relieve Task Force Tarawa. All those aircraft also needed a place to bed down.

Matt, Buss, and Rosie went through the details of tonight's mission. Matt and I had enjoyed our first day off since the 20th of March, and as much as I appreciated the time with Monty and our maintenance Marines, I wanted to get back at it.

Our mission was to push north and be prepared to support the 1st MARDIV's push toward Baghdad from the east. The reports from MAG 39 and 3rd MAW were less than encouraging. Throughout the morning and early afternoon, no fewer than eight Cobras had incurred damage with enemy fire forcing down two of them. Fortunately, those crews had all survived, but many of those aircraft would be out of the fight for weeks or months.

"Sky Chief, Deadly 43, mission number 7043." We got checked in and expected them to push us further north.

Sky Chief was ready for us, "Deadly 43, be advised there are reports of heavy small arms and RPG fire along Highway 6. You are cleared to switch to maroon."

"Matt, will you check us in and put RCT-5's last position in the GPS? I'm going to push us to the west of Highway 6." I wanted to get us out of the expected flight path.

The sun had just set, and we only had about another half hour of flight time before we needed to go to a new FARP—Qualcomm, which was located south of Baghdad and Karbala. Matt had checked us in with the FAC, and we were trying to get a good turnover from him.

The Iraqis, as expected, had put up a formidable defense along one of the few major highways that led into the capital. We noticed dozens of small teams of defenders on each side of Highway 6. They used the "shoot and scoot" approach on advancing armor but also effectively engaged lightly armored Humvees and other supply vehicles with RPGs and heavy machine guns. Additionally, they lit fires on both sides of the road to obscure our visibility and provide themselves cover as they moved.

We had just settled into a ten-minute calm when we heard it. "Break right, break right." Buss had seen it way before I had.

At five hundred feet and 130 knots, I pulled power and rolled into a steep turn away from the stream of tracers that seemed to be following us. I thought if we avoided flying over the highway, we could at least avoid fire from both directions. Still twenty miles south of Baghdad, we saw only houses—no major buildings. Single-story homes and associated fenced or walled courtyards dotted both sides of the highway.

As I continued to shift right, completing a near 360-degree turn, I felt a slight shiver of cold sweat start to form again. Any tracer fire is concerning, but with this fire several hundred meters to our six o'clock, it was less a direct threat and more of a taunt. Only after reflecting on the past few missions did I understand the immediate and guttural response to tracer fire was not only unhealthy but was dangerous. These same and potentially underestimated Iraqi gunners were likely attempting to pull us in lower. Lower to look, lower to seek revenge, and lower to make ourselves an easy target for a much larger weapon.

Despite the potential trap, we were going to take a look and get lower. I had an obligation to conduct reconnaissance to ensure there were no enemy units filling in behind our advancing forces. The simple fact was that we had a mission, and we were going to do it.

"Buss, can you put your IR laser on where you saw that? I'm rolling out about 340. Let's plan to stay high and use the gun." I felt the familiar rush of adrenaline and, simultaneously, felt a knot form in my stomach. I could tell that Matt was ready.

He knew what I would say. "Matt, master arm is going to arm. It's all you, but let's be careful. There's a shitload of houses out there."

Click. Click.

We came out of the turn. The sun had gone below the horizon, and we were still another ten minutes from putting on the NVGs. This was a bad time of day for both the NVGs and the FLIR. It was too bright for the NVGs and too dark to not use them. Plus, we were flying through another 100-degree day. The sun had heated everything. Houses, cars, the highway, rocks, and people were all basically the same temperature. It would take hours for everything not human to cool down enough to quickly pick out targets on the FLIR. Lastly, we had been engaged from our six o'clock position while heading west. We had essentially sky lined ourselves, and that needed to change.

"Matt, you see anything yet?" I knew someone lurked out there.

Matt looked at the FLIR. "I am not seeing anything."

I had seen enough to know we needed to head to Qualcomm and let the night come to us. Right now, we were at a disadvantage. Plus, RCT-5 didn't have any immediate work for us.

I made the call. "Four-four, we're gonna mark the position of the lead LAVs, and then we are outta here to head to Qualcomm. We can't find those shooters from here."

Click. Click.

Buss and Rosie crossed over to our right side. I turned around and headed north. In no more than ten minutes, we found the lead elements of the "Highlanders" of 1st LAR and the tanks of the 2nd Tank Battalion. We knew our support for RCT-5 and the elements of 1st LAR were important, especially as they had pushed to just outside of Baghdad. In fact, RCT-5 had spent yesterday pushing the Iraqi Special Republican Guard's Al Nida Division off Highway 6. Supported by units of the 2nd Tank Battalion, RCT-5 had engaged thousands of determined defenders. Now, they were only a few miles south of the Salman Pak Airfield. Intelligence showed Salman Pak as a suspected training camp and a potential location of chemical weapons.

"Four-four, I see LAVs off the nose. I'm going down for a closer look. Call out any obstacles you see." I released the radio and pushed the nose over.

Click. Click.

This was not exactly a "motivational pass" but more an overflight to let those Marines out on the pointiest end of the spear know that we had arrived. I pulled more power, 100 percent torque, as we dropped out of the dark to three hundred feet and close to 140 knots. We both picked out what we thought was the center point of the LAR formations and overflew them. Then, we came off hard to the right in a climb and made the turn for Qualcomm.

Sergeant Mike McGuire looked up from the commander's seat in his LAV-25 and wondered where those Cobras had come from. The twenty-one-year-old vehicle commander and section leader could only guess. He and his two vehicles had held the left flank of RCT-5 for more than six hours. They had actively engaged, with increasing frequency, a seemingly endless number of fighters throughout the day from across sideroads, the Tigris River, and an expanding crowd of canals.

A proud member of the Camdenton High School "Lakers" class of 2000, Mike had done what thousands of adventurous high school graduates do every year. He had driven to the local recruiting office, listened to their pitches, weighed the pros and cons, and said yes to the Marine Corps.

Mike had left the quintessentially rustic and neighborly community of Camdenton, Missouri, a town of less than four thousand tucked into the southern tip of the Lake of the Ozarks, for adventure. It was clear he wasn't in Camdenton anymore and clear the adventure had found him.

He had seen and experienced everything since arriving in Kuwait in January. He and his tight-knit section of LAV-25s had rolled through the breaches near Safwan. They had seen the destruction and carnage in Nasiriyah, endured an epic sandstorm, and engaged multiple Iraqi units at unknown locations over the past two weeks. He had led when asked to lead and followed when ordered to follow. Tonight, they held their position but prepared for tomorrow's eventual advance on another unknown suburb, another unpredictable borough, another fickle edge town whose unknown loyalties determined the residents' fight-or-flight response. All this led to the eventual push into another major city: Baghdad.

From there was only a guess. After Baghdad, where was it? Kirkuk? Mosul? Fallujah? No one knew. They only had rumors. If the twenty-one-year-old sergeant thought the thirty-six-year-old major who had just flown over his head knew, he would be mistaken.

We would see each other again. Neither of us knew it, but we would rejoin in a few weeks to push deep into the Sunni Triangle and into Saddam Hussein's hometown of Tikrit—as part of an air ground unit called Task Force Tripoli.

The flight into Qualcomm was remarkably routine. The FARP teams had improved with each new expeditionary refueling and ordnance station. Truly incredible. The flow of arriving and departing traffic was better. The marking of the landing spots became more defined. As we flew further north, the climate and topography worked to our advantage. The bleak water-restricted southern provinces of Iraq suffered from near constant blowing sands. As we flew north, the blowing sands and open desert were gradually replaced by green fields and orchards accented by trees, brush, and farmland. We landed at Qualcomm without the normal sand or brownout.

We shut down to refuel and had an hour before Sky Chief expected us to be airborne. So, the four of us met at the nose of my Cobra and game planned the next six hours. First, we needed a simple strategy to minimize our obvious exposure flying over Highway 6. This was less about the ground fire we'd just taken and more about the eight damaged Cobras that were either loaded onto flatbed trucks headed south or shut down at FARPs throughout the country. Secondly, we needed to ensure we remained in a position to support the now defensively postured units of the 1st MARDIV. Lastly, we needed to have a plan to conduct reconnaissance closer to Baghdad and to the flanks of the division.

We made the decision to increase our altitude from the normal three to five hundred feet to a lofty one thousand feet. That would give us better visibility, better reaction time, and clearance over most of the unmarked wires, radio and microwave towers, and other obstacles that had begun to appear randomly.

"Sky Chief, Deadly 43 off of Qualcomm." I checked us in as we took up a position flying southwest of Highway 6 headed in a northwestern direction.

Sky Chief didn't really have a plan for us. He passed us a ten-digit grid that represented the furthest units of the division. The assigned mission involved armed reconnaissance but shaped up to be something different. Off our left wing was the Tigris River, and flying closer to the river allowed us to look at both sides of the highway while keeping a less populated area below us. RCT-5 was still further up Highway 6, and they, along with RCT-7, had marked vehicles with NVG visible glint tape. I looked below, and through the grainy green hue of the NVGs, I began to see vehicles to my right. We were again passing over the defensively aligned armored vehicles of 1st LAR. We continued northwest.

I saw endless miles of suburban sprawl followed by the outline of Baghdad. I didn't relish flying over the nation's capital, a major metropolitan area with nearly six million residents and tens of thousands of Iraqi armored, mechanized, air defense, and infantry units. Even from that distance, we could see continuous streams of tracer fire. The US Army had pushed their 3rd ID onto the outskirts of Baghdad from the west, and USAF, US Marine, US Navy, and coalition fixed-wing aircraft continued to pound targets around the city.

We also had no way of predicting how many foreign fighters had made their way across the porous Syrian border. Saddam Hussein himself and his entire government would not give up easily. Hussein had grossly underestimated the resolve of the Americans and the coalition leadership. His regime was at stake. He had put the survival of everything he'd spent generations building at risk. I suspected he would be as ruthless defending his regime as he had been building and maintaining it.

I certainly didn't know Saddam Hussein. Few Western outsiders had ever met him. I had never studied him or made an effort to discover anything beneath the veneer of the man. His life and his family were of little consequence to me. He had brought me here, and the Ghost had followed. He had brought us *all* here, and for what? He was an arrogant, abrasive, and abusive tyrant. The international pariah had likely tortured, hung, terrorized, and starved his last innocent countryman or perceived political rival. Change was coming—change had already come.

"Matt, can you see enough from here?" I asked.

"Yup. I got a good picture on the FLIR and can see both sides of the road. There's nothing moving. There's nothing moving anywhere," Matt responded. His voice projected a calmness, a matter-of-factness that I didn't quite understand. I could see well enough on the NVGs, but there was Baghdad out there. We had all seen the video clips of literal walls of AAA fire blanketing the sky. If this was the land of Oz, then Baghdad was the Emerald City, a place no one wanted to be.

The further north we went, the more cultural lighting we saw. We also heard other Cobra flights checking in and out with Sky Chief. MAG 39 flights worked to the west and to the north of us. We always expected other flights of Marine helicopters to operate in our area. However, that presented a problem since we didn't always know where they flew, and with no formal deconfliction procedures, we counted on the practice of "see and avoid."

Normally, we would have rules that pushed helicopters to fly at specific altitudes and along predetermined routes to prevent midair collisions. Those rules didn't exist here. We didn't have a Navy E-2C Hawkeye or an equivalently equipped aircraft dedicated to ensuring our airborne safety. So, along with "see and avoid," we counted on Sky Chief to maintain awareness of where we and other flights of Hueys, Cobras, Phrogs, or CH-53s flew. Sky Chief didn't have a radar, so it was up to the senior aviators flying in the back of the KC-130 to plot out positions, listen to our updates, and try to keep us aware of potential dangers. So, I was sure to pass Sky Chief our location and altitude.

Time crept by, and one hour turned into two.

"Four-three, we are bingo." Buss and Rosie were ready to head back to Qualcomm.

I had flown slower than normal, more of a maximum endurance profile since Qualcomm sat comparatively close to Baghdad.

"Sky Chief, Dead 43's bingo. Nothing significant to report. We will be back on station in about an hour." I got the feeling that tonight was going to be a bust. "Four-three flight, let's plan to land from the east. Go trail." I made the call to Buss and followed it up with another call to Qualcomm.

The shutdown and refueling went just like usual. The air had cooled, not significantly but noticeably. It also had a heaviness compared to the south and came with a hint of humidity. The fuel stop went quickly, and we prepared to head back north. "Four-three check."

"Two," came from Buss.

I settled back into the cockpit and rolled the throttles to 100 percent. The rotor blades followed and began their familiar *thump, thump, thump.* Next, I heard an unfamiliar voice. It had clearly come from a helicopter, and from the familiar background noise, it had likely come from another Cobra.

The pilot stated, "Qualcomm, Phaser 31 is a flight of three five miles to the west for landing. We just lost our dash three."

We were in no rush. I called Buss. "Four-four, we are going to wait for these guys to land before we take off."

Click. Click.

"Matt, what did he say? Did he say he lost his dash three?" I became curious.

I saw the lead Cobra land to my left about fifty meters away from us. It was a flight of three Cobras, and based on the Phaser callsign, they were from HMLA 267. I waited until all three had landed before I called the lead Cobra back.

"Phaser, say again your last? We are headed back north to Grizzly. Do you have anything to pass?" I waited a few seconds.

"Deadly, my dash three hit wires or a tower. He is down. Stand by to copy a grid." The voice, calm and businesslike, communicated something that was anything but.

"Send the grid." I was not sure what else to ask.

I immediately got that sinking feeling again, and my right foot began to twitch just enough to remind me that something was terribly wrong. Was his dash three in a field waiting for a pickup? Did Sky Chief know? Was someone sending ground vehicles?

He sent us the grid, and Matt and Rosie both plotted the location in the town of Al-Aziziyah close to where the 1st MARDIV had set up a forward CP.

I needed some more information. "Does Sky Chief know, and was there any communication with them on the ground?"

"They didn't land—they crashed. I told Sky Chief." Those were his last words to us. Only silence followed.

Everyone listening to our brief conversation realized that they had offered all the information they had, and we wouldn't get any more at the moment. We planned to do whatever we could with whatever we had. We had not prepared for that or trained for it, but the shooting war would have to take a temporary backseat.

"Four-four, we are going to take off and roll out one two zero and then turn direct. We are going to climb to one thousand feet. Call on board." I released the radio.

Click. Click.

I needed to hear what Sky Chief knew or had planned. "Sky Chief, Deadly 43 is off Qualcomm and inbound to assume on-scene commander."

There was no response from Sky Chief. We reached a position only about fifteen minutes from the last known location of their dash three. Again, we knew they belonged to MAG 39, and we knew from the callsign that it was a Cobra assigned to HMLA 267, the Stingers—the same squadron and likely some of the same crews that had flown the border post missile strikes on the opening night, engaged targets in Nasiriyah, and supported the fight in all places in between.

HMLA 267 was one of our sister squadrons and had arrived in theater about the same time as 269 but aboard US Navy amphibious ships from California. Their CO was a forty-something Cranston, Rhode Island, native who had grown up in a strong catholic family of eight. Lieutenant Colonel Steve "Woodman" Heywood had taken command of 267 in the fall of 2002 and brought his twenty-seven aircraft and nearly four hundred Marines and sailors across the globe.

Woodman had moved to southern California as a high school senior. With a strong work ethic passed down from his mother and father, he had worked his way through college. He, like so many others, began a career in the Marine Corps after a fateful meeting with a Marine recruiter. Though he had spent most of his career in California, Woodman clearly had an adventurer's spirit. I believe a nomadic gene festers deep in every Marine, and Woodman was no different. He had deployed across Asia and the Pacific, had been an exchange pilot with the British Royal Marines, and was now finally in command of an HMLA.

As a WTI and experienced flight lead, he would lead from the front. He'd led a division through the same insane weather that was the opening night to destroy Iraqi border posts. He had flown multiple missions in Nasiriyah and continued flying missions as the MEF pushed north.

Tonight, Woodman was again on the schedule and pushing his flight north from his headquarters in Kuwait, trying to track and monitor the movement of his crews. His helicopters and aircrews were flying more than two hundred miles north. It would take time for this fateful message to be deciphered and understood.

Tonight was the last night of his new normal. Tomorrow would be an altogether fresh and possibly insurmountable reality. After tonight, death and loss would no longer be something that happened to other people or to other units. Tragedy, frustration, and grief would soon kick in the Stingers' front door. That would be their new normal.

CHAPTER 31

Location: Southeast of Baghdad
Date: 05APR03
Time: 0025L

I wasn't sure what to expect, but we were flying at one thousand feet, and I was pulling almost 100 percent power. With a full load of fuel and ordnance, we flew at only 140 knots.

"Deadly 43, we have a report of a Cobra down in the vicinity of Aziziyah, but we have no airborne search and rescue (SAR) assets or ground assets available." Sky Chief operated with the same information we had.

I responded, "Deadly 43 is about ten minutes away. We will let you know." Then, I spoke to my wingman. "Buss, we are gonna pull maximum power. Once we get there, I think we should set up a high orbit, left turns." I had no other plan.

Click. Click.

It immediately felt like a race. A race for answers. A race to ensure fellow Marines, a duo of fellow Cobra pilots, had a fighting chance. If not a chance to save them, perhaps a chance to account for them. Words couldn't really describe what I knew we all felt. We simply had to try something, regardless of the circumstances. It's what I would hope someone would do for me and Matt or Buss and Rosie.

I just wanted to get there. As much as I respected the Cobra, it was in times like these when I wished we had something simply faster. The vibrations caused by the beat of the rotor blades only intensified as we demanded more from them and the engines. The vibrations increased, the Hellfire and TOW racks wobbled, and the entire airframe seemed to convulse and shiver as I pulled more power. Even the data in my HUD fidgeted with an unnerving display of airspeed, altitude, and heading. The pre-game jitters moved beyond my head and gut—they consumed me. All four of us and our 140-knot Cobras flew anxiously and restlessly, hoping there was a chance. I tried to put out of my mind what we all already knew but wouldn't dare utter.

We had finally arrived at the 267 crew's last known location. I had reduced power and started an easy left-hand turn. The early morning looked as dark as it felt calm. The smoke from the day's oil fires still hung in the air. This reduced our visibility, but we could still look up and see starlight. I glanced down but found nothing. No smoke, no fire, no Cobra.

"Four-four, we are slowing to one hundred knots and looking down into those three open fields. We are not seeing anything."

We did spot a series of unmarked radio towers on our way up. The suburban towns, best described as mud house villages, had unlit towers virtually everywhere. They seemed to climb up to almost five or six hundred feet. I could see pretty well through the NVGs, but with the oil-infused smoke still obscuring visibility, we'd have to depend on the FLIR to find the wire stanchions or radio towers. I needed to keep us at an altitude sanctuary.

Sky Chief broke the silence. "Deadly 43, proceed direct to the northwest in the vicinity of Grizzly and contact Luck on TAD 6. We have a C-130 enroute to assume on-scene commander."

This was not a request but an order. I paused and thought about asking Matt or Buss if we should ignore the request, but I knew that I needed to get us moving north. We had started our second lap to the left at a comfortable one thousand feet and an easy one hundred knots. I turned back for one more pass. I moved the stick to the right, taking out some of the angle of bank to expand the area we could cover.

"Four-three flight, you see anything? Let's keep the turn in, and we will roll out about three two zero." I wanted to get in at least one more turn.

"Deadly 43 copies. Flight switch," I said with chagrin. I let Buss and Rosie in on the plan. "Four-four, we are gonna extend this out to the south and get a long run over the area before we turn toward the north."

Click. Click.

We had only made one lap in the general area but had seen nothing. I would extend that by another two or three minutes. Sky Chief couldn't see us, and another few minutes of searching was exactly what we all wanted and needed to do.

The Ghost stayed close. She was still here, operating day, night, in any weather, and clearly in any place. She remained as fearless, as unmerciful, as unsparing, and as callous as ever. She was everything we thought we had become. Regardless of whether we recognized it or acknowledged it, we had learned from the dark times. In some unexplained way, we had rediscovered how to see and breathe in this darkness. The four of us had developed a growing clarity and coherence that had not previously existed.

As we made our final pass, the now familiar feeling of dread and despair began to infect me. It was a relentless and ruthless disease with no cure. The scene was blurred, but it was clear we were witness to a tragedy. I could also smell her; she was as close as ever. The Ghost had taken another.

Phaser 33, piloted by Captain Ben Sammis and Captain Travis Ford, USMC, in BUNO 161020, was gone. I didn't know either of them, and I felt a pinch of guilt that I hadn't met them. There was always guilt. As if I could have somehow known their fate and magically been the voice of God and warned them—saved them.

If I wasn't careful, the sickening frustration I felt was going to consume me. I took a deep breath. I needed to choke all this shit down. I needed to focus. I turned the flight back to the northwest. We needed to find out how we could help right a few wrongs.

Location: Safwan Hill FARP (Busch Stadium) – Basra, Iraq
Date: 06APR03
Time: 2030L

"Hardman, this is Deadly 23, flight of two. We are on the deck at Busch. Be over your position at time 45. How copy?" My message meant it was 2030L now and we would overhead his position, or close enough, at 2045L.

A thick British accent replied. "Hardman copies. We have work for you."

The FAC was making a game plan for us. We just kind of sensed it.

"Deadly, can you make a few laps around the city and take notes on anything?" He released his radio.

I thought about that for a second. "Hardman, anything in particular we are looking for?"

"Hey, mate, we think we have got enemy strongholds being built in the south and then another up north. Also have you a grid in a few for a suspected armor rally point." He cut off again.

Sounded like some run-of-the-mill armed reconnaissance. "Two-four, we are going to head southeast and then run the city counterclockwise. I think he means he's got some vehicles massing to the north."

Buss and Rosie got it. *Click. Click.*

We pulled out of the FARP with a right turn, keeping Safwan Hill to our left side. I was still amazed at how small it looked now. We made the turn to the south and put the city of one million off our left wing.

Matt saw it first. "Heads up—we got some tracer fire at ten o'clock."

"Two-four copies." Rosie was seeing it, and so was I.

We had been called across the country to support the United Kingdom's 7th Armored Brigade under the command of the United Kingdom's 1st Armored Division. The famous Desert Rats prepared for the final push into Basra. The brigade had fought in and around Iraq's second largest city for more than two weeks and made several daring strikes deep into the city, but the overall plan called for a full push into Basra the next morning. We headed toward the headquarters building at the Basra International Airport, which had been seized by the UK forces.

The show had begun. We conducted three complete laps around the city and saw nothing minus the random but continuous tracers from small arms fire. What we would not know until our following act was how perilously close we had flown to multiple Iraqi Army and Fedayeen positions. Completely unaware, I was the picture of complacency. I was not taking the mission seriously. How could I? The real war was hundreds of miles away in Baghdad, and here we were doing laps around Basra. We were all bored and likely wondering why we had been sent here from Riverfront. The trip here seemed like a waste of time, and I was still unsure why the city was not already under allied control.

Maybe if we found and engaged a few targets, we could get pushed back up north. We needed to get on with it. "Hardman, Deadly 23 is ten miles coming up the east side. Do you have any work?"

From Matt's perspective, the flight from Safwan or Busch Stadium had been less than ideal, and the laps around the city were even more challenging. The familiar blowing winds that kicked up clouds of sand and debris had replaced the cooler and clearer skies of Baghdad. We had flown directly from Riverfront and, after topping off our fuel tanks at Safwan, advanced on Basra.

The weather had worsened, and the moon remained well below the horizon. We had seen the large power lines to the west of the city. These were not local utility lines but four-hundred-foot power lines feeding the city power. As we approached them, they looked even taller. We planned to fly directly over the stanchions, thus avoiding the lines themselves.

Finally, they were ready for us to get to work. We had already burned an hour's worth of fuel.

"Hardman, 23 is over your position. Ready to copy 9-line." I waited for Hardman's response.

The Iraqi 51st Division still had operational units in the area. Even after weeks of fighting, the Iraqi 41st Armored Brigade and the Iraqi 32nd and 33rd Mechanized Brigades still had combat capable units engaging United Kingdom forces day and night.

We copied the 9-line and turned toward the northern parts of Basra. We were closer than I had expected. The targets were reported as T-55 tanks and assorted armored and supply vehicles. That was on the northwest side of the city. It was just west of the University of Basra, which was connected by a series of roads that included Highway 6 and Route 31. Both of those major roads had several highway overpasses and covered locations. They provided excellent places to hide from allied attack fixed-wing aircraft but were vulnerable to low-flying and low-shooting attack helicopters.

"Two-four, we are going to go north and then south on the east of the Euphrates."

I had just released the radio when we saw it. Buss was first to point it out. "Two-three, you see that tracer fire?"

Click. Click.

I noticed something different about Basra—something I couldn't put my finger on. The city should have been much more docile after three weeks of continuous combat and siege, but somehow, I felt a new energy—a nervous energy. Why were we here again? The UK had their own attack helicopters. Where were they? We had not been here in weeks, yet here we flew. To add to the confusion, MAG 39 had had a Cobra forced down by enemy fire earlier in the day. Where were they, and where was that brief?

The Iraqis directed their tracer fire up and to our west by more than a half a mile. With the poor NVG conditions and low visibility, the Iraqis had been shooting at noise. I continued our turn and rolled out to the northwest. The visibility had improved slightly to the north.

Hardman was back. "Deadly, we've got a platoon or so of T-55s two miles to the north of the intersection. We have been exchanging mortar rounds and tank rounds most of the day. This is Type 3 CAS. We cannot observe your fires right now."

That would be new for us. I responded, "Deadly copies."

We had three types of CAS missions. They ran from the most to the least restrictive for the aircrews. Over the past weeks, we had been given very detailed 9-line briefs with defined targets and other instructions designed to protect friendly forces. Tonight, with Type 3 CAS, we would have more freedom to engage enemy targets but also more responsibility to ensure the safety of soldiers of the United Kingdom's 1st Armored Division. Type 3 control meant that Hardman gave us a clearance for multiple attacks with a single engagement subject and specific restrictions.

Hardman knew the target, had previously observed it and plotted it, and had already worked it with his own mortars. In all likelihood, our 9-line had the weapons geometry approved prior to our arrival. The brief Hardman had given us covered the basics of geographic boundaries, targets, final attack heading, and location of friendly forces. The clearance gave us more of a game plan than a called play. Hardman still needed to listen to our communications and maintain abort authority.

Rosie's voice snapped me back to the present. "Two-three, we have a platoon of T-55s two thousand meters to the north."

I let Hardman know. "Hardman, Deadly 23 has the targets. We are in hot from the south with multiple missiles."

"Hardman copies," was his only response.

It was like some Pavlovian response jolted my body as I made the call. It triggered an immediate rush of adrenaline along with a series of other physical responses. I felt my foot begin to tremble just enough to remind me to breathe. Something was happening to me. What that something was, I was not exactly sure.

"Matt, you see them?" I could only see the grainy and greenish outline of roads and the waterways through my NVGs.

Matt could view the Iraqi tanks on the FLIR. "Oh yeah. We have ten plus vehicles up there. The tanks' engines are running, and they are all stopped in a column. They are easy to see on the FLIR. I am going Hellfire."

"Two-four leads in with Hellfire on the easternmost tank. We think we can get the two eastern ones." I let Buss and Rosie think on that.

Buss had already considered that, and from the left side of the formation, they had a plan. "Copy that. We are taking the western two with TOW."

Matt had already coded the missiles with the correct laser code. After that, he would ensure that he entered the same code for our onboard targeting laser. He quickly selected the specific missile he wanted to fire, and once he saw that I had moved the master arm to arm, the missile was gone.

Whooosh.

The flash temporarily blinded me, as the NVGs were overwhelmed by the sudden influx of light created by the launch motor. The missile covered the distance in seconds, making near instantaneous impact. The second missile came off as savagely as the first with the same familiar sights, smell, and sounds. The impact was obvious. I could not see the tanks, but I could see the flames pushing five or more feet straight up from both turrets. I slightly cocked my head to the right and, with my naked eye, could see that white flames had enveloped the tops of the tanks.

At four hundred feet and less than one hundred knots, we crept closer. Matt began to open up with 20mm as Rosie's first TOW impacted something just outside my periphery.

"Two-four's got a second TOW on the wire," Buss relayed.

We recognized them as Soviet-era T-55 tanks of the Iraqi 51st Mechanized Infantry Division, a unit assigned to the Iraqi 3rd Corps based in Nasiriyah. Mechanized with Russian and Chinese supplied fighting vehicles such as the BMP and BTR, both were designed to carry infantry and supplies. T-55 main battle tanks, the ones we now engaged, supported them. Nearly all the Iraqi armored vehicles, though functional, lacked advanced optics for night fighting. They also had unsophisticated and forty-year-old armor that was easily penetrated by both TOW and Hellfire missiles.

The three brigades of the Iraqi 51st Division had been given areas to defend throughout the southern oil fields, Basra, and other locations deemed critical. Most had surrendered, deserted, or been defeated in place by US and UK forces. The 51st Division's commanding general and his deputy had surrendered to coalition forces back on the 21st of March.

That left the remaining units to be led by Saddam loyalists, the Republican Guard, Fedayeen, and the famous Ali Hassan al-Majid, or Chemical Ali. To provide some background, Ali was the first cousin of Saddam Hussein. He had previously served as Saddam's minister of defense and intelligence. He'd also led Saddam's secret police after his rise to power in 1979. Additionally, US intelligence had linked him as the mastermind of Iraq's chemical weapons plans. Ali had notoriously demonstrated his chemical weapons effectiveness both on his own people and on the Iranians over the past two decades.

US and allied forces had distributed decks of cards with Iraq's most wanted holding the highest face cards. Saddam Hussein was the Ace of Spades. Right behind him was Ali, the King of Spades. Despite his high place in the Iraqi government, he remained isolated while charged with defending Iraq's southern sector. It came as no surprise that the formally trained infantry officer would not only survive allied attacks but would counter them with a staunch defense. Ali had managed to secure the city and organize a defense. At the time, we weren't aware that Ali was there and didn't realize how effectively he had organized his defense of Basra.

"Two-four, we are coming off the right." With a blanket clearance from Hardman, we were going to push south and east of the Euphrates.

Click. Click.

We had pulled off the target at about one thousand meters. Below, we noticed a flurry of activity with personnel running and moving in all directions. We had clearly caught the column of armored vehicles preparing for something. Due to the weather or maybe just complacency, they felt confident enough to run their engines at night, essentially in the open air. It made no sense, but we came back for another pass.

I wanted to make sure Buss and Rosie saw what Matt did. "Two-four, Matt counts another eight or ten vehicles and a bunch of foot mobiles there. You concur?"

"Yeah, looks like they were not expecting us," Buss replied.

"Hardman, 23 flight's back in from the south. Two-four, we are coming back in from the same direction. You have the last tank to the west. We are hitting the BMP to the north of the tanks." I released the radio, thinking I had conveyed a simple enough plan.

Click. Click.

I turned back to the east and then moved south along the river with the city off of our right wing. I would extend down another mile or so before turning back east and then to the north.

"Whoa, come left." Buss broke the brittle silence.

I saw it at the same time. Several streams of tracer fire were headed our way but were still way ahead of us. They had clearly come from inside the city. I took a mental note to make our next run from the west of Basra and east into the target if we needed another pass. That would be our last pass onto this target.

We had no balance or deeper understanding of the tactical situation beyond these vehicles. We had no idea whether that unit was the Iraqi's main effort, a diversionary force, a reserve force, or just some unfortunates. We now flew back toward the target, less than a minute out from causing even more destruction and chaos. Even with a limited amount of ordnance and the likelihood that no more Cobras were headed there that night, we needed to ensure we hit the targets that the 7th Armored Brigade wanted to hit.

I called the attack. "Two-three's in from the south." Then, I framed as more of a question, "Matt, you got the BMP with Hellfire and the gun on the vehicles."

I added power and pulled back on the stick to level us just under three hundred feet and ninety knots. I flew the heading that Matt had put into the GPS. I could only see about one thousand meters on the NVGs and counted on Matt to see the targets.

"I got 'em. Master arm to arm."

Whoosh.

The Hellfire's launch motor flashed as the Cobra heaved the missile at the target, leaving one Hellfire remaining. Another immediate impact. The explosion added some needed ambient light to help the NVGs. I could view the impact area and could now see the last T-55, along with several other support or supply vehicles. I identified men running and moving toward the overpass. To my left, I saw another flash. Buss and Rosie had put a Hellfire at the last T-55, and Matt had begun firing the 20mm at the remaining vehicles.

His rounds impacted what looked like a military supply truck, saturating the front of the vehicle until a small fire started followed by a minor explosion. He stopped firing and turned to the northeastern-most vehicle. That one looked more like a pickup truck, and the 20mm HE rounds worked even faster. As we pulled off, I counted no fewer than ten vehicles on fire.

"Two-four, we are coming off east, resetting to the north, and heading to Safwan for gas." I released the radio, then selected the other radio to let Hardman know we were going off station. "Hardman, Deadly 23 checking off station for fuel. BDA to follow."

We passed the destruction of the majority of the vehicles and confirmed we'd destroyed five of the six tanks reported. We never saw a sixth T-55, but Hardman didn't seem concerned. He told us to land at the international airport since they had fuel for us. Plus, the commander of the 7th Armored Brigade wanted to chat with us. *Hmmm.*

CHAPTER 32

Location: 7th Armored Brigade HQ, Basra International Airport, Iraq
Date: 06APR03
Time: 2215L

The approach to the airport presented another refreshing change. It maintained the characteristics of an airport, and we easily navigated into it. We had a controller who pushed us to a parking area and assured us fuel was on the way. Though blowing sands consumed the starlight and the moon hung below the horizon, we could see the single long runway and the taxiways. Fortunately, workers had blown clean most of the sand. We had a routine landing, de-arm, and shutdown.

Brigadier Graham Binns commanded the Desert Rats, and fortunately, he didn't want to see us, but his staff did. I thought about that for a minute and considered why I felt such relief. Maybe it was just my nature to expect a skewering for crossing some undefined line or breaking some unwritten rule, but not tonight. We waited until the UK fuel truck made it to our positions. Then, taking no chances, we refueled the Cobras ourselves.

Even at the late hour, we had garnered more than a few sightseers. We found them to be exceptionally friendly and helpful soldiers, but I respectfully asked them to remain clear of the aircraft and requested that the driver of the refueling truck post someone to watch the Cobras. We kept our body armor on and slung our M4s over our shoulders but left nearly everything else in the cockpit. That included ammunition, helmets, NVGs, maps, etc.

We completely trusted our allies, but there is a universal expectation that, unless it's chained or bolted down, soldiers, Marines, and sailors may attempt to "liberate any gear adrift." That infamously included your wallet, watch, or girlfriend.

Interestingly, there were four UK Lynx AH.7 attack helicopters parked only feet from our Cobras. With a quick look, I noted they were all TOW equipped and NVG capable. The UK had parked them on the flight line, but they were obviously not participating in tonight's show. No sooner had we all noticed the Lynxes than a pilot walked toward us. Surprisingly, it was a US Army major.

He started the conversation. "Hey, fellas. How's it going? You coming from Kuwait?"

"No, we are coming from south of Nasiriyah. What's going on here?" I figured this guy might know a few things.

"Yeah, with all this oil and sand in the air, we can't fly." He sounded disappointed. "I'm the flight leader, here on an exchange tour. We are limited with the Lynx right now. The sand has really hurt the engines, and because of that combined with the smoke, we're grounded."

I really didn't know what to make of this conversation. I certainly didn't want to insult him or his crew, but Buss, Rosie, and Matt all looked at me. I knew what they were thinking. Why the hell were we assigned this mission and not them? Why did we just risk a one-hundred-mile open desert flight on a moonless night to support a unit that already had attack helicopters? It was turning into a more dangerous situation than any of us had expected. Any complacency had been washed away after the first Hellfire shot. Now the kicker—we still had to go back out to execute the mission with the added challenge of dust, towers, debris, Iraqis, and smoke in the air.

We spent a few more minutes talking with the major. Clearly a pro, he was on his second tour with the Brits flying the Lynx. I would have liked to stay there and pick his brain, but our ride had arrived. It made the hair stand up on the backs of all our necks. Never mind the massive high-tension lines that we had dodged on the way in and the obviously desperate defenders in Basra. The time had come to move.

An SUV arrived to drive us to the HQ located near the tower complex a short distance away. After the brief ride, we climbed out of the SUV and entered a full command center. It wasn't long before a staff officer—a major—came out to greet us. We were going to get a brief from his colonel, but first, he invited us to grab some water and sustenance.

The British version of an MRE was a significant upgrade from what we were used to eating. Maybe it was the mustards, or maybe it was the jams or the biscuit. It really didn't matter. Their MREs seemed much more sophisticated and somehow made me feel like we had landed someplace far from our actual location. It was just enough of a touch of elegance to let me relax and step away for a moment.

We had been there for about thirty minutes when the British Army major returned to introduce us to the colonel. From there, Buss and I went into the main operations center while Matt and Rosie grabbed some more food and found a seat.

The operations officer of the 7th Armored Brigade, or maybe his deputy, greeted me. It didn't matter who he was, and I didn't ask. It was as old school as I can remember. Despite having all the technology of a modern CP, complete with projectors and flat screens, he walked me to a map and pointed out our location. Next, he paused, turned, and looked at me and Buss. Surprisingly, or maybe not so surprisingly, he thanked us for being there and for hitting the armor west of the university. Then, without ceremony, he turned back to the map.

He showed us the Iraqi fortified positions, as well as the clear and obvious positions of UK forces, and then highlighted their approaches to the city. The basic plan for the morning had Challenger tanks and Royal Marine commandos attacking from the south with Warrior infantry fighting vehicles and other supporting elements attacking from the north. It certainly was more complex than that, but those were my major takeaways.

The 7th Armored Brigade would lead with Challenger 2 main battle tanks. Those sixty-five-ton monsters were the shock troops of the United Kingdom. Fitted with thermal sights, a 120mm main gun, world-class armor, and multiple 7.62mm machine guns, they were deemed nearly unstoppable by opponents. They certainly posed a serious problem for Ali and his remaining Iraqi armored formation. Those Challenger crews had come prepared.

The names of the units alone dripped with history and conjured up visions of great battles and heroism. The likes of the Royal Scots Dragoon Guards, the Queen's Royal Lancers, and the 2nd Royal Tank Regiment would ride those Challengers into battle.

In direct support, additional armored forces were planned to employ an infantry fighting vehicle called the Warrior. This had a similar mission to the US Army's Bradley fighting vehicle or a Marine LAV-25. Armed with a 30mm cannon and 7.62mm machine gun, they brought infantry into the fight and would remain to provide additional fire support. Those units bore similarly iconic names such as the 1st Fusiliers, the Irish Guards, and the Black Watch. They had received their final briefings and soon positioned themselves to enter the city. An impressive plan, but we also knew they would not be attacking until the early morning. The next few hours would be us, alone, attacking the Iraqi defenders.

We were scheduled to return to Riverfront at 0200L, but there was no way we would make that. From our discussions with the 7th, we intended to launch in about two hours and recon the entire city. We would also look to engage some additional vehicles that had been spotted by their FAC, Bigfoot. Best case, we would return to Riverfront around 0500L.

With that in mind, I realized I needed to get a message back to the squadron informing them of our delay. I could try via Sky Chief but suspected the 7th had communications with the MEF. So, I found the major and asked him if he could get a message through the MEF to MAG 29: "Deadly 23 and 24 are safe on deck (SOD) at Basra International with an anticipated RTB Riverfront no later than (NLT) 0600L."

At that point, Buss walked back up to me with his own message. "Hey, I was talking to their fires guys, and it looks like there are some additional mortar positions and a few other places they want us to do reconnaissance. Two to the north and one to the south."

Buss and I both found a seat. "Copy. I think we are going to plan for a 0130L takeoff. That should let us run to those positions and then come back here or Safwan for gas before we head to Riverfront. We have all the rockets and probably about three hundred rounds of 20mm left. The TOWs were showing some faults; I am not sure about them."

Buss knew what I meant. "We have three Hellfires and two TOWs, and everything else is good. I am ready to go whenever you are." Buss noticed me brainstorming. "What's up?"

I had a lot of thoughts running through my head, but I was not convinced the next sortie would be so easy. "Hey, with all their planning for the major offensive in the morning, we are the only CAS assets on station. Once we take off, the Iraqis will know it's Marine H-1s, and we'll immediately become their number one target. We need to stay above the wires, out of the smoke, and away from the city."

Buss paused and pondered the obvious. "Okay, let's go north first. Feel it out up there with Bigfoot. Then, we can probe in from the south, but any sign of heavy machine guns or AAA, and we are going out west. I think we can shoot missiles from maybe two or three clicks, but nothing more than that."

It was already past midnight when I found the operations officer and told him we planned to launch early and find Bigfoot. I also let him know we should have time for another two hours once we got back and refueled. I gathered up Matt, who was busily talking with a few of the UK soldiers as Rosie looked for our driver.

"Here's the plan. We are going to launch, head east to Bigfoot, and see what he needs. Then, we are going to push back west and south to recon clockwise around the city. If we have ordnance after that, we will refuel and stay for another one point five or so and then head to Riverfront. Buss and I talked about the wires and towers along with the visibility. We will stay high, use missiles, and stay away from overflying the city. You guys have any questions or concerns?"

Nothing. Business as usual. Matt and Rosie were certainly vocal when they needed or wanted to be, but this seemed simple. It was nothing we had not done before, but I started to get that uneasy feeling nonetheless.

"Bigfoot, Deadly 23's with you. We got one point five of playtime. Send your 9-line." I took a bit more of a direct approach because I didn't want another two hours of turning gas into noise.

He passed the grid, nearly the same as the previous one but about eight hundred meters to the north.

"Deadly, be advised, my observer passes that your last runs extended over the top of another reported enemy position. I would recommend you run west to east and stay away from a turn south." Bigfoot released the transmitter.

"Well, fuck me. Where the hell was that information two hours ago?" I muttered to myself but loud enough for my VOX to activate and for Matt to hear. I was tired and had just taken another "go pill," but it had yet to kick in.

Matt didn't waste the chance. "No kidding? If we overflew those Iraqi positions, those guys were smart not to expose themselves. I'm sure they couldn't see us and knew we would have only turned back into them and gone hot."

I considered what Matt had said, and it made sense. We all knew that we overflew unknown and unmarked enemy positions on every flight. We also knew the enemy could shoot at us whenever they chose, but they were smart enough to wait until they had a real chance. A tactical risk versus reward proposition. I had convinced myself of that, but if I were them, I would shoot at me at every opportunity. I shoved that thought away.

Matt pushed the tempo now. "That position is just south of Highway 6 and across the river from what looks like a power station. All four TOW missiles look good. I am going to lead with TOW. I see a bunch of vehicles there, and they are all hot on the FLIR."

I took note. Hot meant they were running engines, not a normal thing at zero dark something on an otherwise calm Monday morning. I dropped the power and pushed the nose over.

Matt beat me to the radio. "Go master arm to arm. I've about a dozen vehicles off the nose." Pause. Pause. "Okay, ahhhhh, I see a bunch of troops there with trucks and a couple of what looks like BMPs." His tone was just slightly elevated, and his clarity exposed the effects brought on by a jolt of adrenaline.

I called the FAC. "Bigfoot, Deadly 23 is going hot to the north. Two-four, PGMs on the armor, then 20mm on everything else."

I could feel my right foot begin to twitch; it gently bounced off the pedal. This was simply too easy. Was this the trap? I continued to scan to my right with Buss and Rosie to the left.

Whoosh.

The TOW came off the rail. Again, I could almost hear the *tick, tick, tick* of the missile's fins moving as Matt made adjustments. I could only sit and wait. It would just take seven or eight seconds of flight time, but it felt much longer. I could see the back of the missile snake its way to the target. Matt was the pilot, and he skillfully flew it past the steel beams underneath the highway and into the BMP.

"Two-four's in hot," Buss relayed.

Whoosh.

The missile left 24's wing only a second behind Matt's trigger pull, but the Hellfire quickly beat the TOW to the target. It announced its arrival with an ear-splitting explosion. That was no armored vehicle—it must have been a supply truck or something with a lot of fuel in it. The light opened up the view.

I tried to quietly let Matt know I would follow his missile with a pod of 2.75-inch rockets. I could see the target area well but wanted to let his missile impact first. We saw twenty vehicles in the open in an area the size of three or four football fields. That must have been their supply or rally point.

The Iraqi defenders were not going down without a fight. It started with one spark, then two more, and then a fourth, fifth, and sixth in rapid succession. As the tracer fire came up toward us, no one needed to say anything. Both cockpits were busy putting missiles into targets, and there was nothing we could do about the fire headed our way. It definitely wasn't random. It came off our nose, clearly from the place where we had just put two missiles. I was still no expert on tracer fire, but I classified that as AK-47 or other small arms fire. We believed in "big sky, little bullet" logic, which counted on one or several little bullets not being able to hit us in the vastness of the night, but I still planned to put one pod of 2.75-inch rockets into the location of the AK fire.

I pushed the first rocket out, selecting singles with one push for one rocket. The reverberation, although slight, was followed by another and then another. Matt went back to the gun as the rockets impacted the area of the AK fire.

Chug. Chug. Chug. Chug.

My focus was drawn to the target area where I saw at least five vehicles fully engulfed in flames. With the added light, I was seeing more detail, and it became obvious how effective we were. I could also see how our hapless and exposed enemy was floundering under our repeated attacks. Unfortunately for them, this was far from over.

"Two-four, let's extend east across the river and then north. Second run from east to west." I cut the transmission, expecting a response.

I listened but heard nothing from Buss and Rosie. If they had responded, I didn't hear them. I continued to look down to the left. With Buss and Rosie to our right, just fifty meters off my wing, they continued to empty 20mm rounds on target. They likely hadn't heard me over the noise of the cannon.

After turning to the east, no further away than two hundred meters, I added power, checked our altitude and airspeed, and then waited for a few more seconds before turning to the left. I rolled out of the turn, heading almost due west.

"Bigfoot, 23's in hot from the east."

"Copy, Deadly," came the response from Bigfoot.

I keyed the radio again. "Two-four, we are going to expend all remaining rounds on this pass, minus one missile and hopefully a few rounds of 20mm."

Click. Click.

Saving 20mm was an unrealistic request and completely out of character, but something in my head told me to keep an offensive capability. Saving a missile was easy. We only carried eight missiles, and you could look outside the cockpit and count the ones remaining if you struggled with math. There was a 20mm ammunition gauge in the front seat of the Cobra, but it was notoriously inaccurate, and no one ever trusted it. I rolled out heading west with maybe a few degrees of northern windage.

Whoosh.

The TOW missile came off as soon as I armed the system. Matt had identified the target and had the trigger down, almost saying, "Let's go."

Another TOW immediately followed that impact.

Whoosh.

Off to the right, Matt and Rosie had already put one TOW out and would likely fire another Hellfire. I waited. I could see the AK-47 barrel flashes and then the tracers from the target area. *They are only shooting at the noise,* I kept telling myself. I looked through the HUD to ensure I started level at four hundred feet and eased the nose over into a shallow dive, wings level, ball centered.

Another missile sailed past our right wing—Rosie's last TOW. I continued to track Matt's final TOW. Once it impacted, I opened with a volley of three 2.75-inch rockets. The rockets were fired a bit prematurely and were not quite as accurate as the last pass.

The pitch and tone of the rockets heading from under the wing to the target remained familiar. We waited for the visual report, which confirmed our rockets had found their target or had at least gotten close—close being a continuous point for debate. That had been a three-thousand-meter run-in, and Matt had had more than enough time to open with the gun. We were likely only six hundred meters out when I selected the last of the rockets and rippled them.

"Two-three's coming off to the right," I warned Buss.

I knew he and Rosie flew on my right side, but we wouldn't overfly the target or come left over the city.

Click. Click.

"Bigfoot, Deadly 23 and flight, mission complete. We are RTB. Prepare to copy BDA."

We gave Bigfoot a verbal description of the targets engaged, the number of targets we likely destroyed, and an estimate of the remaining enemy forces in that specific area.

"Thanks, fellas. That was fantastic work. Come back anytime. Safe travels." Bigfoot had signed off. The British were always so polite.

"Two-four, we are headed to Busch for gas and a quick debrief. Switch Busch. Matt, you have the controls whenever you're ready." I released the radio.

My right foot continued to fidget, and my left eye had begun to show a weird sign of strain. The muscle fluttered, causing my eye to partially shut and reopen every few seconds. I chalked it up to dehydration, go pills, and a little fatigue, but it had started a few nights before and had gotten progressively worse.

Accommodative eye fatigue, I would learn later, causes a spasm of the eye muscle. It is generally associated with conditions that force the eye to accommodate or focus and refocus constantly. NVG flying is its fertile field. We had read about that during our initial NVG qualifications and again for our instructor qualifications. At the time, I wasn't sure what it was, and I sure as hell wasn't about to say anything to anyone.

We found Busch Field calm and gave them their only business. It was a UK-run FARP but exceptionally well organized and managed. We shut down first and then dragged the fuel hoses to our aircraft.

We had one Hellfire left and likely about one hundred rounds of 20mm. Buss and Rosie had one Hellfire and one TOW and around the same amount of 20mm, but neither of us had any rockets. It was still hot and dry, and that bullshit southern wind had whipped up. At almost four in the morning, I could tell that we all wanted to simply sleep on the ground and fly back in a few hours, but that was not in the cards. As much as I wanted to rest, we needed to get back to Jalibah and get those aircraft checked out, rearmed, and ready for the morning launch.

"Buss, you're good taking us out of here and getting us home?" I asked in my most passive yet challenging tone.

Buss never missed anything. There was a reason he was a MAWTS-1 instructor. More importantly, he knew I would not have asked if I didn't need a break. Even though it would be a short break, it would still be a challenge. The weather had continued to degrade. The winds had picked up. The familiar lack of horizon waited for us.

By four thirty local time, we were airborne. Matt flew from the front seat and had us tucked in close on Buss's right wing. I enjoyed working as a "dash two copilot." Meanwhile, the weather worsened; it could have been March 21st again. I watched Matt, Buss, and our altitude, airspeed, and heading in the HUD. It may have been the longest short flight of the deployment.

CHAPTER 33

Location: Salman Pak East Airfield (Yankee), 15 Miles South of Baghdad
Date: 11APR03
Time: 1815L

"Deadly 15, check." We were a long way from Riverfront.

"Two," Buss chirped.

We watched our plane captains signal us out of the FARP after we had been rearmed. Matt saluted, we added power, and I pushed the nose over. The Cobra accelerated quickly. I looked behind me to see Buss closing the distance. I added some left stick and turned directly toward Baghdad. The weather had made a turn for the better, and the moon would finally make its first appearance. We had spent the better part of the day working out of our new home.

It was just past sunset on the 11th. We had completed our fourth sortie of the day, and after having refueled, we would continue flying into night. The tempo was markedly slower than when we had left Baghdad some six days ago. The missions had turned into convoy escorts and visual reconnaissance, but we were too savvy and too cynical to believe the war over. Not one member of Deadly 15 flight believed that, and we all tightened up our game every time we flew into Baghdad proper.

As we passed into downtown Baghdad, we felt as vulnerable as we ever had. Below us, a massive flow of people moved about. It was as though the entire city had emptied into the streets to welcome, observe, or plot. US and coalition military vehicles moved or were parked on every street, and Marines attempted to patrol while surrounded by exuberant Iraqis. State Department, Army, Marine, and other US government agency helicopters flew everywhere with no one coordinating the movements in or out of several key LZs.

Boomer had made some key decisions for MAG 29 over the past week. He had seen the US Army's 3rd ID smash into the ribcage of the last Special Republican Guard units in southwestern Baghdad while I MEF counterpunched their way into Baghdad from the southeast.

With the fight moving further and further away from Riverfront, he, his staff, and squadron commanders had hatched another inventive plan to again move the MAG closer to the fight. This plan included flying ten Cobras and four Hueys two hundred miles further north and establishing a MAG forward headquarters at Salman Pak or Yankee Stadium. They also included a detachment of Phrogs for CASEVAC and resupply, along with CH-53Es flying in critical supplies and support equipment.

The MEF and a majority of the RCTs began to focus on the capital and finding the now absent Saddam Hussein. This was also very Clausewitzian. By securing the capital, decapitating the leadership, and breaking the will of the people, they should end the war.

I had spent the past two days at Riverfront, packing up and packing out the maintenance detachment. It was up to Monty and the team to take the right tools, supplies, and Marines for the trip. I had several days to unwind, pack my gear, open mail, write letters, and watch CNN or BBC coverage of the war. I took note when I saw the Iraqi people tearing down the statue of Saddam Hussein in Firdos Square with the help of a Marine M1A1 tank. It was the most overt symbol of the fall of Saddam and his regime.

We planned for MAG 29 and HMLA 269 to continue supporting the RCTs in and around Baghdad and to support an innovative use of LAV-25s. The 1st MARDIV quietly husbanded a majority of their LAR assets. They intended to assemble a regimental-sized combat unit composed primarily of LAV-25s. Major General

Mattis's assistant division commander would command this new force.

Brigadier General John Kelly was no stranger to the ideas of maneuver warfare and was a former LAR battalion commander himself. Just one more of the dozen or so Basic School instructors of mine who had found themselves here. He was put in command of Task Force Tripoli. This was shaping up to be an interesting ride.

Location: 10 Miles South of Tikrit, Iraq
Date: 13APR03
Time: 1720L

Deadly 67, mission number 0705, had checked on station just south of Tikrit with Gump, the FAC with "B" Company, 2nd LAR. He was one of the multiple FACs embedded with portions of 1st, 2nd, 3rd, and 4th LAR battalions. Tripoli had brought hundreds of vehicles and thousands of Marines north. It included artillery, supply, infantry, and communications units, along with a handful of Navy SEALs.

"Six-seven flight, let's push east of Highway 1. We have the lead LAVs off the nose." Our CO, Jeff "Huey" Hewlett, finished the call with a turn to the left.

I responded, "Two."

They had assigned Matt and I as Huey's wingman. Buss and Rosie weren't flying that day, and since we had pushed to Yankee, there had been a mixing of the crews. To be honest, I didn't relish flying off Huey's wing. It wasn't necessarily because the "old man" posed any specific challenges. It was more about my preferences. We had developed habit patterns, and I liked to do things in specific ways.

There were little things Huey wanted his pilots to do that were sometimes not followed to the letter of the law. He would soon learn I treated his tactical directives as more advisory in nature than absolute. One example was a mini-HUD that went over the lens of the NVGs and repeated everything from the backseat HUD to both pilots. He believed these were important to wear. We knew them to be helpful, but also to be cumbersome and disorienting. I didn't use it, and I didn't check to see who did.

The same was true for the helmet-mounted sight. The 20mm gun could be aimed via directional signals generated by a metal rail attached to the top of the helmet. There was also an additional cord associated with powering the system that was attached to the helmet. When either pilot pulled the action bar, an electric signal was sent to slew the gun to where the helmet was "looking." This sounded like a great leap in technology and efficiency, but it was legendarily unreliable and inaccurate. I mean, never in the dozen years I had been flying Cobras had it ever worked as advertised.

Combined, these ad hoc systems added a significant amount of extra weight on my head and neck. So, the helmet sight idea was also flushed; Huey just never knew it—or if he did, he didn't say anything. Likely the latter.

We sensed that Tikrit might be the last big battle of the war, and there was a push to get some of our junior pilots more experience. With that, they'd recalled our on-loan MAWTS-1 aircrew. We expected them to go to Kuwait within the next few days.

Matt and I had spent the previous day flying off the CO's wing, but the mission had been one dry well after another. Today's mission had already taken on a different flavor. Sections launching earlier in the day had reported engaging Fedayeen units, the Ba'ath Party militia, and the remaining organized forces of the Al Nida Special Republican Guard Division. The home of Saddam Hussein seemed like the most likely place for a final showdown.

"Deadly 67, we have reports of artillery, supply trucks, and AAA about ten clicks to our north to the east of Highway 1. Stand by to copy grid." Gump had some work for us.

Matt had the grid in the GPS, and we headed inbound. Those targets seemed to be located between the lead LAR elements and the follow-on convoys of the still advancing Task Force Tripoli. We didn't know how they had found those targets. It could have been from LAR units, drones, fixed-wing aircraft on station, or other sections returning.

Huey and I didn't care where the intelligence had come from. We pressed north.

To our east, we could see Tikrit, a small city by Western standards, flanked by the Tigris River. A series of prodigious palaces and compounds littered the river. Each one looked more luxurious and opulent than the last. If Adolph Hitler and the senior Nazi party officials had had the Eagle's Nest and Berchtesgaden, then Saddam Hussein and his Iraqi military elite had Tikrit. It was the northern tip of what would become known to thousands of Marines, sailors, airmen, and soldiers as the Sunni Triangle.

Bordered to the south by Baghdad and to the west by Ramadi, the Sunni Triangle represented the cultural center of the Sunni-dominant population and Saddam Hussein's power base. The Al Anbar Province also held the provincial capital of Ramadi and the influential city of Fallujah. Anbar Province was the country's largest province. It was a massive expanse of land with a history that dated back thousands of years. Thousands of years of legends, traditions, memories, rivalries, and frustrations. The famous Silk Road included these same paths, connecting the east to the west, and led from the borders of Saudi Arabia to Syria, Jordan, and places beyond.

The weather looked as clear as it had ever been. The moon would rise in about three hours, and Matt and I flew as dash two. I could feel a weight slowly lifting off of me, if only temporarily. The targets sat west of the highway and south of the major airfield in Tikrit. As we approached, we dropped to three hundred feet and accelerated slowly with no major obstacles, minus the phone and electric lines that were strung on each side of the highway. At thirty feet or so, the phone lines presented no threat, but we remained vigilant anyway. I kept a lookout for wires and towers and didn't pay as much attention as I should have to the target area. We arrived on top of the position before I knew it.

"Gump, Deadly 67. We have the targets in sight. Wings level." Huey waited for a response.

"Deadly, you are cleared hot." Gump said nothing else.

I looked off the nose and saw ten to fifteen Iraqis, all running back toward their artillery pieces. These were D-20s, 152mm artillery pieces that could hit the main convoy of Task Force Tripoli if they had the proper spotters in place or had preplanned fire missions. We had somehow, unbelievably, caught them unprepared. Huey pulled hard to the right and then went into a slight climb.

He called the attack. "Six-eight, run in three three zero, going guns and rockets on the vehicles. I'm pulling left."

"Two."

I could feel the tension build. My right knee began to gently bounce, and the signal continued to spread until my right foot began its familiar tapping, adrenaline surging through my veins. Trying to take a deep breath and focus, I added power and crossed behind Huey. After pulling out of the turn, I launched into a slight climb.

"Matt, master arm's going to arm. Let them shoot first, and we will adjust off that. Once you're off the gun, I'm going rockets on those trucks." I was still looking through the HUD when their rockets impacted the first D-20, and then another pod hit the second one.

We had chosen to lead with the gun. Matt began pouring 20mm into the truck just outside of the semicircle that was their firing position. We pushed closer, and from less than five hundred meters, I selected a seven-shot pod, aligned the reticle on the second truck, and mashed the thumb trigger. The destruction was immediate, but the explosion was unexpected. I responded with a hard pull to the west as Matt began to engage the tree line where the infantry or artillery men had sought cover.

"Gump, Deadly 67 requests an immediate reattack." Huey had already turned inbound, and I needed to catch up fast.

As we pulled off, I could clearly see a half dozen kneeling or squatting Iraqis with AKs to their shoulders. Our first pass had clearly not deterred them. Their flight-or-fight response had evidently opted for fight.

We needed to let Huey know. "Hey, Boss, you see those guys in the tree line?"

I moved the master arm back to the standby position and cut hard inside their turn. Damn, Huey pulled a lot of power. Eventually, I passed behind his tail and then pulled into an even more aggressive turn and simultaneous climb. I understood his urgency. We had caught them unprepared, and he wanted to destroy the guns and supplies while we still had the initiative. We had yet to have any SAMs or RPGs fired at us after that night in Nasiriyah, but our intelligence reports said these forces would be better equipped. They were certainly more motivated, and I was expecting more sophisticated weapons.

"Six-eight, go fifteen seconds in trail. We are going to use the same run-in heading. We will take out the last supply truck and try to get rockets on the other D-20. You focus on that tree line." Huey had a more detailed plan, and it made good sense.

I responded, "Two."

If it had worked once, why not try it one more time? As I began my turn, I had a brief flashback to Nasiriyah and felt an immediate appreciation for the trust that Buss and Rosie had in us. I had put them through similar repeated attacks. I'd exposed them to Iraqi ground fire as I pulled both of them over the same pieces of terrain from the same direction multiple times. I knew this was different, but the discovery was humbling. I was humbled to discover that Buss and Rosie not only trusted me, but they believed in me. They believed I would get them through anything, the same way I knew Huey would today.

The second pass proved as effective and as destructive as the first. We had expended nearly one thousand 20mm rounds and another twenty-eight rockets on an artillery unit that had fired their last rounds. The tree lines absorbed every round we had left in the ammunition can, and the spinning of the barrels signaled that they were done. I didn't notice when it happened, but at some point between the first rounds impacting the target and landing at the end of the night, my foot stopped bouncing.

The succeeding seven hours followed a similar routine of rearm, refuel, and then attack selected targets pinpointed by the air officers and the FACs of Task Force Tripoli. For the FACs, official unit callsigns had long given way to personal callsigns; it had always been a subtle but welcome deviation. Cybil, Jake, Disney, Mudduck, Sideshow, Gump, and a host of others were our guys, all aviators, just not in a cockpit on that tour.

Cybil would serve as our last FAC. We had worked with him in Nasiriyah and several unknown places in between. He was as talented and as aggressive as they came. Captain Jimmy "Cybil" Brown, the San Jose State graduate, had served with 2nd LAR since 2002 and knew their mission and capabilities as well as any.

As LAR units made their move to the north of Tikrit, we followed. We watched when asked to watch, attacked when told to attack, and simply maintained a presence. Maybe my original thoughts of being a debt collector or repo man had once again morphed. Maybe we were watchdogs. I needed to think about that.

The sunset brought along no specific changes for the flight, except in Huey's case. With every hour into darkness, he seemed to gain more energy, more confidence. I had talked briefly with his copilot, Johnny Ginn, during our last fuel and rearming stop. He'd said he was glad we were here and encouraged us to keep up the pace.

Every CO wants to be up flying and leading from the front, but the reality is that COs at the level of lieutenant colonel are sometimes most effective pushing out their best crews and then orchestrating the fight inside a headquarters alongside the air group commander and other squadron commanders. It's one of the realities of command.

That was not the case tonight. Tonight, Huey pressed the pace and challenged us to keep up stride for stride. He may have forgotten that Matt and I were now world-class marathoners, and no one would or could outwork us.

With the sun long set and the new moon waxing slowly, the darkness finally resembled the sanctuary it had represented in the past instead of the prison it had been more recently. We completed our last refuel at a FARP located near Tikrit South airfield and then began the one-hundred-mile trip back to Yankee. We edged off the road by about a half mile to the east.

The road to Salman Pak was unfamiliar, but we tracked south along Highway 1. We passed Samarra, the town where the "Wolfpack" that was 3rd LAR had rescued the remaining POWs from the US Army's 507th Maintenance Company and two Apache pilots who had been shot down in late March. Then, we passed by Balad, a major Iraqi air base, before swinging east to avoid Baghdad. The light levels had improved the NVG conditions. This all simplified our turn into and landing at Salman Pak.

Matt and I had kept up an easy banter on the flight back. The fact that we had again landed after two in the morning was almost expected. What I had not prepared for was the complete lack of admiration or elation Matt and I felt for the night's missions. It had been great to fly with Huey and Johnny Ginn. They were a tight and talented crew, and we now had a bond with them, but it had just been different. Flying without Buss and Rosie felt strange. They would have appreciated this first night with improved visibility.

We sat down in the GP tent we had erected at Salman Pak. This was our all-in-one ready room—an intelligence, operations, and logistics center and squadron lounge. With Huey and Johnny Ginn already sitting for the debrief, Matt and I pulled up a camp stool and listened. It was a needed break. The statistics proved indisputable and credible, all recorded by our gun cameras, but we experienced a sense of weariness and indifference that bordered on apathy.

We had destroyed fifteen tactical targets, including three missile systems at the Al Sahara Airfield, the location of the former Iraqi Air Force Air Academy. The list continued with artillery tubes, supply trucks, several AAA pieces, and unspecified numbers of infantry. We had fired TOWs, Hellfires, 2.75-inch rockets, and 20mm rounds with near impunity. The importance of the mission was somehow overshadowed by the perceived ease with which it had been executed. Maybe that should have been worrisome.

After completing the debrief, we headed for our cots. Matt and I ended the night having eclipsed our one hundredth hour of combat flight time in just the past twenty-three days and nights. Excluding our day off for maintenance and the sandstorm of March 25th and 26th, we had flown every day.

Location: Tikrit North Airfield (Al Sahara), Iraq
Date: 14APR03
Time: 1445L

Deadly 03, 04, and 05, also known as mission number 0703A, consisted of a flight of three: two Cobras and a Huey. Captains Andy Dyer and Scotty Atwood piloted the Huey with Corporal Ken Deal and Sergeant Bob Poindexter serving as the crew chiefs. Deal and Poindexter had seen it all. They had flown with Andy on the opening night, been downtown in Nasiriyah, and lived with multiple RCTs for days at a time. They shook hands with colonels and generals, ferried reporters, delivered wounded Marines to safety, and put thousands of rounds down range when it mattered. We felt privileged to have one of them on the .50 caliber heavy machine gun and the other on the 7.62mm minigun.

We also had Buss and Rosie back on our wing, and if ever I had felt a sense of invincibility, it was that day. We were supporting Task Force Tripoli for a third time, and we suspected it would be the most adventurous day in the Sunni Triangle.

The late morning brief at Yankee brought a few strange things to light. For one, we had Iraqis waiting at the front gate of the compound with Cokes and smokes. It hadn't taken long for the local kids to realize a free market was waiting to be exploited. It only took a few Marines puffing on Sumer king size cigarettes and drinking warm twelve-ounce bottles of Coca Cola for the senior enlisted Marine to quickly ban such transactions.

Another oddity happened as we walked to launch the flight back to Tikrit. I stopped and took a hard look at the Cobras lined up. They were some seriously ugly babies, but not in our eyes. Flying off *Saipan* only a few weeks ago, they'd looked like they had just come off the production line floor. But now, after weeks of constant use and nothing to clean them with, they looked tired. There were oil slicks down both sides and hydraulic fluid stains on virtually every panel, along with rocket, missile, and cannon soot covering the remaining spaces. They looked anything but new, but yet, they looked amazing.

We'd heard rumors that another HMLA was heading for the theater. That morning, we received confirmation that the "Gunfighters" of HMLA 369 had landed in Kuwait a day or so earlier. We were happy to know more forces would soon arrive. I had friends in that squadron, another cast of characters with callsigns like Stump, Ziggy, Meat, and Mouseboy. It comforted us to know we had more support, but that likely meant our higher command might send us somewhere else. We didn't know if they'd send us north, west, or east, but without saying it, we understood change was coming again.

The high-pitched whine of the Cobra engines provided that familiar and welcome sound, which was immediately followed by vibrations as the turbines spun faster. More fuel, more air, and more fire continued to mix. The blades began to spin. More vibrations followed as the main rotor blades started cutting through the air. The noise grew with the methodical buildup of the rotor blades' speed. The smell of fresh exhaust permeated the cockpit as I pulled the canopy closed.

If I close my eyes, I am still in that cockpit. I can still hear it as if it were yesterday—that statement of power, purpose, and unfailing commitment. The sound alone is a memory that triggers yet another memory. It's a sensory seal or cap that, when removed or twisted, reveals the sights, sounds, and smells of another world. Damn, I really miss that world.

We soon had all three helicopters checked in on the radios and were taxiing for takeoff. We were experiencing an almost cool, springlike morning. The ramps, clear of sand and dust, had more than enough open space to be used as a runway. We had reduced our ordnance loads over the past two days, dropping the nineteen-shot 2.75-inch rocket pods for seven-shot pods and dropping the lower TOW rack so we only carried two TOW missiles. We kept four Hellfire missiles and six hundred rounds of 20mm. The Hueys also dropped down to one seven-shot 2.75-inch rocket pod but kept several thousand rounds of .50 caliber and 7.62mm ammunition on board. No naivety among us.

The one o'clock takeoff from our new home in East Baghdad was as carefree as I could recall. The Huey kicked out to the east of the formation as we headed north. It was the ultimate safety blanket. With four more sets of eyes, a sensor for the copilot, and a crew chief hanging on each gun, they were capable of addressing any immediate threats.

I called for the switch. "Zero-three flight, switch Sky Chief."

Buss chimed in with, "Two."

"Three," added Andy.

We flew east of Highway 1 but stayed west of the town of Baqubah. Baqubah didn't pose any real threat to us, and I'm not even sure whether Marines had made it there, but the residents acted like kids not picked for the kickball team. Every day and every night, we had flown close to the city, and they had tried to engage the 269 aircraft. After the 12th, we had marked it as an impromptu "no fly zone." They hurled RPGs, SAMs, AAA, and small arms fire from ranges that had no hope of hitting us. Maybe they didn't get the memo, but we wouldn't take the bait.

"Zero-three, you see that target at three o'clock level, one finger below the horizon?" It was Buss and Rosie.

I looked to the right but saw nothing except one of the many small military outposts that dotted the desert. Some were located on the outskirts of towns; others, inside the towns. They could have been police, army, or tax collectors, but all had a clear set of walls sealing them from the outside, and most had distinctive flag poles and government vehicles. I looked further, and then I saw the "target." *Hmm, should I authorize this?*

"Zero-five, you think you can get that?" I said in an obviously challenging tone to Andy.

Immediately, I heard Andy respond, "Ohhh yeah, we can definitely get that."

I turned hard to the right and set up an overhead pattern. I didn't have to say anything else. The Huey had already banked right and was heading toward the target. Buss and I set up the overwatch position as Andy and Scotty positioned the Huey just above. I could see the crew chief trying desperately to haul the target into the cabin of the Huey; it was putting up an impressive fight. This was no normal target. It was no high-value target for the intelligence community. It was no direct threat to us, but it certainly had intrinsic value, which would be measured in bragging rights that would last years. Hmmm, maybe it was worth the risk?

Thirty seconds passed.

Forty-five seconds passed.

One minute passed.

It was nerve-racking. If they hit the target with the main or tail rotor, or if even a gust of wind blew them too close, it would be catastrophic. This was now officially a bad idea, but that impressive and valuable target remained. Andy and Scotty, both excellent pilots, held a position much closer to the situation.

We needed answers. "Matt, you think they are close?"

Heads down, he answered, "Ahhh well… It looks like Corporal Deal has almost sealed the deal."

I needed to audible the play before it went any further south, but before I could make the call, the nose of the Huey pitched down and slid left. I wasn't sure what had happened. They continued to descend. Neither pilot said anything as the nose-down attitude immediately turned into a flare. I feared the worst as a massive cloud of dust followed. We all held our breath.

The radio cracked. "Hey, we are sending Corporal Deal over this wall, and he's gonna personally secure the target."

Click, click was about all I could muster.

I could feel my heartbeat in my fingers. I looked down to see the twenty-two-year-old sprint the hundred yards from the Huey. He jumped, caught the top of the wall, and then pulled himself over. He disappeared for a few seconds and then re-emerged at full speed, heading toward the target. If you can recall Lieutenant Spears from *Band of Brothers* as he sprinted through German lines to find Dog Company and then return, this is what it felt like to me. There were no Iraqis firing at Corporal Deal that we saw, but the comparison bears some merit.

The next few seconds ticked by in dog years. The target looked secure, but no one knew for sure. Then, the same happened in reverse with Deal scaling the wall and running back to the sanctuary of the Huey. He secured himself and the target inside.

"Zero-five has the precious cargo on board, and we are lifting." Andy dropped the news in his typically calm and cool tone as he pulled power.

We watched from our perch as the Huey emerged from the ground dust and climbed up to join us. Once again, we turned and headed north. The entire evolution may have taken three minutes, but it took three years off my life. I was glad it was over and made a note to never do that again.

"Sky Chief, Deadly 03, mission number 0702 alpha, off Yankee." We needed to be prepared to do some real work.

Sky Chief was ready. "Deadly 03, contact Cybil on maple."

We made the frequency switches and checked in with Cybil as requested, heading directly to Tikrit. We knew that Cybil was with 2nd LAR and likely the northernmost force of Task Force Tripoli. He provided a welcome voice.

He didn't have much work for us, so we took the initiative to do reconnaissance inside the same place where the CO and I had engaged multiple targets the night before. Al Sahara Airfield was a massive complex complete with barracks, headquarters buildings, destroyed training aircraft, and other facilities that marked it as an Iraqi Air Force training center. It looked empty with no one inside the compound. A ghost town.

As I passed over Al Sahara, I thought that we needed to take a closer look. The feeling of dread had been replaced with a feeling of success after having secured the last target, so I felt the need to find another. I knew what air bases looked like, and I wanted to find the headquarters building. After just one more lap, I found it.

"Zero-three flight, I am going to land and check out one of these buildings. You stay airborne." I had already decided. "Matt, I'm going to hop out and take a look inside that headquarters building," I said, already having slowed into a ten-foot hover. From there, I touched down, lowered the collective, and grabbed my M4. "Matt, I'll be right back."

Matt asked, "What exactly are you going to do?"

Without bothering to respond, I opened the canopy, hopped out, closed the canopy behind me, and jogged through the front door. I knew this was a bad idea, but curiosity of all things had called me to land and explore. Maybe seeing this war from one thousand feet had left me wanting. Maybe it was an unrecognized challenge that drew me toward it. Maybe the fatigue played a role, or maybe I was just being stupid. Regardless, I fearlessly entered the building.

To my right, I found a staircase to the second floor. Straight ahead, framed pictures of Saddam Hussein stared back at me. There were dozens of canvases lining the wall up the staircase. All of them had Saddam in every position from his classic Stalinesque pose with his right hand in the air to another that portrayed him as a falconer complete with birds.

As I climbed the stairs, I could almost hear my heartbeat. I opened the double doors at the top and stepped through. I had only taken three or four steps when I heard the door behind me kick open.

Andy and Buss had been talking with Matt, who had given them the only facts he had. I had landed, hopped out with an M4, said I'd be right back, and jogged into the headquarters building. I had not been seen since. Andy made the call. He would land and send in a crew chief while Buss kept eyes out.

It was round two for Corporal Deal. He grabbed his own M4, and as the Huey landed, he tracked my steps inside the headquarters. He saw what I had seen on his way in and heard someone on the second deck. Then, he picked up his pace, and as he pushed through the double doors, he froze as I turned to face him.

"Hey, sir. What the hell are we doing?"

What I was doing was obvious. We had stumbled onto an Iraqi officer or aviation cadet's barracks. Deal and I opened the wall lockers to find all the contents in pristine condition. We found uniforms, dress caps, helmets, and everything you would expect in a military academy but nothing of intelligence value.

We needed a game plan. "Let's grab some of these items, along with a few of those pictures downstairs, and get out of here."

"Roger that, sir."

We took a few pieces and then pulled down and rolled up several of the canvases before making our way back to the Huey. As we walked out the door, Sergeant Poindexter greeted us. His look said, "Really? This is what you were doing?"

He snagged a few of the items I had in my hands, walked back to the turning Huey, and tossed them in. After returning to the rear seat of the Cobra, I strapped in, did a quick radio check, and took off. I was not sure what I'd thought I would find. Saddam's chemical weapons blueprints? Cases of stamped Iraqi gold bars? Anything? Something? Anyway, it was time to refuel.

The trip to Tikrit South airfield went by quickly, and we made the routine landing next to the fuel trucks. Taking in my surroundings, I was amazed at the mini zoo around the airfield. Someone had penned up gazelle, zebras, ostriches, and other animals I couldn't identify. In the middle of all this destruction and chaos, I found it hard to picture this as part of a normal city—a city with schools, children, shops, restaurants, businesses, and apparently a zoo.

The refuelers told us this was the site of one of Saddam's son's palaces, and this was his zoo. Even if it was the personal zoo of Saddam's youngest son, Qusay, it was something so odd, something so *Alice in Wonderland*, it only begged more questions. We were getting just a peek into a world that was otherwise unlike any place we had ever been. The zoo had gold-plated roofs in the stalls for the animals. Plus, there were out-of-place marble statues and detailed masonry adorning random outbuildings.

I turned back toward the two other aircraft that had shut down. I needed to come clean to the entire group, especially the two NCOs. We all met at the tail of the Huey. I had not made the best choices after I'd spotted the first target and then again after I'd landed at Al Sahara. I began to launch into my confession, but the group quickly interrupted me. No one cared, and no one wanted to hear my reasoning. What they really wanted was to see what I had found. I asked Deal to bring it out with the hopes of having a memento or two for the squadron and maybe something for each of us.

Before Deal had a chance to display anything tucked inside the Huey, Andy came around the corner. He had the "target" in his hands. The three-by-five Iraqi flag that had been secured by Deal was now on full display. It certainly hadn't been worth the risk, but that was old news. Next, Deal came out of the Huey with a few uniform items and several of the Saddam pictures.

I opened the conversation. "Gents, this was not my finest hour, but we have a few items here. I'll roll the pictures up and keep them in my tail boom. You guys can keep the rest in the Huey. Any questions?"

It wasn't exactly Nazi gold from Hitler's Eagle's Nest. No state secrets or things of any extrinsic value. Something still seemed wrong about landing and doing a one-man recon. I should have pushed down any ideas of grabbing a few souvenirs when I'd seen there was nothing of value in the headquarters, but I had an undeniable sense that the war would soon come to an end. I wanted something so I wouldn't forget. Something that I could touch and feel that would make it all real. It was no excuse, but the deed had been done.

CHAPTER 34

Location: Yankee FARP – Salman Pak, Iraq
Date: 15APR03
Time: 0020L

"Deadly 03 flight, we are gonna call off station and make the turn south. Zero-five, will you check us out with Cybil? I'll call Sky Chief and get our routing back to Yankee." I knew my voice sounded tired.

Scotty responded, "05."

The day had turned into a beautiful central Iraqi night, where we could see as well as we ever had. Gone were the continuous blowing sand, low visibility, and moonless nights. A growing sliver of moon, a visible horizon, rivers, greenery, buildings, and other contrasting terrain had replaced those other things that made flying so difficult. Also missing in Tikrit was the sense of an ambush or hidden battalion of Iraqi armor. I couldn't put a finger on it, but that place looked too sophisticated and polished. Too well designed and built. Just too *something*.

A sense of control had returned. We'd all emerged from the insanity that was the south and from the ambiguity that had been a part of every flight to find a pseudo resort town. On the other hand, when we flew over Baghdad, Basra, or Nasiriyah, we could sense it—a feeling that fate called and we only had a matter of time. Tikrit was to Baghdad what the Hamptons were to New York City. It was a place where the populace simply didn't seem to want to fight back. Whether true or not, I had a growing sense that we held more control over the outcome than we had ever given ourselves credit for.

"Zero-three flight, I'm coming right. We are going to fly well east of the highway and stay away from Baquba." I waited.

Click. Click.

Click. Click.

I settled into the hour flight back to Yankee. We had fired only a few rounds over the past three sorties. The city had been quiet, but we'd heard multiple sections of fixed-wing aircraft check on station as we'd swapped FACs from Cybil to Disney to others looking for work. Those fixed-wing aircraft must have been pushed west or north. We had finally moved to the south and east of Tikrit, conducting visual reconnaissance. I'd feared complacency had settled in, the sure sign of impending doom for any aviator, but every call, every turn of the flight, had remained tight and characterized by a sense of purpose and a clear focus.

Howdy, Pez, Flash, and Country had checked in with Cybil a few hours earlier as well, and maybe they would have more luck. From the radio transmissions, it seemed Cybil intended to push air assets further west and to the north to spy anything coming down Highway 1. His plan was to detect, as unlikely as it seemed, any yet undetected Iraqi units moving in from the west. Maybe Cybil knew something the rest of us didn't because his instincts were usually spot on. Tikrit would soon reveal a tell. There would be one last attempt to astonish, to amaze, and to exact some form of retribution on the Americans. Our last flight of two Cobras was led by Howdy, and neither he nor anyone in that flight could have anticipated what was about to happen.

We had left Tikrit and made the turn back on Highway 1. The work with Task Force Tripoli had been routine. We'd executed intelligence gathering, overwatch, radio relay, and convoy escort missions. Each part was important work, and we had hopped between units most of the day and well into the night.

"Yankee, Deadly 03, flight of three, ten minutes out," we announced.

We made the turn out to the east and set up for a straight-in approach to our flight line. In front of us lay Baghdad. The city of six million never disappointed. The lights of the city had slowly returned over the past week, resuming some semblance of normalcy. We landed in a trail formation—that is, in single file.

After the three of us performed the shutdown ritual and went into our makeshift maintenance spaces, Monty walked up. Over the past weeks, I had asked Monty to do some fact finding. We'd eventually have to quantify everything. It's the nature of things. There are always those looking for numbers to validate a story.

"Morning," said Monty. "How are we doing? I've got most of the information you were looking for. Let me know and I'll bring it over."

I gave him a thumbs up and took a seat on one of the camp stools we had brought with us. MRE boxes turned on their sides made up the remainder of the seats. Before long, Monty returned and handed me a folder. It surprised me that he had gotten it because he knew if I wanted something, I would get up and find it myself. He knew what the file contained. He had worked like a detective, slapping the mountain of evidence down in front of the suspect. It would make for quite a read.

I opened the folder and began to skim the topics and digest the numbers. It was black and white, but it painted a picture using every color in the rainbow. The evidence, damning yet optimistic. The statistics, appalling yet alluring. The aggregate, fantastic and nearly unbelievable. Still, the numbers remained incomplete. After tonight, we would fly combat missions from Yankee for another week and from our final Iraqi-based FARP located in Al-Kut for nearly another month.

I pulled the camp stool into the corner, found a large plastic bottle of water, and started to read. Since leaving Riverfront for Tikrit, the fourteen helicopters had flown 308 sorties and nearly five hundred hours. This didn't include the aircraft we still had flying out of Riverfront. Since March 20th, the squadron had launched 647 TOW and Hellfire missiles. Hueys and Cobras had fired 5,600 2.75-inch rockets. Cobras had expended sixty-four thousand rounds of 20mm, and the Huey crews had delivered a mind-numbing 227 thousand rounds of .50 caliber and 7.62mm ammunition. This was more ordnance than had ever been fired in combat in the history of our squadron, all done in less than a month. It was not bravado; it was a ruthless and cold number—a fact.

Those munitions had been invested in almost seven hundred tactical targets. That included more than an Iraqi Armored Division's worth of destroyed T-55, T-64, and T-72 main battle tanks, along with three battalions' worth of armored fighting vehicles.

As I flipped the page, I suddenly felt as though I were being watched, like someone had just peered over my shoulder and judged. The Ghost scurried about somewhere, nodding her head as I read the next page of statistics. She let me know I would not get away with it. A confirmation that while our first statistics seemed impressive, opposing forces existed, just as dedicated and potentially deadly as ever.

The first number was thirty-seven. This represented confirmed holes and recorded damages to the eighteen Cobras. That included impacts from 23mm cannon shells, along with damage from 12.7mm and 7.62mm machine gun fire. I knew we had been lucky, but I dared not think about it. I didn't want to somehow jinx us. It was an alarming number and one that would likely continue to climb. Our Hueys had fared better, but we would continue to find previously unrecorded and unrecognized holes, scarring, and pieces of Iraqi bullets in aircraft. This would happen even after we returned to the US.

I had just finished reading through the file when my two wingmen, Deadly 04 and 05, made their way into the tent. Now, we could finally conduct a debrief. Though we had landed about an hour ago, I'd wanted everyone to have a chance to eat, relax, and prepare to talk about the mission and what we were planning for tomorrow.

As it turned out, 269 operations had already written the flight schedule and begun executing it for today with the next day posted as well. I read it and felt that creeping uneasy feeling of the inevitable.

Buss was leaving, and I would lead the division of three with Howdy and Pez as my wingman with Andy and Scotty as the other.

For Buss, Matt, and Rosie, the flight schedule for the 16th marked the third major milestone of this seemingly endless deployment. The first was the not inconsequential jump of an entire air group from *Saipan* to Riverfront. That transition had tested and strained the squadron in ways we could never have predicted. The two thousand flight hours the squadron had flown over the nearly four-week period was as unprecedented as it was unimaginable. The jump from Riverfront to Yankee, an operation that would have taken months to plan in peacetime, had been executed in fourteen hours, and now we looked at a sequel.

Our MAWTS-1 augment aircrew were going home. Buss, Murph McKay, and our Huey crew chief, Staff Sergeant Ryan Leighton, were all flying back to Kuwait. I couldn't imagine not having them in the ready room. I couldn't remember a time when they weren't there. Just another signal or warning that the times were changing.

CHAPTER 35

Location: Salman Pak East Airfield, Iraq
Date: 15APR03
Time: 0250L

We had just completed our debrief when the sound of two Cobras let me know that Howdy and his section had returned for the night. It would take another hour for them to make their way into the tent, but I wanted to hear how things had gone after we had checked off station. Howdy and his crew of Flash, Country, and Pez stowed their gear and entered the single GP tent around 0345L. Even at that late hour, we wanted to put the final punctuation on another long day.

Howdy walked in with the trio of pilots in tow. "Gentlemen, how's it going?"

The six of us sat on a combination of camp stools and MRE boxes and waited for Howdy and his crew to take a similar pose on the remaining MRE "chairs." I could see they were all amped up a bit, perhaps the lingering effects of go pills.

I asked, "Hey, Howdy, we are just finishing up here. You mind if we listen to what you guys did up there? Looks like we are all going back tomorrow."

Howdy kicked it off this way. "No sweat. Okay, I'll run this back from the check-in, but back me up on the details."

Flash shrugged, and Buss and Rosie gave a similar motion.

With the mission fresh in his mind, Howdy kept the stream of consciousness flowing. "Things seemed like they were slowing down when we checked in with Sky Chief, but overall, the last mission was anything but slow. We flew up to Tikrit without issue and took small arms and AAA fire just like every night flying near Baqubah. They didn't get the memo to fucking knock it off already."

I tried to get comfortable while Howdy continued. "We get to Tikrit and go through the hot pits to top up with gas at Sammis Field and take the flight back up to Sky Chief to check in for possible follow-on tasking. Then, it all started to happen."

I lowered my head and looked over at Pez, Flash, and Country. They were leaned over with their eyes closed, almost as though they were back in their cockpits. I glanced at everyone else in the room and noted they were doing the same thing. They were listening and visualizing the events.

"Deadly 31, this is Sky Chief. Report airborne out of Sammis and proceed up to the west of Tikrit. Contact Cybil on TAD 27 for follow-on FAC(A) mission."

"Deadly 31, copy that. I'm lifting and turning immediately north, five hundred feet and one hundred knots. Call on board."

Now, I looked directly at Flash and then back at Howdy as he continued. "I had very specific opinions on this mission, and this was the exact scenario where I knew we could really help. We could see further than Cybil, and we could expand his battle space further than he could affect. We know FAC(A) work is all about flexibility and agility. I thought we needed to be less formal and more adaptive."

I knew exactly what he meant. The training to be a FAC(A) was tedious and exacting, and it demanded devotion to doctrine almost to the point of zealotry. Howdy essentially said they needed less chalk talk or scripted plays and should instead adopt the mindset of joining a pickup game.

Howdy took a breath and went on. "I checked us in with Cybil. We knew he had been engaged for the past hour. Cybil was right where Sky Chief said he'd be—north and west of Tikrit in a defensive coiled position, screening toward the west."

"Cybil, Deadly 31, overhead flight of two, for your work."

"Copy, Deadly 31. I have you in sight with a lot of fixed-wing CAS aircraft coming to work a bunker and ammunition complex about five miles to our southwest. We had no joy getting the last flight to get eyes

on the target. Need you to FAC(A) and work those jets on target. How copy?"

Howdy replied, "Deadly 31 is enroute and will advise. I have the marks and control."

Cybil understood. "Copy, Deadly 31. You have control. Good hunting. Be safe and report back to me with BDA."

We were all looking at Howdy. It was clear he had a lot more he wanted to tell us. Taking another breath, he resumed his story. "Just as soon as we transited the five miles to the target area, we saw what looked like a large ammo dump with bunkers and buildings and well-developed storage. I told Dennis to put a Hellfire into the largest building. He did, and we got immediate secondaries, which means these structures were likely filled to the rafters with explosives. His missile impact and explosions served as a great mark for the arriving CAS aircraft."

Pez jumped in, glancing around at all of us. "Then, we just started having jets checking in. There were probably ten to twelve all at once. There were Navy F-14s and F-18s and Air Force F-16CJs. It was nuts."

Howdy nodded in agreement, then kept the recount moving. "There was no organization, and they were all eager to drop and shoot, so I stacked them at one-thousand-foot intervals from twenty-five thousand to thirty thousand feet. I had to keep asking for callsigns of who was at the bottom of the stack of jets because it was hard to keep track of."

Flash and Country took the brief pause to add their perspective. "We provided local security as well as put rounds into the target area to keep the jets' eyes oriented on the targets. Howdy and Pez were preparing to run the jets into the bunker complex."

Howdy keyed his radio. "Alright, who's at the bottom of the stack at twenty-five thousand?"

The F-16 pilot responded, "JOPPA 15, flight of two F-16CJs, two-thousand-pound bombs each and two AGM-88s each with twenty minutes of playtime."

"Twenty minutes!" exclaimed Howdy. "Holy shit—that's not much. We need to get moving."

The other flights echoed JOPPA 15's low fuel state for playtime.

Howdy made a decision. "Alright, 99 aircraft, listen up. We are going to run you all south to north with an egress to the west and back into the stack at thirty-one thousand or greater with you responsible to deconflict coming back into the stack. Our LASER code is one-two-two-one for all munitions. Do you copy?"

"All the jets answered up and confirmed the plan," Howdy continued. "So, we ran the first section across the target with Dennis picking out different impact points while I asked the jet 'in the chute' to confirm his laser code."

"Laser on," said Howdy.

Joppa 15 responded, "Contact the target."

Howdy called, "Roger, you are cleared hot."

The first impacts were the most violent. Two-thousand-pound bombs were anything but discreet. Each bomb carried nearly one thousand pounds of composite explosives. By the time the second bomb found its mark, the secondary explosions inside the compound had spewed fireballs three hundred feet into the night sky.

What followed were immense clouds of smoke drifting to the north. Almost mystically, they began to rain down debris behind the flight. Deadly 31 and 32 were inside the fragmentation pattern but also committed to this almost untenable position. They needed to keep working the jets into the target. At a distance of 3,500 meters, they nearly missed the three armored vehicles making their way toward Cybil.

I looked around the tent as we all stared in a combination of disbelief and astonishment. I noticed that we had all leaned in a little closer as Howdy shared the final details. "We worked the remaining F-16CJs and the Navy F/A-18s and F-14 Bombcats with pretty good success. We fired every missile, every rocket, and every round we had available. We just couldn't get any closer. Finally, low on gas, we checked off station."

He ended the brief abruptly, or at least it seemed abrupt to me. That was it? We knew he had more, but it was almost four thirty in the morning. I looked at Flash. He cocked his head, signaling that he knew there was more to that story. I waited to catch the eye of Pez or Country. When I finally did, a more formal gaze replaced their normal sarcastic smirks, indicating, "It's late, and it was no big deal—just another night."

I got the sense that we were somehow interlopers intruding on their very private and personal debriefs. They'd made no mention of the three Iraqi BMPs, which had maneuvered to engage Cybil's company of LAVs from 2nd LAR, that Cybil had reported were destroyed by Deadly 31 and 32 earlier in the evening. No mention that the actual number of jets was closer to forty. No mention that they had engaged a major munitions hub reportedly secured by the Iraqi Special Republican Guard.

Howdy had stopped talking long enough to hear the deafening silence that followed. The effects of the go pills had certainly begun to fade but not for those of us listening. We knew we had just heard something exceptional, something clearly out of the ordinary. The simplicity of the debrief had also made it significant. The emotion was evident and clear. I could feel the dangers and fear. All right there. Almost tangible enough to touch.

Witnessing the body language and reactions of his crews made each point more remarkable, more impactful. It had long become part of the HMLA subculture to be harder on ourselves than required. Yes, we sometimes walked with a swagger, but this job needed confident people. Ironically, we gave ourselves little praise, and the past few weeks had made that clear. We didn't talk about what we did well or fawn over what we believed we had accomplished. Rather, we discussed our missteps and mistakes and what we would do to get better.

There were no holy scrolls recounting the heroic acts of anyone, no glowing multi-page reports of tank engagements, CASEVAC missions, or critical fire support to Marines in close contact with the enemy. That was not and had never been in our DNA. We accounted for our missions with numbers and recorded them on government-issued paper. There were only spreadsheets that listed mission number, flight time, location, and ordnance expended. Nothing else.

To hear Deadly 31 and 32's mission recounted validated what I knew but refused to acknowledge. We had absolutely played a key role in that war, and what we had seen and done was worth repeating. I began to flash back to the countless acts of selflessness by Matt, Buss, and Rosie that I had witnessed. Professional vanity only allowed us to acknowledge such acts with a quiet comment or a quick joke, but I understood what they had done was not as common as we had convinced ourselves.

I thought back to the night Fuzzy had flown hundreds of miles to get a wounded Marine to Riverfront. I thought about Spike leading us into Al-Hay. I thought about Buss leading us in Nasiriyah. I thought about Sergeant Mike McGuire with 1st LAR. I thought about our Huey crew chiefs defending Marines while strapped into a Huey and firing their machine guns out of side doors. I thought about Andy Dyer and his crew rescuing his downed wingman. I thought about Woodman and his pilots and our other sister squadrons and their crews. I thought about the FACs and the FARP teams. I thought about friends leading infantry and armored units. Every day, they woke up ready to poke the bear. They never hesitated, they never flinched, they never faltered.

What Howdy had said was especially important for his crew as well. We'd finally heard someone verbalize our design. What we had been purpose built to do. The honesty in his words was only matched by an unquestionable integrity. No bravado, no proverbs, no analogies. Nothing but the recall of a purportedly routine mission that had just ended minutes before but likely felt like it had been flown years ago by someone else. There was a collective sense of disbelief that I knew all ten of us felt. A rawness drove this story, and it could only be expressed by someone who knew the stakes, who had witnessed the darkest side of this war, and who respected the finality of it all. A deeper truth remained buried in those words.

I watched Flash, Country, and Pez. They all nodded, and I could see their minds running wild. *Did we just do that?* They hung in mental suspension, somehow unable to move forward from their thoughts.

Play. Pause. Rewind. Play. Pause. Rewind.

This morning, now the early hours of the 15th of April, was much like the early morning of the 21st of March. Andy, Howdy, Pez, Flash, Country, me, Matt, Buss, and Rosie were just talking and sitting on MRE boxes in a GP tent—the same way it had started some twenty-seven days previously.

The moment was not lost on anyone. For all the unknowns, and despite the enigmatic character of the war, we had irreversibly turned the tables. That Ghost had vanished with nothing left to fear except us. We had become the Ghosts.

Never again would I underestimate the power of personal connections; the impact of shared experiences; the effects of trauma, fear, hopelessness, and despair on our collective will. We'd learned to not only survive but to thrive. As aviators, we would all eventually leave that country with a grounding in combat aviation—nothing more and nothing less. As leaders, we'd leave with a dozen lifetimes of lessons. We had refused to accept the story as she had written it. Instead, we'd persevered to rewrite our own endings.

EPILOGUE

We would fly for more than another month in Iraq, gaining another one thousand flight hours by the time *Saipan* pulled anchor and set sail for the Mediterranean. The move by MAG 29 to Salman Pak would not be their last. We were happy to see a new HMLA in theater. It meant we were one step closer to leaving. With major combat operations grinding to a slow stop, we were expected to backload or reembark onto *Saipan* and go home soon.

By the end of April, we had completed operations in Tikrit and made the next jump to Al-Kut, a city tucked east of Baghdad only thirty miles from the Iranian border. We'd reconnected with Task Force Tarawa, who had positioned themselves at the former Iraqi Air Force base and in the surrounding urban sprawl. We flew another twenty helicopters from MAG 29 to execute a variety of combat missions to include CAS, CASEVAC, and resupply, along with escort missions. The days and nights blurred together as the collective fatigue on Marines and machines began to take its toll.

We would remain in Al-Kut until the middle of May, and then we'd slowly begin to backload to *Saipan.* During this time, we experienced a feeling best described as a mix of desperation and anticipation. We were tired and becoming lazy and complacent. We could not get back aboard ship fast enough. We knew this war was over. Not *over* over, but over for us, and only for now. Boomer and the commanders up and down the MEF chain of command were already planning. Some units were being sent home immediately while other units were extended until fresh units from bases and stations across the globe could arrive.

The days began to drag, and the Marines started to get testy with each other, impatient with the mundane and intolerant of routine. We needed to go. By the end of May, we had landed the entire squadron back on *Saipan,* and Fuzzy's HMM 162 had also rejoined us. Boomer and his staff had all reembarked.

With the outline of Kuwait City in my rearview mirror, I was already looking forward to passing back through the Suez Canal. *Saipan's* destination was Naval Station Rota in Spain. I had made several stops here on previous deployments and looked forward to some green grass and cold beers.

Unlike most "wash-downs" done in port, we did them on the way to Rota, not while in Rota. We would conduct a complete freshwater wash of every aircraft and every vehicle while at sea. We would also begin conducting forensic inspections of each aircraft, preparing them for the eventual flyoff in about three weeks. We also initiated the much-needed writing of after-action reports on everything from weapons performance to the quality, endurance, and reliability of critical components and systems.

Life back on *Saipan* gave me a chance to finally reestablish a routine. I could exchange emails with my wife and four kids and let my parents and others know we were headed back. So much had changed, but we were all excited to return home.

I found comfort in knowing all the neighborhoods in Jacksonville, North Carolina, experienced similar excitement. The small North Carolina town had been comparatively quiet for the past five months. The 2nd MEB had deployed along with another two MEUs. Except for the normal traffic of everyday shopping and kids going to school, the pace and vitality of Jacksonville had ebbed. With the departure of nearly every sailor and Marine, the town had sat nearly idle.

After 148 days at sea, the USS *Saipan* pulled into Naval Base Rota, Spain, on Friday, June 13th. Captain Hackney, as always, had kept her word. There would be some work while docked pier side, but the hardest work had already been completed while at sea. A liberty port provided time for her Marines and her sailors to take some much-deserved and needed time off.

Officers and enlisted sailors and Marines had been given their limits. That included what to wear, what time to be back on ship, where and how far they could travel, where not to go, and what not to do. I was just happy to make regular trips to the gym and sleep in a bed.

As the 1MC loudspeakers declared liberty on *Saipan*, Howdy and I grabbed a cab into El Puerto de Santa Maria, a lazy coastal town known for great food and a few good beach bars. We had been given strict instructions to keep a low profile and be back aboard ship or off the streets by 0200L. That was a pipedream. As the day turned into night and the night turned into early morning, the Marines packed the streets. Those same Marines stayed out well past curfew, and some would stay out until the sun came up. Rather than take names, we bought more beers.

The morning of the 14th was a continuation of the 13th. I was tired and hungover and needed to find some more money. It was a marathon now.

Howdy and I had made our way to an outdoor café and were just uncorking a little hair of the dog at about 0800L when Boomer walked by with several of his staff.

No kidding. He slowed down just enough to identify that the nearly slumped over bodies were two of his majors. In a glance, he confirmed we were alive, noted the two large bottles of red wine, and then gave us his typical smirk and head nod. They walked off without saying a word.

AFTERWORD

The Devil in the Triangle

Location: Fallujah, Al Anbar Province, Iraq
Date: 24JUN04
Time: 1420L

"Flares, flares, flares. Break right, break right." The call had come too late.

They had seen the smoke plume only a second before the missile impacted the lead Cobra just behind the number two engine. They watched, they waited, and they held their breath. There was no way the human eye could be expected to give warning to a missile traveling at nearly 1,100 miles per hour.

"Jettison all the ordnance. The throttles are closed. I'm going to level off at one hundred feet. Prepare for a hard impact," Tramp called out.

BUNO 163939 or Coyote 41 had just taken a direct hit from a Russian-made SA-14 into the right engine. The crippled AH-1W of HMLA 775 was crashing. It was only a matter of where and how hard. It was up to the pilot to determine whether they had any chance of walking away. Tramp was flying, and he had prepared his entire career for this moment. He was one of only a few uniquely qualified pilots who could execute a high-speed low-level autorotation.

"Tramp, keep coming right. Keep coming right. We gotta get closer to the cloverleaf," came from his copilot, "Kaddafi."

They were headed directly into downtown Fallujah, but they needed to turn east and try to glide as far outside the city limits as possible. The missile's impact had destroyed the number two engine and had sent shrapnel into engine number one. The number one engine was, nearly simultaneously, winding down. If they could not find some open space to crash, there was no chance of surviving the impact, much less escaping. Friendly lines were more than five hundred meters to the east.

"Pull up! Pull up! We need to get closer to…" Kaddafi made his last call.

The Marines from 1st Light Armored Reconnaissance (LAR) had seen the entire tragedy unfold and immediately put their idling LAV-25s into gear. They held the far-right flank of the 1st MARDIV and sealed the exit to the Sunni Triangle's flashpoint, Fallujah. They would turn onto the highway that, though barricaded, led directly into the insurgent center of the city. The LAR Marines' radios barked with additional orders as they accelerated toward the expected crash site.

It would be a while before I got the call that we had lost another aircraft, this one to a shoulder-fired SA-14. This would make it the third Cobra destroyed. The Cobra, along with four additional Huey aircrew wounded in the cockpit and still more wounded after taking mortar fire to our flight line, painted an alarming mosaic. There was something else here at work. Why couldn't I see it?

The Sunni Triangle was full of contradictions. The history, the mysteries, the tragedies, and the injustices all combined to form a political and cultural timebomb. Perhaps it was exploding right in front of me? There was no way I could tell. Who was looking at each piece of the puzzle, and were these events more carefully orchestrated than we thought? If they were, then by whom? And if random…well, there are no coincidences here.

ACKNOWLEDGMENTS

To my wife, Jennifer, the love of my life and my best friend. She has selflessly supported me and shepherded our family through countless moves and what seemed like endless deployments. To our four children, Katherine, Cassandra, Eric, and Caroline. Like so many military families, they all endured deployments, moves, new schools, and lost and then found friends. They have grown into amazing adults who live with a sense of purpose and integrity. I could not be more proud of them.

To those who spent hundreds of hours meeting with me over the past years. Your insights and time spent listening, recalling, encouraging, and supporting *Ghosts of Baghdad* was invaluable—thank you.

Major General Julian D. Alford, USMC (Ret.)
Colonel John "Buss" Barranco, USMC (Ret.)
Lieutenant Colonel James "Cybil" Brown, USMC (Ret.)
Colonel Aaron "Chet" Brunk, USMC
Lieutenant Colonel Andy Dyer, USMC (Ret.)
Captain Tom "Diesel" Frosch, USN (Ret.)
Colonel Doug "Spike" Hardison, USMC (Ret.)
Lieutenant General Robert "Fuzzy" Hedelund, USMC (Ret.)
Captain Ted "TAG" Heflin, USN (Ret.)
Colonel Jeremie "Hank" Hester, USMC
Colonel Jeff "Huey" Hewlett, USMC (Ret.)
Lieutenant Colonel Steve "Woodman" Heywood, USMC (Ret.)
Tim Iacofano

Lieutenant Colonel Jeff "Stinky" Prowse, USMC (Ret.)
Colonel Brian "Howdy" Kennedy, USMC (Ret.)
1st Sergeant Ryan Leighton, USMC (Ret.)
Captain Michael McGuire, USMC (Ret.)
Colonel Sam "Country" Meyer, USMC
Lieutenant Colonel Hugh "Darkhorse 1-6" Mills, USA (Ret.)
Lieutenant General Robert "Boomer" Milstead, USMC (Ret.)
Brigadier General Scott "Scooter" O'Mera, USMC (Ret.)
Colonel John "Johnny-O" Ostrowski, USMC (Ret.)
Major Dennis "Pez" Pyszczymuka, USMC (Ret.)
Lieutenant Colonel Eric "TAG" Price, USAF (Ret.)
Rear Admiral Don "DQ" Quinn, USN (Ret.)
Lieutenant Colonel Mike "Flash" Richman, USMC (Ret.)
Colonel Julian "Chicklets" Rivera, USMC (Ret.)
Michael "Rosie" Roseberry
Major General Gregg "Sweet Pea" Sturdevant, USMC (Ret.)
Vice Admiral Jerry Unruh, USN (Ret.)
Lieutenant Colonel Marc "Vino" Weintraub, USMC (Ret.)
John Weisman
Colonel Matt "Wilde" Ziegler, USMC

To my publisher, Andy Symonds, and his entire team at Ballast Books. What an amazing team. Special thanks to my editor and sounding board, Darren Sapp, along with Lauren Green, Breanne Beightol, Mimi Bark, and Kayleigh Rucinski. Thank you all.